Fast Food, Fast Talk

Fast Food, Fast Talk

SERVICE WORK AND
THE ROUTINIZATION OF
EVERYDAY LIFE

ROBIN LEIDNER

University of California Press

Berkeley • *Los Angeles* • *London*

Part of Chapter 5 has been previously published as "Serving
Hamburgers and Selling Insurance: Gender, Work, and Identity in Interactive Service Jobs," *Gender & Society* 5 (June 1991):
154–77.

University of California Press
Berkeley and Los Angeles, California

University of California Press, Ltd.
London, England

Library of Congress Cataloging-in-Publication Data

Leidner, Robin.
    Fast food, fast talk : service work and the routinization
of everyday life / Robin Leidner.
      p. cm.
    Includes bibliographical references and index.
    ISBN 0-520-08169-2 (cloth). — ISBN 0-520-08500-0 (paper)
    1. Insurance companies—United States—Employees—
Case studies.   2. Food service employees—United
States—Case studies.   3.Work environment—United
States—Case studies.   I. Title.
HD8039.I482U65   1993
331.25—dc20   92-38004
                                         CIP

Printed in the United States of America

9 8 7 6 5 4 3 2 1

The paper used in this publication meets the minimum
requirements of American National Standard for Information
Sciences—Permanence of Paper for Printed Library Materials,
ANSI Z39.48-1984. ∞

Contents

Acknowledgments

My study of the routinization of interactions showed me that although standard formats may militate against sincere expression and personal connection, they do not make them impossible. I hope that despite the standard form of these author's acknowledgments, readers will understand that my gratitude to the generous and able people who helped bring this book into being is more than routine.

The management and workers of Combined Insurance and McDonald's, most of whom must remain anonymous, made the research possible, and they have my sincere appreciation. Bob Meyerhoff and Bob Anderson of Combined Insurance deserve special mention. They arranged for my access to the company and did everything possible to help with the research. Frank Gowens of McDonald's was extremely helpful, as were the owner of the franchise I studied and the staff at McDonald's Chicago regional office. I am particularly indebted to those trainers and workers at both companies who accepted my presence and my inquisitiveness with good humor.

I was lucky to have had the advice and support of wonderful friends, teachers, and colleagues as I researched and wrote this book. Their ideas, questions, criticisms, and suggestions helped me avoid many pitfalls and rescued me when I insisted on plunging into others. They deserve some of the credit for the creditable features of this book, but they are not responsible for its flaws.

I have been given more than practical and intellectual support. Since PMA, the Positive Mental Attitude that Combined Insurance believes is crucial for success, is not a prominent part of my emotional makeup, those whose encouragement, good cheer, understanding, and faith helped me along have my heartfelt gratitude.

The members of my dissertation committee at Northwestern provided all the assistance that one could expect of a committee, but none of the arbitrary dicta or other impediments that one might fear. Andrew Gordon and Charles Ragin contributed ideas and inspiration. Carol Heimer, who chaired the committee, and Arthur Stinchcombe both went well beyond the call of duty, offering good food and friendship in addition to good judgment and guidance. Others whose interest, advice, and editorial skills helped me with the dissertation were Martha Bays, Arlene Kaplan Daniels, Krishna Das Gupta, Marjorie DeVault, Rosanna Hertz, Christopher Jencks, James Rosenbaum, and John Walsh. I thank Northwestern University, the National Science Foundation, and the National Graduate Fellowship Program of the United States Department of Education for financial support of my graduate education.

Fred Block, Charles Bosk, Jerry Jacobs, Ruth Milkman, Carmen Sirianni, and Vicki Smith all read the dissertation and provided excellent suggestions on how to revise it. Since my arrival at the University of Pennsylvania, Demie Kurz and Vicki Smith have been unfailingly sisterly and stimulating companions. Andrea Katin, Jane Mansbridge, Kathy Mooney, and Lauri Perman have also provided emotional support, practical assistance, or both, and Naomi Schneider has been a patient and supportive editor.

I am especially grateful to Annette Lareau, the miracle worker whose understanding, intelligence, and practicality helped me to abandon the struggle for PMA and develop instead the mental attitude that actually allowed me to finish the book, OKMA. Finally, a few people deserve special mention for having managed to put up with me from dissertation drafts to publication. My parents, although bemused by this seemingly endless process, have been unfailingly supportive of my efforts, for which I am deeply grateful. Sam Kaplan, my dear and dependable friend, has bolstered my sometimes precarious confidence, cheered and entertained me, read many drafts, polished my prose, and helped me get organized when I was most muddled. To borrow the elegant conclusion of E. B. White's *Charlotte's Web,* "It's not often that someone comes along who is a true friend and a good writer." Sam is both.

1

Working on People

The logic of work routinization is simple, elegant, and compelling. Adam Smith's famous discussion of pin manufacture laid the groundwork: instead of paying high-priced, skilled workers to do a job from start to finish, employers could split the job into its constituent parts and assign each task to minimally qualified workers, thus greatly reducing costs and increasing output (Smith 1776). Frederick Taylor's system of scientific management, aimed at removing decision making from all jobs except managers' and engineers', pushed the division of labor still further. Routinizing work processes along these lines offers several benefits to managers. First, designing jobs so that each worker repeatedly performs a limited number of tasks according to instructions provided by management increases efficiency, through both greater speed and lower costs. Second, it results in products of uniform quality. And its final and most enticing promise is that of giving management increased control over the enterprise.

These systems for dividing and routinizing work were conceived for manual labor and were first widely implemented in manufacturing; therefore most sociological work on routinization has been based on studies of this sector (e.g., Blauner 1964; Burawoy 1979; Sabel 1982). As the clerical work force grew in importance, the principles of routinization were applied to what had been considered "brain work," transforming some clerical functions into rote manual tasks and reducing the scope, variety, and opportunity for decision making in many jobs (see Braverman 1974; Garson 1975; Glenn and Feldberg 1979a; Mills 1951). In recent years the service sector has come increasingly to dominate the U.S. economy (Mills 1986; Noyelle 1987; Smith 1984), and the routinization of jobs that require workers to interact directly with customers or clients—what I call "interactive service work"—has been expanding as well, challenging

1

employers to find ways to rationalize[1] workers' self-presentation and feelings as well as their behavior. As routinization spills over the boundaries of organizations to include customers as well as employees, employers' strategies for controlling work affect not only workers but the culture at large.

Although many of the rationales, techniques, and outcomes associated with routinizing other kinds of work are applicable to interactive service work, the presence of customers or clients complicates the routinization process considerably. When people are the raw materials of the work process, it is difficult to guarantee the predictability of conditions necessary for routinization. Organizations attempting routinization must try to standardize the behavior of nonemployees to some extent in order to make such routinization possible (see Mills 1986). It is part of the labor process of many interactive service workers to induce customers and clients to behave in ways that will not interfere with the smooth operation of work routines.

In addition to the issues of deskilling, autonomy, and power already associated with work routinization, the routinization of interactive service work raises questions about personal identity and authenticity. In this sort of work there are no clear distinctions among the product being sold, the work process, and the worker. Employers of interactive service workers may therefore claim authority over many more aspects of workers' lives than other kinds of employers do, seeking to regulate workers' appearance, moods, demeanors, and attitudes. But even when management makes relatively little effort to reshape the workers, interactive service workers and their customers or clients must negotiate interactions in which elements of manipulation, ritual, and genuine social exchange are subtly mixed.

Routinized interactive service work thus involves working on people in two senses. The workers work on the people who are their raw materials, including themselves, and the organizations work on their employees. These processes can be problematic, both practically and morally. This book explores these practical difficulties and moral and psychological stresses through case studies of two

1. Here, as in Max Weber's work, "rationalization" means the use of abstract rules and precise calculations to organize social action to meet given ends.

2. For managerial views on the distinctive features of interactive service work, see, e.g., Lovelock 1988; McCallum and Harrison 1985; Normann 1984.

organizations that have taken the routinization of interactive service work to extremes, McDonald's and Combined Insurance.

ROUTINES AND RESISTANCE

The literature on work routinization is centrally concerned with the relative power of employers and workers. Braverman's influential account of work routinization as a process of deskilling (1974) presents the struggle for control in its starkest terms. When workers rather than employers are most knowledgeable about how best to accomplish tasks, management does not have absolute control over the work process: how long tasks take; how many people are required to do a job; how much work can reasonably be completed in one shift. When management determines exactly how every task is to be done, it loses much of its dependence on the cooperation and good faith of workers and can impose its own rules about pace, output, quality, and technique. Moreover, since the removal of skill from jobs makes workers increasingly interchangeable, management's power to dictate wages, hours, and working conditions is expanded.

Among the most serious criticisms of Braverman's account is that it overstates the capacity of management to get its own way (Friedman 1977; Littler 1990; Thompson 1989). Historical and sociological research has documented the capacity of workers acting individually and collectively to resist managerial plans in ways that affect how routinization is implemented or even undermine it altogether (e.g., Edwards 1979; Halle 1984; Montgomery 1979; Paules 1991). The amended picture depicts workplaces in which the interests of workers and employers are, almost invariably, directly at odds, with outcomes determined by the resources each group has at its disposal in the struggle for control.

This revised account is still inadequate, however, for understanding interactive service work. There, the basic dynamic of labor and management struggling for control over the work process is complicated by the direct involvement of service-recipients: customers or clients, respondents or patients, prospects or passengers.[3] All three parties are trying to arrange the interactions to their own advantage,

---

3. There is no commonly used term for the nonemployees involved in service interactions. I will frequently use the inelegant term "service-recipients" for this generic category, since, unlike "customers" or "clients," it can include people involved in noncommercial or nonvoluntary interactions. It is not an ideal term,

whether they want to maximize speed, convenience, pleasantness, efficiency, customization of service, degree of exertion, or any other outcome they feel to be beneficial. And in many instances the interests of workers are at odds with those of management. Telephone companies want each operator to handle as many calls as possible, while operators prefer a less harried pace; employers insist that the customer is always right, while workers who deal with the public want to defend their own dignity when faced with customers who behave outrageously. In other circumstances, however, workers' and management's common goals, especially their mutual interest in exerting control over service-recipients, are at least as salient as their differences.[4] For example, commission salespeople are as eager to maximize sales as their bosses are, and nurses and other medical workers want patients to cooperate with hospital regimens. Whether workers ally themselves primarily with service-recipients or with management in a given situation depends on the type of service being rendered, the design of the service system, and the preferences of those involved.

This variability suggests that we need a more nuanced understanding of the meanings of routines for workers than the sociological literature provides. There is a high degree of consensus among analysts on how routinization affects workers: it oppresses them. It robs their work of interest and variety, it eliminates the opportunity for workers to use and develop their capacities by solving problems and making decisions, and it prevents them from deriving self-worth, meaning, or deep satisfaction from work by detaching it from workers' wills (see, e.g., Braverman 1974; Garson 1975, 1988). Routinizing interactive service work seems to extend this oppression to deeper levels. Hochschild (1983) has shown in the case of flight attendants how regulating what she calls "emotion work" legitimizes employers' intervention in the very thought processes and emotional reactions of workers, alienating workers from their feelings, their faces, and their moods.

---

however, since some types of participants, such as survey respondents, do not receive any service.

4. The point is, not that the contradiction between the interests of workers and management under capitalism disappears under some circumstances, but merely that in a given work process both parties may have interests that are served by a similar outcome.

The heroes of the historical and sociological literature on routinization are the workers who resist, those who do not allow the "time-study man" to observe them (Montgomery 1979: 115), who refuse to smile (Hochschild 1983), or who insist on their right to their own style (Benson 1986). The literature seems to assume that those who do not resist are nevertheless discontented. It is true that some workers report themselves to be satisfied with their tightly scripted jobs, even to enjoy them. Such workers, a theoretical embarrassment to critics of routinization, can be understood in two ways. One possibility is that management has succeeded in duping them, perhaps by leading them to value the limited rewards available to them, perhaps by persuading them to accept at face value managerial schemes that merely give the appearance of choice or influence to workers (Howard 1985). The other is that the workers' satisfaction reflects the absence of an alternative model or vision of what work can be, a void which leaves workers with no basis for comparison that would make clear how paltry are the satisfactions for which they have settled (Mills 1951).

Rather than assuming that workers who do not resist routines are either miserable or duped, it would seem more fruitful to consider whether there are circumstances in which routines, even imposed routines, can be useful to workers. In the case of interactive service workers, this question is closely tied to how the interests of the three parties to the service interactions—workers, management, service-recipients—are aligned. Workers have good reason to embrace any imposed routines they see as expanding their ability to control service interactions. The insurance agents I studied, for example, believed that their routines gave them power in sales encounters and helped maximize their sales commissions. When workers do not see the routines as enhancing control over service-recipients, they are more likely to resist standardization, as did many of the fast-food workers I studied. Some, however, accepted and even welcomed tight scripting, for, in addition to sparing them some kinds of effort and clarifying the standards for good work, the routines could act as shields against the insults and indignities these workers were asked to accept from the public.

Although the presence of service-recipients can provide a motivation for workers to cooperate with routinization, managers of interactive service workers are not necessarily more successful than other types of managers in seeing that the work is done according to their designs. Even when workers do their best to implement routines as management would like, there is no guarantee that service-recipients will do the same. A major feature distinguishing routinized interactive service work from other kinds of routinized work is the requirement that the behavior of nonemployees be standardized to some extent. In some circumstances service-recipients do their best to fit smoothly into routines, perhaps because they believe that doing so is the surest way for them to get the service they want, perhaps because they feel they have little choice. Some service-recipients, however, resist routines.

Resistance is especially likely when the service-recipients have not chosen to become involved in the interaction (as in many types of sales), but it is also common when the service-recipients do not believe that compliance will get them the outcome they want, either because they think the routine is badly designed or ill-suited to the circumstances, or because they want customized service. Even cooperative service-recipients can inadvertently upset routines if they are unable to understand how the routine is supposed to work, if they are unable to play their part correctly, or if the routine is ill-suited to their situation. The workers of both McDonald's and Combined Insurance dealt with some service-recipients who were cooperative and some who were not, but their typical experiences differed sharply. The counter workers dealt exclusively with people who had already decided to do business with McDonald's, most of whom were very familiar with the service routine and wanted to play their parts smoothly. The insurance agents called on "prospects," many of whom would have preferred to be left alone and some of whom made clear that they did not want the service interaction to proceed at all.

In any setting, whether service-recipients are more eager than workers to see that the routine is followed correctly or are motivated to keep the workers from carrying out the routine at all, their behavior is never entirely predictable. Organizations have a variety of means of standardizing service-recipients' actions. Cues in the setting, printed directions, and taken-for-granted norms may provide sufficient order, since tailoring behavior to meet the needs of anonymous, bureaucratic organizations is a common enough experience for most adults in the United States. When the task is more difficult or the service-recipients more recalcitrant, it is likely to be up to interactive service workers to guide or pressure them to behave in organizationally convenient ways. As Stinchcombe (1990a) has noted, "ethnomethodological competence," the capacity to make use of unspoken norms of behavior to control interactions, is an occupational qualification for many jobs. By scripting interactions, employers can try to limit their reliance on the ethnomethodological competence of their workers.[5] The routines of Combined's agents were expressly designed to give the agents control over the sales interactions, showing them how to use words, gestures, and demeanors to overcome resistance. At McDonald's, in contrast, the routines were intended to constrain the workers more than the customers. While these two sets of workers had different organizational weapons at their disposal, both had to face some service-recipients who seemed intent on thwarting the routines or on interfering with the workers' preferences about how to proceed.

Interactive service workers are located on the boundaries of organizations, where they must mediate between the organization and outsiders. They have to try, simultaneously, to meet their employer's requirements, to satisfy the demands of service-recipients, and to minimize their own discomfort (see Glenn and Feldberg 1979b; Lipsky 1980; Prottas 1979). Corporate spokespeople, employee trainers, and other professional cheerleaders frequently make the case that the interests of the three groups are harmonious, since all benefit from efficient and amicable service interactions. In fact, though, there is a great deal of variation in how closely the preferences of the three parties are aligned. The degree of congruity of interests determines much of the character of an interactive service job: its degree of difficulty, the nature of jobholders' incentives and disincentives, and the quality of relations between workers and service-recipients.

The rules set down by management often require that interactive service workers displease service-recipients, either because the routine does not allow workers the flexibility to meet customers' requests, because the service-recipient does not want to participate in the interaction at all, or because the logic of the routine runs counter to interactive norms. Service-recipients can become frustrated by their inability to get what they want, and they may perceive the workers as pushy, unresponsive, stupid, or robot-like. In

---

5. Problems arise, however, when strict routinization prevents workers from using the ethnomethodological competence they already have.

any case, even if the dissatisfaction felt by the service-recipient is attributable to the rules set down by the employer, it is likely to be experienced by the service-recipient as the fault of the worker, and it is the worker who has to deal with the problem. Interactive service workers thus serve as buffers, absorbing the hostilities consumers feel when organizational routines do not meet their needs or expectations (Glenn and Feldberg 1979b: 12–13).

In interactive service work, as in other kinds of work, understanding employers' designs for routinization is only the first step in understanding how the routines function in practice. We must also examine how employers try to persuade or coerce the relevant actors (in this case, service-recipients as well as workers) to cooperate and how the behavior of these actors, and other contingencies, alter the routines in action. In interactive service work, the patterns of shared and opposed preferences among the three parties to the interactions are crucial determinants of the outcomes, including the degree to which workers and service-recipients resist organizational attempts to standardize their behavior.

ROUTINE INDIVIDUALITY

In speaking of workers and service-recipients acting on their preferences, I do not mean to imply that they are necessarily guided by conscious decisions about how to maximize material interests. Among the greatest obstacles to successful routinization of interactive service work, and among the most troubling difficulties it raises for participants, are tensions between the self-conceptions of service-recipients and workers and the ways they are treated and are called upon to treat others. The practices of routinization call into question taken-for-granted norms about social interaction and deeply felt beliefs about authenticity, individuality, and personal integrity. Not only does the routinization of interactive service work complicate the problems of alienation traditionally associated with the elimination of self-direction from work, but it alters cultural understandings of acceptable conduct toward others and manipulation of self.

Employers who routinize interactive service work seek to legitimate intervention into areas of workers' lives usually considered to be the prerogative of individual decision-making or to comprise aspects of individual character and personality. Employers may try to specify exactly how workers look, exactly what they say, their demeanors, their gestures, their moods, even their thoughts. The means available for standardizing interactions include scripting; uniforms or detailed dress codes; rules and guidelines for dealing with service-recipients and sometimes with co-workers; instruction in how best to think about the work, the service-recipients, and oneself; and manipulation of values and attitudes through consciously constructed corporate cultures and through training programs that provide indoctrination. Surveillance and a range of incentives and disincentives can be used to encourage or enforce compliance (see, e.g., Albrecht and Zemke 1985; Biggart 1989; Fuller and Smith 1991; Hochschild 1983; Howard 1985; Van Maanen and Kunda 1989).[6]

The routinization of human interactions is undoubtedly disconcerting, and reports or satires of the latest instances are common in popular culture. *Harper's*, for instance, regularly documents examples of routinization in both commercial and private life. The sources of these reports are varied, and the routines were designed to serve a broad range of purposes, which are not always the purposes of those to whom the standardization is applied. The script for operators of a New York phone-sex service, for instance, specifies that they tell callers whose time is up, "Sorry, tiger, but your Dream Girl has to go. . . . Call right back and ask for me" (December 1990: 26). A letter-writing kit for military personnel provides parents with a monthly schedule of sample topics and messages for letters to their children, such as these ideas for January: "Tell about your coldest day. Draw your favorite snowman's face. P.S.: 'Keep warm!'" (May 1991: 28). The guidelines on personal appearance for employees of Walt Disney World include the dictum, "Fingernails should not extend more than one-fourth of an inch beyond the fingertips" (June 1990: 40). Managers who are not sufficiently wily by nature can consult a pamphlet on how to inspire fear with "power strategies based on the unknown," such as inquiring, "Wasn't that tried someplace else, where it flopped?" (March 1991: 24). Timid people uncomfortable with mingling can turn to the section on "Great Opening Lines" in *How to Work a Room* for such suggestions as "Are you

---

6. Since disgruntled interactive service workers are often well-situated to sabotage organizational objectives through their treatment of service-recipients (see Benson 1986; Fuller and Smith 1991), their employers may be more inclined than others to court workers' consent using persuasion, indoctrination, and incentives rather than to enforce standardization through coercion.

alone by choice or by chance?" (January 1990: 26). And tongue-tied lovers with no Cyrano to do their wooing may subscribe to a romantic monthly letter-writing service, so that they need only insert the name of their beloved in the prepared text that begins "My dearest, sweetest F3" (February 1989: 26).[7] *Harper's* prints these texts without interpretation or comment, other than droll headlines such as "The Relationship Is in the Mail" and "The One-Minute Machiavelli." Whether readers are amused or appalled, they will presumably see something ludicrous in the excerpts. Collectively, these excerpts tell us that no detail is too trivial, no relationship too personal, no experience too individual, no manipulation too cynical for some organization or person, in a spirit of helpfulness or efficiency, to try to provide a standard, replicable routine for it.

These scripts and instructions make various kinds of assumptions, some more morally problematic than others, about the actor and the target audience, but they raise interconnected questions about the status of the self and the treatment to which others are entitled. When scripts and rules of self-presentation are imposed on workers, the questions concern the relative boundaries of legitimate employer intervention and worker autonomy and privacy. Disney World employees are asked to fit themselves to a corporate image that has been specified down to the fingernails. The phone-sex operators are not strictly limited to scripted conversation, but they have to manage to combine expression of erotic interest and involvement with attention to profit maximization and bureaucratic details of time-keeping. They, like virtually all followers of scripts, have to dissemble. So do people who choose to use scripts in personal or professional life for mingling, letter-writing, or corporate game-playing. This acting, whether it involves the simulation of a feeling that is entirely absent or merely the pretense that the expression of an emotion is spontaneous, involves a degree of emotional self-management and a willingness to be less than straightforward with the intended audience.

7. The original sources for these excerpts are: training manual for operators of 970-LIVE, a phone-sex service in New York City; the instruction booklet for the Military Edition of The Write Connection Program, created by Positive Parenting of Phoenix, Arizona, at the request of the U.S. Navy; "The Disney Look," guidebook for employees of Walt Disney World; Susan RoAne, *How to Work a Room: A Guide to Successfully Managing the Mingling* (New York: Shapolsky Publishers, 1988), 89; "The Office Manager's Handbook of People Power Strategies," pamphlet published by Prentice Hall Professional Newsletters, Englewood, N.J.; letter mailed to subscribers of Incurable Romantics, New York, 1988.

The deception of the audience is sometimes completely self-interested (the "power strategies"), but it may be intended generously (the letters to children). The fact of the scripting or emotion work need not always be hidden. The phone-sex callers, we may assume, are aware that their Dream Girls are acting as part of their job, although to get the most out of the service the callers may persuade themselves otherwise. In other circumstances the script works only if the audience is persuaded that the interaction is not planned, manipulative, or routine at all, as in the display to a loved one of apparently spontaneous and sincere feelings. Almost all scripting of interactions, regardless of motive and degree of deception, is based on some unflattering premises about the intended audience. Routinization assumes that people are largely interchangeable, that they are not deserving of sincerity, possibly that they can easily be duped, assumptions that are more offensive in some contexts than others.

Since the targets of scripted exchanges are also participants, they must decide what stance to take in response. When the scripting is obvious, they can choose to play along or not, perhaps withdrawing their participation, perhaps trying to make contact with the actor instead of the role, perhaps judging the skill of the performance. They may not mind the scripting—the carefully rehearsed mingler may sound stilted to the listener, but who doesn't in such situations?—or they may take offense—"Does he expect me to fall for that line?" Service-recipients may appreciate routinization if they feel that it offers reliable service, relieves them from the obligation to provide any emotional investment in the interaction, or ensures equitable treatment to all.

However, in many cases service-recipients resent being treated as interchangeable. They are more concerned with satisfaction than with equity, and they want to feel that they are engaged in a real conversation with a real person who listens to them. As Roman (1979: 15) warns in a book on telemarketing:

> Paradoxically, as the consumer has become part of a conditioned mass market, he or she has also become more demanding in insisting on being regarded as a unique individual whose own special personal needs must be attended to.

It is indeed a challenge to construct scripts for dealing with someone who "regards himself as a highly special individual and will react favorably only to those who treat him as such" (Roman 1979: 15), but employers have gamely sought ways to graft personalizing touches onto standard interactions. In such cases, part of the employees' work is likely to be sugar-coating or concealing the routinization.

When the service-recipient has any doubt about the spontaneity or uniqueness of the interaction, choosing a response can be tricky. If one assumes sincerity and responds accordingly, there is the danger of being a trusting fool, allowing oneself to be manipulated. Suspicion and aloofness, on the other hand, cut one off from potentially gratifying human contact. Responding in kind to surface cues despite recognition that the situation is contrived, an interim strategy, is problematic as well. It signals acceptance of the terms of the interaction although one might in fact resent them.

And what about the actors themselves? What does participation in routinized interactions do to their sense of self? Employers who manage the self-presentations and emotions of employees are aware that they must pay attention to the relation between the workers' self-conceptions and their behavior on the job. While airlines try to get their flight attendants to throw themselves fully into the cheerful, solicitous, unresentful persona assigned to them (Hochschild 1983), the employers of the phone-sex operators are apparently conscious that role distance (Goffman 1961b) can provide protection from any demeaning implications of fulfilling others' fantasies. "Remember," they counsel in the "Professionalism" section of the employee manual, "you are not your character on the phone" (*Harper's*, December 1990: 27).

Sociologists need not believe in the existence of unmediated emotional responses or of an inviolate individual with a stable core of self in order to recognize that participation in routinized interactions presents dilemmas of identity. When such participation is a condition of employment, as it is for many interactive service workers, these dilemmas are everyday concerns.

First, there is the problem of managing the disjunction between actions and feelings. Hochschild (1983: 7) argues that workers whose emotions are managed by their employers become alienated from their feelings in a process parallel to that described by Marx of the alienation of proletarians from the actions of their bodies and the products of their labor. These workers thus have difficulty experiencing themselves as authentic even off the job, for they lose track of which feelings are their own. As Wharton and Erickson (1990: 21) argue, "An essential facet of experiencing one's self as real is the congruence between action and self-feeling regarding that action." How able are workers to maintain a sense of self when their actions do not reflect their feelings, or when their feelings are manipulated to produce the desired effect?

Second, there is the question of the content of the routinized behavior, the ways the worker is required to act. Some workers' routines call upon them to take on characteristics they may value, such as patience, good cheer, or self-confidence, but in other cases the required behavior is more problematic. Because we read character from actions, workers who must behave in ways they ordinarily would not somehow have to reconcile the contradictions between their self-conception and their behavior. Can they manipulate people without thinking of themselves as underhanded and disrespectful? Can they stifle their ordinary responses without thinking of themselves as doormats? The problem of detaching oneself from the implications of work behavior is not unique to interactive service workers whose jobs have been routinized. All interactive service workers—salespeople, clergy, teachers, doctors, waitresses, and so on—face similar tensions, whether or not their jobs are scripted and standardized. But routinization calls attention to the inauthenticity, thus heightening the discordance between workers' self-identities and the identities they enact at work.

Problems of identity are raised by how interactive service workers are treated as well as by how they behave, and routinization can shape the interactive style of service-recipients. Sociologists do not generally hold that identity can be created and maintained autonomously. As Cooley's idea of the "looking glass self" (1902) and Mead's elaboration of the sources of self in interaction (1934) convey, people's self-conceptions are shaped by the treatment they are accorded. A sense of self is formed in childhood, but throughout life it remains vulnerable to messages from others. If car salespeople are treated with suspicion (Lawson 1991), phone solicitors with rudeness, restaurant servers with condescension or familiarity, domestic servants as non-people (Rollins 1985), how will they react? Certainly they need not accept the implied judgment of the service-recipients. But they must construct some means of defending themselves from demeaning treatment or some account that allows them to accept such treatment without thinking of themselves as demeaned. Hochschild (1983) stresses the difficulties of protecting oneself from the implications of treatment on the job, but Hughes

(1984 [1970]) and Rollins (1985) show how "the humble" can salvage a sense of control and self-esteem or even construe themselves as superior to "the proud." My account acknowledges both workers' agency in interpreting their own behavior and the treatment they receive from others, and the constraints that the conditions of employment set on the possible range of workers' interpretations and responses.

Routines may actually offer interactive service workers some protection from assaults on their selves. Where workers are often exposed to rude, insulting, or depersonalizing treatment from service-recipients, routines can make that treatment easier to bear. Workers who follow scripts need not feel that they are being personally attacked when they are subjected to slammed phones, nasty comments, or tirades about poor service. Employers often provide training in how to think about and respond to poor treatment. Philadelphia's parking authority workers, for example, receive instruction on how to react to being spit on by people angry at receiving a ticket (Matza 1990: 19).

Whether or not workers appreciate all or some aspects of routinization, they have available a range of possible responses to it. They may reshape their self-concept to fit what they see as a positive new identity (see Biggart 1989 on direct sales workers); hold on to their own identity but set it aside at work, where they assume a new "situational identit[y]" (Van Maanen and Kunda 1989: 68); try to alter or vary the routine to reflect their own will and personality; distance themselves from the work role by willing "emotional numbness" (Van Maanen and Kunda 1989: 69); or interpret their own behavior and the treatment they receive in ways that are positive or at least neutral. Which of these responses are used depends not only on the workers' personal characteristics but also on the nature of the service interactions designed by their employers. Almost inevitably, however, their jobs require them to take an instrumental approach to their own identity and to relations with others.

THE RESEARCH

I did not choose to study McDonald's and Combined Insurance because I thought they were typical interactive service organizations. Rather, both companies took routinization to an extreme, and I was interested in examining how far working on people could be pushed. I believed that extreme cases would best illuminate the kinds of tensions and problems that routinizing human interactions creates, and that a study of long-established and successful companies would provide clues to the attractions of routinization and the means by which managers can overcome the difficulties of standardizing workers and service-recipients.

Although these two companies both pushed routinization almost to its logical limits, their public-contact employees did very different kinds of work and had different kinds of relations with service-recipients. The companies therefore adopted dissimilar approaches to routinization, with distinctive ramifications for workers and service-recipients. McDonald's took a classic approach to routinization, making virtually all decisions about how work would be conducted in advance and imposing them on workers. Since Combined's sales agents worked on their own and faced a broader range of responses than McDonald's workers did, their company had to allow them some decision-making scope. It did create routines that were as detailed as possible, but it pushed the limits of routinization in another direction, extending it to many aspects of workers' selves both on and off the job. It aimed to make a permanent, overall change in the ways its agents thought about themselves and went about their lives.

At each company, I collected information through interviewing and participant-observation. I examined routinization at two levels. First, I learned as much as I could about the company's goals and strategies for routinization by attending corporate training programs and interviewing executives. Next, I explored how the routines worked out in practice by doing or observing the work and by interviewing interactive service workers.

At both McDonald's and Combined Insurance I received official permission to do my research. The managers I interviewed, the trainees I accompanied through classes, and the workers I interviewed, observed, and worked with were all aware that I was conducting a study and that my project had been approved by higher levels of management.[8] The customers I served and observed were the only participants who did not know that I was collecting data.

I carried out my research at McDonald's in the spring through

---

8. Pseudonyms are used throughout the text, except for top-level officials of McDonald's and Combined Insurance.

fall of 1986. I began by attending management training classes at corporate headquarters. Next, managers at the regional office arranged my placement at a franchise that was apparently chosen largely on the basis of its convenience for me. The manager of the franchise arranged for me to be trained to serve customers; once trained, I worked without pay for half a dozen shifts, or a total of about twenty-eight hours of work. I then conducted structured interviews with workers who served customers, obtaining twenty-three complete interviews, as well as several that were incomplete for a variety of reasons. I also spent long hours hanging around in the crew room, where I talked informally with workers, including those not in customer-service jobs, and listened as workers talked with each other about their job experiences and their reactions to those experiences. I supplemented the participant-observation and worker interviews with interviews or informal talks with most of the franchise managers and its owner, with management trainers, with a former McDonald's executive who had been in charge of employee research, and with numerous former employees and current customers of McDonald's.

Most of my research at Combined Insurance was conducted in the winter and spring of 1987. I received permission to study the work of its life-insurance agents and was assigned a place in a training class. When the two-week training period ended I was put in touch with a regional sales manager who arranged for me to work with a sales team. (See Chapter 4 for a discussion of ways this team may have been atypical.) Because one must be licensed to sell insurance, I did not actually do the agent's job, but I spent a week and a half in the field with the sales team, going out on sales calls with each of its members in turn. Since these daily rounds included a lot of time spent driving from one prospective customer to another, I had ample opportunity for informal interviews with the agents. I also conducted a formal interview with the sales manager, and I attended an evening team training meeting and two morning team meetings, one of which was attended by the district manager. In addition, I interviewed several Combined Insurance executives, including a vice president in charge of introducing a new sales presentation, a regional sales manager, the director of market research and one of his assistants, and a manager responsible for developing sales routines and materials.

In the summer of 1989, I conducted follow-up interviews at

Combined Insurance to learn about major changes the company had made in its life insurance products and sales approach. I reinterviewed the director of market research and the man who had been the regional sales manager but who now was responsible for overseeing one-half of the company's life-insurance agents. I also interviewed two regional sales managers, one the man who now managed the region where the sales team I had studied was located, and one located in a part of the country where the new sales system had been introduced more recently. The follow-up research allowed me to learn about the subsequent careers of the agents I had known and, more important, to find out how the agents' jobs and the company's results had changed under the new sales system.[9]

I supplemented my research at these two companies by gathering information on other kinds of interactive service work through interviews, site visits, and examination of employee scripts. I visited a Burger King training facility and interviewed a training manager there; I interviewed an executive from Hyatt Hotels and attended an orientation session for Hyatt workers; and I interviewed people who worked, or had worked, as an AT&T customer service representative, a waitress, a door-to-door canvasser, and a psychologist.[10]

OVERVIEW

Chapter 2 lays out the main obstacles to routinizing interactive service work and the strategies organizations have employed to try to overcome them. One obstacle arises from the difficulty of defining quality in the provision of services. Routinization is intended to ensure consistency in the quality of work, but, as Garson (1988: 60) asks, "Is a more uniform conversation a positive good?" Can consistency be equated with high quality? Since workers cannot be separated from products in interactive service work, the question next arises: how much intervention in workers' lives is justifiable in order to ensure a uniform appearance, attitude, and work process?

A separate problem is that the raw materials of interactive service work, people, are never entirely predictable, and routinization makes sense only if stable conditions of work can be guaranteed. Given the intrinsic fluidity, negotiability, and indexicality of interaction

9. See Appendix 2.
10. For further details of the research process, see Appendix 1.

(see Prus 1989a), how can prepared scripts replace flexible individual response? A service interaction must work on two levels: as a work process with a specific goal, and as a human interaction. The danger in routinizing human interactions is that if workers do not, or are not allowed to, respond flexibly, form may come to supersede meaning, thus increasing the likelihood of failure on both levels. In other words, rigid routines strictly enforced can actually prevent workers from doing an adequate job, harming both customer satisfaction and employee morale (Koepp 1987b; Normann 1984).

Employers have responded to these dilemmas in several ways, as I show in Chapter 2. First, they employ a variety of strategies intended to reduce the unpredictability of work specifications by standardizing the behavior of service-recipients. Second, they try to overcome resistance to mass-produced service by finding ways to personalize routines, or to seem to personalize them. Finally, in circumstances where too much unpredictability remains to make it possible to dispense with worker flexibility, employers may use a strategy I call "routinization by transformation," which is intended to change workers into the kinds of people who will make decisions that management would approve. Chapter 2 concludes with a discussion of how managers' and workers' efforts to control interactive work processes are complicated by the participation of service-recipients.

Chapters 3 and 4 provide descriptions and analyses of how McDonald's and Combined Insurance, respectively, go about routinizing the work of employees who deal with the public. Each chapter gives an overview of the company, describes its training process in detail, and examines how the routines work out in practice, noting how actual working conditions and procedures compared to the companies' stated policies and goals.

The processes of routinization at McDonald's and Combined Insurance were similar in many ways, despite the dissimilarity of their products and organizations. Both companies were faced with the two basic challenges of routinizing interactive service work: to standardize the behavior of employees, and to control the behavior of customers. Both companies paid close attention to how their workers looked, spoke, and felt, rather than limiting standardization to the performance of physical tasks. Emotion work was an integral part of serving McDonald's food and selling Combined's insurance, and smiling was a job requirement shared by the food-service workers and the insurance agents. Both groups were expected to behave deferentially and to try to please their customers.

Nevertheless, the jobs were dissimilar enough to allow a comparison of differing approaches to routinization practicable in different circumstances. Some of the major distinctions between the two cases were the extent of efforts to affect workers' personalities, the gender of the workers, and the degree of supervision. Moreover, the companies' routines varied greatly in scope and content, since interactions at McDonald's are briefer and less dependent on workers' initiative than insurance sales calls. Many of the differences between the two jobs stemmed from differences in the predictability of service-recipients' behavior and demands. This variable influenced the complexity of the work routines and the nature of the relations between workers and service-recipients. Where the behavior of service-recipients is relatively unpredictable, interactive service workers may be responsible for getting them to cooperate, as was the case at Combined Insurance.

Mills regards customers as subordinates of service providers (1986: 121), but the extent to which they were experienced as such varied greatly in these cases. Both the food-service workers and the insurance agents had to sell and to serve, but their jobs differed in the emphasis placed on each. Service-recipients therefore played very different roles in the interactions. At McDonald's the work was done for them, while at Combined Insurance the work seemed to be done to them. Variation in the nature of the worker-customer relation helps explain several important differences between the two cases, including differences in the types of attitudes workers were expected to cultivate, the range of personal qualities subject to standardization, the scope of decision making left in the job, and workers' reactions to routinization.

As Chapter 5 shows, the two cases also differed markedly in how the interests of managers, workers, and service-recipients were aligned. These variations were determined in part by managers' decisions about how to set up routines, how to compensate workers, and how to balance customer satisfaction with efficiency and profitability. Both companies tried to ensure that the workers would take the customers' interests as their own, while defining the customers' interests in ways that were organizationally convenient, but the degree to which the three parties actually shared interests varied. At McDonald's, customers and managers generally had similar preferences about how the interactions were to proceed, which limited the workers' range of action. Combined's agents and management, by contrast, shared an interest in controlling prospective customers in order to maximize sales. For this reason, Combined's agents' routines enhanced their power over customers, while McDonald's workers' limited theirs. In each setting, however, there were many specific situations in which the interests of the three parties parted from these general patterns, and these shifting stakes helped determine the outcomes of the carefully planned routines imposed by management. Chapter 5 documents how those routines worked out in practice.

Throughout the book, the relevant contrasts are not only those between these two jobs, but also those between routinized interactive service work and other kinds of routinized work, and those between routinized service interactions and nonroutinized interactions. The special character of routinized interactive service work is the focus of Chapter 6, which examines the ramifications of routinization for authenticity and identity, including gender identity. I discuss the dilemmas raised for workers' sense of themselves and the range of workers' responses to routinization. These responses varied both between the two companies and, especially at McDonald's, within the company. In each setting, some workers resisted in various ways the identities imposed on them, and others embraced the routines and willingly took on the persona prepared for them by the company.

The degree to which workers can benefit from embracing routines depends largely on the kinds of relations among workers, managers, and service-recipients that routines set up. How particular individuals weigh the benefits and drawbacks of the routines and how they respond to them is more complicated. The meanings workers assign to their own behavior at work and to that of the managers and service-recipients they work with are to some degree fluid and indeterminate. Workers interpret actions, their own and others', and the interpretations they construct, often with the guidance and influence of their employers and their peers, can heighten or mitigate dissatisfaction, allow for some satisfactions and close off others, and lead workers to evade or to embrace their imposed routines.

To underline the importance of interpretation in shaping workers' responses to their jobs, Chapter 6 provides an extended analysis of the construction of gender meanings in the two jobs. I show that when jobs are segregated by gender, workers can interpret similar job characteristics as suitable either for men or for women, as they try to make sense of the existing pattern of employment or to bolster their sense of entitlement to the job. Despite the scripting of their words and actions, both they and the public can interpret workers' behavior as expressing preexisting gender differences that account for the gendered division of labor.

The concluding chapter draws out the implications of routinizing service interactions, arguing that employers who standardize these labor processes exert a cultural influence that extends beyond the workplace. Their organizational control strategies reach deeply into the lives of workers, encouraging them to take an instrumental stance toward their own personalities and toward other people. Moreover, service routines subject people who are not employees of service organizations to organizational efforts to standardize their behavior. Through participation in encounters that violate the norms of social interaction even as they exploit those norms, service-recipients learn not to take for granted that the ground rules that govern interaction will be respected. As they adjust their expectations and behavior accordingly, the ceremonial forms that bolster individual identity (Goffman 1956) and social cohesion (Durkheim 1965 [1915]) tend to be treated as indulgences rather than obligations.

My analysis of interactive service work addresses several shortcomings of the literature on work and routinization. Sociologists of work have not kept pace with the rapid shift of jobs out of manufacturing. Despite some excellent studies of service jobs (e.g., Biggart 1989; Hochschild 1983), generalizations about work under capitalism have not been recast to encompass interactive service work. The enormous increase in the proportion of the labor force engaged in service occupations is widely acknowledged, but models derived from industrial work continue to guide the thinking and research of theorists of the labor process.[11] In these models, workers and

---

11. Braverman (1974) set the pattern. He acknowledged the significance of the rise in service employment but stressed similarities in how manufacturing, clerical, and service jobs have been organized to deskill workers. Although many defects in his analysis have been identified and corrected by subsequent writers (e.g., Burawoy 1979; Edwards 1979; Littler and Salaman 1982), Braverman's emphasis on the general attributes of labor under capitalism and the common features of work in different settings still characterizes much discussion in this field. Two recent reconsiderations of labor-process theory (Knights and Willmott 1990;

capitalists (or managers) are the relevant parties, the creation and
sale of a product is the focus of analysis, and workers' attitudes
and emotions are relevant only insofar as they affect willingness
to accept the conditions of work. When these models are applied to
interactive service work, we find that some of the basic analytic distinctions fit awkwardly at best and that important areas of inquiry
are overlooked. The role of service-recipients in the labor process is
not analogous to that of either workers or managers, for example,
and the manipulation of participants' selves cannot be satisfactorily
analyzed as a form of deskilling.[12]

My approach to analyzing routinization takes from the labor-
process tradition its emphases on concrete work practices and on
issues of control and autonomy. Early work in that tradition has been
criticized for overstating employers' success in imposing work
routines and for assuming that these routines necessarily serve the
goals management intended (see Littler 1990). Such oversimplifica-
tions are untenable when applied to interactive service work, where
not only workers but service-recipients vie with management in a
three-way contest for control and satisfaction. My analysis highlights the various means by which each party tries to exert control
and the shifting patterns of alliance among them, allowing for a
relatively fine-grained consideration of outcomes. In sharp contrast
to the traditional picture of routinization, my analysis shows that,
in some situations, service routines provide workers and service-
recipients with benefits that help account for their frequent acquies-
cence in managerial designs.

A major shortcoming of labor-process theory is its unsatisfactory

---

Thompson 1989) fail to explore the theoretical difficulties raised by service work.
Noyelle's recent work (1987) generates useful propositions about service firms, but
he gives little attention to the nature of the work process or to workers' experiences.

12. Although sociologists have been slow to give full weight to the distinctive
aspects of labor processes in service jobs, the management literature on service
work has boomed. Some early work on managing services stressed the possibilities for extending industrial methods of production and assessment to service provision (e.g., Levitt 1972). Soon, however, writers advising managers
came to focus on the peculiar attributes of service work, examining such questions as how to define quality in a service, how to manage customers' expectations, and how to inspire front-line workers (Albrecht 1988; Cziepel, Solomon,
and Suprenant 1985; Heskett, Sasser, and Hart 1990; Lovelock 1988; Mills 1986;
Normann 1984). This trend suggests that controlling service work poses problems
that methods applicable to other kinds of work do not address. However, the
management literature, focusing on technique, treats a relatively narrow range
of issues.

treatment of workers' subjectivity. Braverman's work (1974) excluded this topic altogether, and subsequent theorists have too often limited it to class-consciousness and consent or resistance to oppressive structures of work (Burawoy 1979; Thompson 1989).[13] As Hochschild (1983) showed, questions of subjectivity are not separable from the analysis of actual work practices in interactive service work, since workers' identities are actively managed by employers. Hochschild emphasized the distress felt by workers subjected to organizational exploitation of their feelings and personalities, but I find that not all workers resist the extension of standardization to their inner selves. Rather, many attempt to construct interpretations of their work roles that do not damage their conceptions of themselves (cf. Hughes 1984 [1951]; 1984 [1970]).

I do not take the position that the routinization of service work and the standardization of human personality that it can entail are in fact benign, benefiting workers, customers, and companies in a happy congruence of interests. Often, these manipulations are invasive, infantilizing, exasperating, demeaning. But if we are to understand how routinization works in service jobs and what outcomes it produces, we need an account of the relations among routinization, skill, control, interaction, and self that is both more precise and more subtle than we have yet been given. These outcomes of routinization are felt throughout society as participants adjust their assumptions about the norms guiding social interaction. The study of interactive service work thus provides a bridge between the sociology of work and broader examinations of culture and society.

---

13. Knights (1990) and Willmott (1990) take on the challenge of integrating subjectivity into labor-process theory.

2

How Can Work on People Be Routinized?

Employers routinize work both to assure a uniform outcome and to make the organization less dependent on the skills of individual workers. When satisfactory outcomes can be obtained by unskilled or semi-skilled workers, the organization benefits through lower labor costs and increased managerial control (Braverman 1974). The related goals of establishing quality control and lowering the skill levels necessary to complete tasks are achieved by determining in advance exactly how each task is to be done and then instituting a system of control that persuades or coerces workers to follow the predetermined routines.

Routinization appeals to employers of interactive service workers for the same reasons that it attracts employers of manufacturing and clerical workers. The routinization of interactive service work is not a new phenomenon—the work of telephone operators, for example, was routinized by the first years of the twentieth century (Norwood 1990: 33)—but it is becoming increasingly widespread. With the rapid expansion of the service sector in the United States in the postwar period (see Albrecht and Zemke 1985; Mills 1986; Smith 1984), the cost and quality of interactive work have assumed greater significance in many organizations, making it more attractive to try to apply the principles of routinization developed for use in manufacturing work to human interactions.

In interactive service work, however, routinization cannot so readily accomplish its intended goals. When routinization is applied to human interactions, difficulties arise in creating products of uniform quality and in decreasing organizational dependence on workers' skills. As was discussed in Chapter 1, in jobs where the outcome or product of the work is not easily separable from the quality of the interaction, quality control is not a matter of standardizing products but of standardizing the workers themselves. This involves extending organizational control to aspects of the workers' selves that are usually considered matters of personal choice or judgment. Furthermore, the goal of uniformity is itself problematic in interactive work. Since good service is often equated with "personal" service, standardization may undercut quality in human interactions.

Employers become less dependent on workers' skills when they are able to prespecify exactly how the work is to be done. In interactive service work, the presence of customers or clients who are integrally involved in the work process introduces a degree of unpredictability that makes routinization difficult. Standardizing the work may be impossible unless the behavior of these nonemployees can be standardized as well.

For routinization to succeed, then, interactive service organizations must work on people—both their workers and their customers or clients—to bring their attitudes and behavior into line with organizational needs. This chapter elaborates the problems inherent in such a project and describes some of the strategies interactive service organizations use to make routinization work. '

QUALITY CONTROL IN INTERACTIVE SERVICE WORK

In manufacturing work, quality control means assuring that all of the products created meet a minimum standard. The work process and the personal characteristics of the workers are clearly distinguishable from the products they make, and quality is a property of the products. Routinizing manufacturing work involves standardizing the workers' movements so that they will most efficiently produce items that meet the organization's standards.

Almost all interactive service jobs have both an interactive and a noninteractive component. For example, fast-food servers greet customers, take orders, and collect payment (interactive work), and place orders, gather the requested items, and put them in a bag or on a tray (noninteractive work). Even work that is almost entirely interactive, such as providing psychotherapy, involves offstage noninteractive tasks such as completing forms. The process of routinizing the noninteractive components of the work differs little from the process of routinizing manufacturing or clerical jobs. Frederick Taylor's principles can be applied to assembling hamburgers as easily as to other kinds of tasks, and the quality of the products can be evaluated apart from the qualities of the workers who created them.

For the interactive parts of the work, routinization and quality control are more complicated, because the distinctions among the product or outcome of the work, the work process, and the worker may be blurred or nonexistent. In many kinds of interactive work, employers cannot introduce specifications for the products or instructions for the work processes without trying to standardize the workers themselves. If the successful completion of the work depends on how workers look, feel, and speak as well as on what they do, then employers' intervention in these matters can be justified as a legitimate interest in quality control. Chase (1978: 140–41), for example, writing in the *Harvard Business Review*, encouraged managers to think of workers' personal attributes in that light:

> Managers have long recognized the desirability of having "attractive" personnel greet the public in such job classifications as receptionist, restaurant hostess, and stewardess. . . . Any interaction with the customer makes the direct worker in fact part of the product, and therefore his attitude can affect the customer's point of view of the service provided.

There are three types of interactive service work in which the success of the work depends on the quality of the interaction, and therefore on the personal attributes of the worker. In one type, the interaction is inseparable from the product being sold or delivered— for instance, in psychotherapy, prostitution, or teaching. In the second type, a product exists apart from the interaction, but a particular type of experience is an important part of the service. For example, patrons of Playboy Clubs expected titillation and deference as well as food and drink (see Miller 1984; Steinem 1983), and airline passengers, who buy tickets primarily to get from one place to another, are promised friendly service on their journey (Hochschild 1983). Finally, in some jobs the interaction is a crucial part of the work process even though it is not part of a product being sold or provided. The success of salespeople, fund-raisers, bill collectors, and survey interviewers depends on the workers' ability to construct particular kinds of interactions.

In all of these kinds of jobs, workers' looks, attitudes, demeanors, speech, and ways of thinking can be integral to the work process and outcome. The jobs all require what Hochschild (1983) calls "emotion work," that is, the work of creating a particular emotional state in others, often by manipulating one's own feelings. Such work may be necessary because it is part of the service being sold—for example, a flight attendant is not doing her job properly if she is not smiling—or because the worker's task cannot go forward without it—a family-planning counselor may not get the information she needs unless she is perceived as nonjudgmental (Joffe 1986). To routinize the interactive parts of service jobs, including emotion work, organizations can use uniforms or other controls on personal appearance, scripts, rules about demeanor and about proper ways to treat customers or clients, and even far-reaching attempts at psychological reorientation.

Some employers routinize service delivery through rigid scripting, but leave the management of the emotional texture of the interactions to their workers.[1] Others go far beyond scripting, shaping workers' personalities, attitudes, and styles. Three factors determine whether employers choose to routinize emotion work. First, they must believe that the quality of the interaction is important to the success of the enterprise. If workers can accomplish their tasks acceptably regardless of the quality of the interactions (as can cab drivers, unlike telephone solicitors) or if the organization is assured of a steady demand for its services regardless of the quality of the interactions (as are government agencies, unlike restaurants), employers are not likely to be much concerned with establishing a consistent quality of service interaction.

Second, employers will routinize service interactions only if they think workers will be unable or unwilling to conduct the interactions appropriately on their own. If employers do not believe emotion work requires any special skills, presumably they will not routinize that part of the work. If they believe that particular kinds of personal attributes are necessary to do the work well—good looks, empathy, assertiveness—they can try to hire people who have those qualities, perhaps using such characteristics as gender and social class to judge whether proper attitudes and skills can be taken for granted. If the interactive task is more difficult or if workers with the desired attributes are unavailable or too expensive, employers may choose routinization.

Finally, the nature of the service dictates whether routinization in fact can ensure quality control. When the tasks are too complex or context-dependent to be standardized, organizations must depend on the skills of more expensive workers.

1. The survey interview project described in Appendix 1 is one example.

LIMITS TO THE ROUTINIZATION OF
INTERACTIVE SERVICE WORK

Work routines are sets of tasks that can go forward without significant decision-making on the part of either workers or higher authorities (Stinchcombe 1990b: 32–72). In highly routinized jobs, such as that of the assembly-line worker, virtually all decisions about how the work is to proceed have been made in advance. Workers each need to know only one basic routine; they do not need the broad range of knowledge and skills that would be necessary if they had to deal with unexpected circumstances. The relations among the various routines carried out by individual workers are also settled by the managers and engineers who establish in advance how the system works as a whole. Stinchcombe likens this kind of rigid routinization to batch computer processing (1990b: 35). Once it is underway, the work progresses according to predetermined decision rules, and no adjustments are made during the processing.

Stinchcombe argues that managers can prespecify work to this extent only under conditions of predictability and stability. Four main sources of instability tend to inhibit routinization: unstable markets, unstable product specifications, unstable technologies, and variable raw materials, parts, or environments (Stinchcombe 1990b: 66). It would not be worthwhile to create an inflexible system for manufacturing a particular kind of product unless there were a large and stable demand for products of that precise specification, and an inflexible routine could not work smoothly unless the technology, raw materials, and environment of the work were consistent.

More flexible systems are required when conditions are less stable, because more decisions must be made in the course of the work process. Such work may be done by skilled craft workers or professionals, who are familiar with a variety of routines and know how to choose among them according to circumstances. Alternatively, the work may be divided so that the parts of the job that are highly routinized are carried out by semi-skilled workers and decisions about which routines and subroutines to use are made by higher-level workers. Flexibility can thus be lodged either in the work of individuals or in the productive process as a system. Stinchcombe compares these sorts of work processes, where there are numerous decision-making points in the work, to interactive computing (1990b: 36). Interactive work systems are, by definition, less highly routinized than batch ones, in that not all decisions are pre-specified. These systems are better able to respond to unstable or unpredictable conditions than are batch work systems.

Service work that involves dealing with people is inherently interactive in Stinchcombe's sense. The conditions of such work are never wholly predictable, because task specifications are largely determined by the behavior, attitudes, and demands of the people who are the raw materials of interactive service work. Because of this uncertainty, we would not expect strict routinization of interactive service work to be practicable. Mills (1986: 61) goes so far as to say that:

> the tendency of organizations to reduce independent actions by their participants in order to minimize exceptional situations, as one would encounter within manufacturing organizations, is hardly meaningful within service operations in which clients/customers are actively involved.

In addition to the difficulty of predetermining how work should be done under conditions of uncertainty, employers of interactive service workers face another dilemma when they standardize human interactions. Such routinization is intended to create interactions of uniform quality, but, as was noted above, consumers may dislike uniformity in interactions. Successful routinization can establish a floor, a minimum standard, of civility and helpfulness in an organization's service interactions. This is no small accomplishment. Indeed, most consumers have been subjected to rude or incompetent service frequently enough to appreciate such a guarantee. However, customers or clients often feel resentful when it is clear that a worker is reciting lines from a script and that everyone is being treated exactly alike, not only because the routine may not be able to provide exactly what they want, but also because they experience the regimentation as dehumanizing and alienating. The phrase "Have a nice day," now a standard conclusion to service interactions in the United States, is a good example of the limits of scripting interactions. Introduced to make service interactions seem less mechanical, the phrase now often has the opposite effect. Its fatuousness and patent insincerity when delivered automatically seem symbolic of organizational efforts to sugar-coat the essential emptiness or manipulativeness of their relations with the public.

Even when the scripting of service interactions is less obvious, it can still be disquieting. Especially where emotion work is involved, service-recipients may be uncertain about the character of their interactions with service workers: are they "real" or mass-produced? For example, Hochschild (1983: 89) quotes an airline passenger's observations about flight attendants:

> When you see them receiving passengers with that big smile, I don't think it means anything. They have to do that. It's part of their job. But now if you get into a conversation with a flight attendant . . . well . . . no . . . I guess they have to do that too.

The passenger plainly believes that interactions that are not genuine—that is, sincere, spontaneous, and uncoerced—are inherently less valuable than genuine ones even if they are not conducted in a way that seems mechanical. They "don't mean anything" precisely because they are produced by organizations for their own reasons. In this case, the problem is that, to the extent that the interactions do not seem standardized, they are manipulative.

These problems suggest that uniformity is incompatible with high quality when human interactions are involved. Human interactions that are mass-produced may strike consumers as dehumanizing if the routinization is obvious or manipulative if it is not. To state the issue in terms of Stinchcombe's prerequisites for routinization, product specifications can never be completely stable for many kinds of service work because only custom-made products will do.

Two kinds of difficulties, then, suggest that interactive service jobs cannot be successfully routinized as thoroughly as manufacturing and clerical jobs can. First, routinization requires stable and predictable working conditions that cannot be guaranteed when people are the raw materials. Second, uniformity of output, a major goal of routinization, seems to be a poor strategy for maintaining quality control in interactive service work, since consumers often perceive rigid uniformity as incompatible with quality.

Nevertheless, employers of large numbers of interactive service workers have not been content to forego the organizational benefits of routinization. They have gone forward with routinization based on three strategies for dealing with these problems. The first is to try to minimize the variability of working conditions by standardizing the behavior of nonemployees, inducing customers and clients to behave so as not to interfere with organizational routines. The second is to try to minimize service-recipients' resentment of routinization by concealing it or infusing it with some semblance of authenticity. The third, used when variability remains significant or when customization is especially important, is an approach to routinization not anticipated by Stinchcombe. When it is impossible to eliminate decision making from a job, some organizations try to standardize the workers' characters, personalities, and habits of thought so that they will make the sorts of decisions the organizations prefer. Rather than hire more knowledgeable and more expensive workers, these service organizations try to transform their trainees in a deeper way than is usually associated with job training. Routinization is thus extended, not by further reducing the autonomy workers have on the job, but by trying to standardize more and more aspects of the workers' lives. In the following sections, each of these approaches to routinizing interactive service work will be discussed in turn.

OVERCOMING OBSTACLES
TO ROUTINIZATION

REDUCING UNPREDICTABILITY

The conditions of stability and predictability necessary for routinization are not entirely independent of an organization's activities. For example, ever since Ford introduced the Model T, manufacturers have tried to shape consumer demand so that uniform products are acceptable and inconvenient desires are suppressed. That is, organizations try to create a market with uniform product specifications. Persuading customers or clients to limit their demands so as not to interfere with the smooth functioning of routines is even more crucial to interactive service organizations, because these nonemployees are actually part of the work process. Customers who do not behave as expected have the same effect on service organizations that ill-fitting parts or unusual specifications have on assembly lines. They hold up the work process, making it impossible to carry out routines and often requiring the intercession of higher-level workers.

Most adults in the United States are sufficiently well socialized to know, in general, how to behave in interactions with service workers so as to fit into organizational routines. They make appointments, if required, and do not appear at other times; they wait their turn to be served; they do not order items that are not on the menu; they refrain from causing scenes. In many cases, though, organizations need to take an active part in arranging for the compliance of non-employees. This effort is necessary: (1) when clear norms do not exist or are not understood by service-recipients;[2] (2) when organizations want to define proper behavior more precisely than general social norms do; or (3) when customers or other service-recipients have reason to want to disrupt the usual routine because it does not meet their needs.

Some means of channeling customers' behavior into patterns that are convenient for the organization are perfectly straightforward: a sign in a diner that says "No Substitutions"; velvet-covered ropes that show moviegoers where they should line up; a closed door labeled "Employees Only." Subtler means may be just as effective. Details of the setting can be manipulated to influence the attitudes and actions of customers or clients. For example, the garish colors and uncomfortable plastic seats often found in fast-food restaurants may discourage patrons from lingering over their meals, and taste-ful, expensive-looking physicians' offices inspire deference.

Customer compliance can also be organized through the labor processes of employees who face the public. Thus workers' routines, which require stable conditions, can actually help to create and sus-tain those conditions. The routines standardize customers' behavior in two ways. First, when interactions are openly, obviously routin-ized, customers can see that they are expected to limit their demands to a predetermined range. They are less likely to insist that their wants be met when it seems that to press for satisfaction would mean "holding things up," "making trouble," or "demanding extra favors," or when it is clear that the service worker is not trained or author-ized to handle special requests. In this case, the very fact of routin-ization helps standardize the behavior of nonemployees.

Second, the content of the interaction routines can be designed to prevent inconvenient behavior or to return a "misbehaving" cus-tomer to compliance. For example, flight attendants are trained to repeat, "I know just how you feel" to calm passengers who are furi-ous about a missed connection, a cold meal, or any other failure in

---

2. For example, Katz and Eisenstadt (1960) describe an Israeli bus driver who had to get out of his bus to demonstrate proper boarding behavior to recent immigrants.

service, because this empathic response makes it harder for passengers to sustain even well-founded indignation (Hochschild 1983: 140). Scripts used by salespeople or other service workers whose clients are not necessarily motivated to cooperate are even more controlling, designed to make it easier for workers to impose their agendas on customers. For example, the workers whose job is to sign up students for a bartending school are scripted to say, "I have appointments available at 2:30 and 4:00; which would be better for you?" rather than "Would you like to come in to see the school?" (International Bartending Institute, n.d.)

In situations where clients or customers are relatively powerless, they may of their own accord try to fit into the organizational routines (see Dewar 1978). In these circumstances interactive service workers need not play such an active part in organizing compliance. Thus Lipsky (1980: 57) writes of workers in government agencies:

> Street-level bureaucrats are not required to command. Clients control themselves in response to the superior power of the workers. This is not to suggest that clients are docile because swift retaliation would result from noncompliant behavior. Rather, compliance in most street-level bureaucracies may be said to result from the superior position of the workers, their control over desired benefits, and their potential capacity to deny benefits or make their pursuit more costly.

Similarly, the less competent clients and customers are to judge how the service should be carried out (because the service is understood to require special expertise), the more likely service-recipients are to submit meekly to the routines imposed on them (see Goffman 1961a).

When service-recipients have more power, workers may have to use a variety of techniques to encourage compliance with organizational routines. The cheerful friendliness that so many United States service businesses try to standardize in their workers is one such technique. This approach not only creates a pleasant atmosphere (quality control) but also makes it harder for consumers to demand satisfaction (organizing compliance), since it is difficult to be angry and insistent with a determinedly friendly worker. More forceful measures are sometimes needed to allow the workers to carry out their routines successfully. When the nonemployees involved are least likely to cooperate, because their interests differ from the workers' or organizations' interests and they have the power to withdraw from the interaction, organizations can design routines that include what Cialdini (1984) calls "compliance techniques." These are devices, such as the classic salesman's foot-in-the-door, that minimize the service-recipients' ability to withdraw from the situation or impose their own agenda on the interaction.[3]

Standardization of the behavior of service-recipients may include getting them to do part of the work. Routinization allows organizations to save money by breaking down tasks into less complex parts that can be done by lower-priced workers. Many service organizations go one step further, setting up the work systems so that tasks previously done by paid workers are made the responsibility of consumers. In fast-food restaurants, self-service gas stations, and supermarkets, for example, fitting into organizational routines means performing what Glazer (1984) terms "involuntary unpaid labor." Glazer describes how the introduction of self-service systems in grocery stores involved a "work transfer" to shoppers of such tasks as finding the desired items, gathering them and bringing them to the counter, and unloading them from the cart. Similarly, a major difference between fast-food outlets and other restaurants is the amount of work customers are expected to do. In these cases, the routines are established not merely to provide services to consumers but also to induce the consumers to provide services to the organization. Business writers urge managers to take advantage of the presence of customers and clients as part of the labor process in interactive service work. For example, "Look to Consumers to Increase Productivity" is the title of a *Harvard Business Review* article (Lovelock and Young 1979), Normann (1984) includes a section on "Making the Client Productive," and Silpakit and Fisk (1985) offer advice on "'Participatizing' the Service Encounter."

Standardizing the behavior of service-recipients, then, is one strategy for making routinization more workable by minimizing uncertainties in the conditions of labor caused by variability in both the behavior of customers and the treatment they desire. Problems remain despite standardization, however, because customers and clients may equate quality with greater customization of service interactions than the companies will allow.

---

3. As is discussed below, organizations design routines that help workers to control service-recipients' behavior, but customers and clients can also exercise control.

PERSONALIZING ROUTINES

Since consumers often resent routinized interactions, perceiving them as mechanical or phony, organizations can try to design routines that have some of the qualities of more spontaneous interactions. The extent of the routinization may be disguised or merely made more palatable by the emotion work of the service workers. Sometimes it is the workers' job to deliver with simulated sincerity lines that are clearly scripted, as when flight attendants assure passengers, "Next time your plans include air travel, make it American and we'll make it a pleasure." Sometimes the workers are expected to personalize highly routinized interactions with eye contact and a smile, which supposedly constitute "treating the customer as an individual." In other cases, the idea is to hide the routinization from service-recipients, to make them believe that the conversation is not scripted. Interactive service workers may have to walk a fine line between not doing enough emotion work and thereby offending customers or clients by making them feel that they are not being treated as people, and trying too hard to seem personally involved in the interaction and thereby offending customers or clients by being perceived as insincere and manipulative.[4]

When "personal touches" are themselves routinized, it is part of the interactive service workers' job to hide the scripting through persuasive acting. For example, Marriott bellhops were instructed to notice and comment on the home city of the guests whose bags they carried, to make the patrons feel welcome (Hostage 1975).[5] Employees of Gloria Marshall Figure Salons were given sample speeches to flatter potential clients: "Mary, I love your suit. I really admire how professional you dress . . . where do you buy your clothes?" (Lally-Benedetto 1985: 8). The idea in these cases was for workers to make customers feel welcome by establishing a seemingly personal relationship with them.

In other situations, the idea is not to bolster the ego of the customer

---

4. Aware of this problem, Sydney Biddle Barrows, "the Mayflower Madam," advised the prostitutes in her employ that although it could sometimes be appropriate for them to fake an orgasm, they should not go overboard ("Don't go and splatter yourself all over the ceiling"), because their clients were sophisticated men who would see through such histrionics (Barrows with Novak 1986: 77).

5. The bellboys were also supposed to mention the virtues of the Marriott in that city.

but to emphasize the personal involvement of the worker in a way that makes it harder for service-recipients to express dissatisfaction or to refuse to comply with the routine. Thus Gloria Marshall provided their figure "counselors" with a whole page of "Encouraging Phrases" to say to customers who had gained weight since their last visit, including, "Mary, have I failed you in some way?" (Gloria Marshall Figure Salons, n.d.) The script for the International Bartending Institute's salespeople actually included a routinized reference to violating the routine, implying that the worker was doing the customer a special favor by signing her or him up without a full deposit (International Bartending Institute, n.d.):

> BUT MORE IMPORTANT THAN THAT /[6] if I put you down for that class and you can't get back in here with your deposit / at 2 p.m. / when you say you will / I can get myself in a lot of trouble. (SMILE) So please don't say you can / if you can't / OK?

Personalizing routines and disguising routinization can mitigate the problem of alienating consumers by treating them mechanically. In effect, these techniques improve the quality of the interactions. If service-recipients discover the scripting, however, through a line poorly written or delivered or a routine repeated exactly as they have heard it before, they are likely to be resentful of having been manipulated, especially if they were taken in by the routine and responded as though they were having an authentic conversation. The strategy of hiding routinization or making it more palatable with personalizing touches thus does not completely solve the problem of variable product specifications in service interactions.

ROUTINIZATION BY TRANSFORMATION

These two strategies used by interactive service organizations to overcome obstacles to routinization—standardizing service-recipients' behavior and personalizing routinization in standard ways—are both designed to allow employers to predetermine how tasks should be carried out, minimizing the discretion left to workers. In some sorts of interactive service work, however, it is impossible to remove all significant decision-making from the job. When prespecification has been extended as far as possible but workers' discretion is still required, employers may then try to transform their workers into the

6. Slashes indicate where the worker should pause.

sorts of people who will make decisions the employers would approve. The effort to train workers to deal with varied situations may include teaching them a variety of routines and a set of decision rules that govern when to use each routine. This strategy may seem more like skills training than routinization, but to the extent that the process involves transforming workers' characters, personalities, and thought processes so that their reactions to variable work situations will be predictable, it is in fact another form of routinization, one that extends more deeply into workers' psyches than does task prespecification.

This sort of effort to transform workers is likely to be most extensive when workers' discretion is most important.[7] Several factors can contribute to the difficulty of eliminating dependence on workers' discretion. First, reliance on workers' discretion is related to the extent of customization necessary for a service interaction to be considered of high quality. When it is most important for workers to respond to the varied demands, attitudes, and behavior of particular customers or clients, employers will find it most difficult to predetermine all significant decisions. Customization is likely to be especially important when the interaction itself is the product being sold.

Similarly, the more difficult or complex the interactive task is, the more the specifications of the work will vary and the more difficult it will be to eliminate the need for workers' discretion. For example, it will be harder to prespecify all the steps of selling a product to people who may not want to buy than to prespecify all the steps of selling a product to people who have sought out the opportunity to buy. In the former case, the customers are less likely to be willing to cooperate and more likely to resist the routine. Their behavior will be relatively varied, and salespeople will have to make decisions on the spot about how to respond.

Finally, dependence on workers' discretion is necessarily increased if they work without managerial supervision or are otherwise relatively free of direct organizational control. In such cases, the workers have discretion both over how hard they work (which relates to the system of control, discussed below), and over how they manage the work (since no higher-level workers will be available to handle

---

7. The alternative to routinization through personal transformation under such circumstances is to hire more expensive skilled or professional workers.

unusual situations). Employers therefore have to trust that workers will be motivated to work hard and also that they will be able to deal with a variety of situations independently. Biggart's work on direct-sales organizations (1989) supports this point. Formal controls are especially weak in these businesses, both because the salespeople are widely dispersed and because they are usually independent distributors rather than employees. Direct-sales organizations have responded to the lack of formal controls by instituting a variety of practices that encourage distributors to control themselves in the companies' interests.

Under these sorts of circumstances, ensuring the quality of interactions is not merely a matter of prespecifying workers' attitudes and demeanors on the job, but also of transforming the workers into the sorts of people who will make the desired decisions. The more the success of the interactive routines depends on the motivation and flexibility of workers, the more routinization through personal transformation may be instituted as a supplement to routinization through prespecification (see Biggart 1989: 136–38).

One of the most extreme examples of routinization by transformation is provided by Amway Corporation (see Butterfield 1985), whose distributors are responsible for both selling Amway's numerous products and enrolling new distributors. Amway goes far beyond providing distributors with routines for doing their work. The company tries to affect their lives in a global and permanent way, molding them through a process it calls "duplicating." There is no part of distributors' lives that Amway does not see as relevant to the success of the business, and therefore none is immune from corporate influence. Amway tries to shape the workers' family lives, political convictions, religious beliefs, personal goals, and self-concepts. It encourages distributors to break off ties with friends or relatives who are critical of Amway, calling them "stinking thinkers." Butterfield compares this standardization of thought, feeling, and way of life to cult indoctrination.

Even when the organizational intrusion into workers' lives is less far-reaching than it is with Amway workers, the training process can resemble such transformative experiences as political reeducation, Marine boot camp, professional education, and religious rebirth as much as ordinary job training. The intent is partly to impart skills and knowledge, but partly to make deeper sorts of changes that will affect the workers both on and off the job. The standardization of workers' attitudes and characters clearly has a dual purpose. It is intended both to make them better able to carry out their work interactions successfully and to make them more devoted to their work and their organization.

Interactive service organizations are not the only employers to take an interest in workers' personalities and attitudes. Edwards (1979) describes the increasing intrusion of corporations into their workers' identities as an effect of the transition from simple and technical means of control of work to bureaucratic control of work. He argues (1979: 148) that when workers' efforts are extracted through elaborate systems of rules, including rules about the grounds for promotion and for punishment, employers establish more control over workers' personalities and values than when their efforts are extracted through direct exhortation or force or through the design of equipment:

> Bureaucratic control tends to be a much more totalitarian system—
> totalitarian in the sense of involving the total behavior of the worker.
> In bureaucratic control, workers owe not only a hard day's work to
> the corporation but also their demeanor and affections.

In Edwards's analysis, however, the interest of the corporation in workers' attitudes is related only indirectly to the production process. He argues that the types of attitudes bureaucratic organizations reward—rules orientation, habits of predictability and dependability, and internalization of the enterprise's goals and values—all relate to the functioning of the control system rather than to the work itself. In other words, they influence the workers' willingness to work hard, not their ability to complete their tasks satisfactorily (Edwards 1979: 148–51).

In interactive service work, by contrast, the workers' character and personality traits clearly are directly related to their ability to do their jobs. The efforts of employers of interactive workers to standardize such traits are therefore often more direct than Edwards's description indicates, and the attitudinal and expressive requirements much more specific. They can also be considerably more far-reaching. Some organizational programs for standardizing workers amount to a different form of worker control altogether, distinct from direct, technical, and bureaucratic means of control. While interactive service organizations may use all of those means as well, those organizations that attempt deep transformations of workers are trying to make such external controls unnecessary by persuading workers to control themselves.[8] They provide "inner justifications" for obedience to organizational demands, which, as Biggart points out using Weber's categories, can be at least as effective as "external means" of control (Biggart 1989: 128; Weber 1946 [1919]: 78). In fact, when management is dependent on interactive service workers to provide good-humored and accommodating service to customers, indirect means of control are less likely to be counterproductive than overt and intrusive ones (Benson 1986; Desatnick 1987; Fuller and Smith 1991).

Labor historians remind us that the extension of corporate control over work methods through routinization has generally met with resistance, because working-class cultures provided alternative frameworks of belief about workers' dignity, rights, and responsibilities (see, for example, Benson 1986; Gutman 1977; Montgomery 1979). Even when struggles over the labor process ended with employers controlling work methods and pace, workers remained free to distance themselves emotionally from their now-demeaned work. Edwards (1979: 148) describes, though, how "the breathing space was reduced" under bureaucratic systems of control, as workplace culture was transformed "to express less of the workers and more of the firm." The diminution of workers' breathing space is even more drastic when, as in routinized interactive service work, employers directly subject workers' attitudes, demeanor, self-concept, and ways of thinking to standardization. Benson's work demonstrates that when management is dependent on workers' expertise in dealing with customers, workers' culture may be a powerful impediment indeed to managerial control. But where extreme routinization lessens workers' leverage or where management successfully inculcates its own values, workers' culture may be stunted or co-opted.

Since the effectiveness of service workers' efforts to resist managerial demands depends in part on the nature of their relations

---

8. Simpson (1985: 418) adds occupational control and self-control to Edwards's list of systems of worker control. In the former, "an occupational group controls its own members"; this control system is typical of some professional interactive service jobs. Simpson describes self-control as "a residual category in which individuals control their own work, as is true of self-employed proprietors." The employer-directed transformations described above are a very different form of worker self-control, even though workers in both situations may feel autonomous in their work.

with customers or clients, it is clear that a thorough understanding of the dynamics of control in service work requires a more complicated model than Edwards's. The involvement of service-recipients in the work process replaces the two-way struggle between management and labor with a triangular pattern of shifting allegiances and interests among workers, managers, and customers. Benson's comment (1986: 284) about department-store saleswomen, managers, and customers applies to interactive service work in general:

> Each of these three major groups pursued its own ends in opposition to pressures from the other two, but under the right conditions would ally with one another against the third.

Managers may use a variety of means to channel the behavior of service-recipients, including providing workers with routines that minimize the likelihood that customers and clients will fail to understand or fail to comply with organizational requirements. The organizationally provided routines are not workers' only means for exercising control over customers, however. When workers' interests depart from those of management or when workers have scope to use their own techniques to forward ends they share with management, they may act independently or collectively to manage customers. Their methods may range from the use or withholding of personal charm and effort, to the provision or denial of useful information (Benson 1986; Prottas 1979), to vengeful retaliation against particularly obnoxious troublemakers. Hochschild (1983: 114) describes an incident in which a flight attendant spiiled a Bloody Mary onto an offensive passenger's lap, and Van Maanen and Kunda (1989: 67) describe quite violent guerrilla tactics even in the utopian confines of Disneyland, including the "seatbelt slap" and the "rather ignoble variants of the 'sorry-I-didn't-see-your-hand' tactic." The types and degrees of independent leverage workers have over customers are determined by the rigidity of their routines, the closeness of supervision or surveillance, the design of compensation and incentive systems, and the customers' own power.

Not only do organizations design routines that help workers to control service-recipients' behavior and workers try to enhance that control through informal means, but customers and clients can also exercise control over workers. In many kinds of interactive service work, the service-recipients act as informal supervisors of the service workers. Customers as well as managers can reprimand service workers for dawdling or avoiding work or behaving rudely. When the work is highly routinized, customers and clients may be well aware of what constitutes adequate work and may feel free to criticize workers who do not perform satisfactorily.

The degree to which service-recipients can control workers and how free they feel to exercise their control vary with the expertise the service requires (Goffman 1961a), the service-recipients' dependence on the particular worker or organization to meet their needs, the relative status of the parties involved, the workers' incentives for satisfying the service-recipient, and the ease with which the service-recipient can take complaints over the worker's head. Edwards (1979: 18) states that the three functions of control systems are to direct work, to evaluate work, and to discipline and reward workers. Service-recipients may control workers in all of these senses. In many settings they direct the work by specifying their preferences or demands; their involvement in the service interaction puts them in a position to evaluate the worker, especially if the connection between work activities and service outcomes is well understood and immediately observable (Mills 1986); and they can reward or punish workers through their grateful thanks or sneering insults, cooperation or intransigence, tips or complaints to workers' superiors. Fuller and Smith (1991) show that businesses are increasingly coming to rely on reports from consumers, which they call "off-site management," to control workers. To the extent that service-recipients have the same criteria for good work that employers do, they can reinforce the other means of worker control in place. To the extent that service-recipients' preferences and demands differ from those of management, they can make the position of interactive service workers even more difficult.

Service-recipients can use the same means of control in dealing with managers that they use with workers, in addition to the collective and abstract control they can exercise by taking their patronage elsewhere. In fact, Fuller and Smith (1991) argue that consumer surveys and other means of off-site management are used by corporations as much to control middle management as to control workers. However, the brunt of consumers' dissatisfaction is commonly borne by interactive service workers, not by the managers responsible for designing the systems and routines that exasperate their patrons (Glenn and Feldberg 1979b). Not only may the service worker be the only target available, but the service-recipient may actually perceive the problem as the fault of the worker rather than of bosses or the system they designed. They see an incompetent waitress, not a restaurant that saves on labor costs by refusing to hire enough workers. As Glenn and Feldberg point out (1979b: 12–3), workers without the authority to alter policies can be quite useful buffers for absorbing the hostility of dissatisfied customers. The more intransigent the policies, the more service-recipients (or, as they may perceive themselves, victims of service organizations) may be driven to extreme and disruptive forms of behavior to try to get around them (Dewar 1978).[9]

Because customers and clients are directly involved in the interactions being standardized, the routinization of interactive service work challenges their individuality and cultural autonomy as well as the individuality and autonomy of the workers. Just as workers' opportunities to sustain identities and outlooks independent of bureaucratic control and corporate logic are diminished by the routinization of interactive work, so too are opportunities for authentic human interaction diminished overall as more social space is taken up by prefabricated interactions.

The chapters that follow will examine how routinization has been carried out in two kinds of interactive service jobs. In one case, routinization has been carried to an extreme through the prespecification of virtually all decisions. In the other, workers retain significant decision-making power, but many more aspects of their selves have been subjected to standardization. I will discuss how the companies arrange for customer compliance, how successful they are in controlling the behavior of their workers, and how the workers reconcile their own sense of identity with the identity imposed by their employers.

---

9. New York City's parking authority, for example, has found it necessary to put Plexiglas and heavy-gauge metal mesh between their workers and motorists who have had their cars towed (Geist 1987).

3

Over the Counter
McDonald's

Organizations have many ways of obtaining the cooperation of participants, ranging from persuasion and enticement to force and curtailment of options. All organizations "hope to make people want to do what the organization needs done" (Biggart 1989: 128), but when they cannot count on success in manipulating people's desires they can do their best to compel people to act in the organization's interests.

Organizations choose strategies that rely on socialization and social control in varying mixtures that are determined by the aims of the organization, the constraints set by the organizational environment and the nature of the work, and the interests and resources of the parties involved. In service-providing organizations, upper-level management must concern itself with the wishes and behavior of service-recipients and various groups of workers.[1] For each group, service organizations try to find the most effective and least costly ways to get people to act in the organizations' interests, proffering various carrots and sticks, making efforts to win hearts and minds, closing off choices.

Organizations that routinize work exert control primarily by closing off choices. There is much room for variation, however, in what aspects of the work organizations will choose to routinize, how they go about it, and how much freedom of decision making remains. Moreover, even when routines radically constrain choice, organizations still must socialize participants and set up systems of incentives and disincentives to ensure the compliance of workers and customers.

---

1. Suppliers, competitors, and other parties outside of the organization are also relevant actors, but organizational efforts to control their behavior will not be considered here (see Prus 1989b).

Both McDonald's and Combined Insurance take routinization to extremes. Both include predetermination of action and transformation of character, but the emphasis differs greatly in the two organizations. McDonald's stresses minute specification of procedures, eliminating most decision making for most workers, although it does make some efforts to standardize operations by transforming the characters of its store-level managers. Combined Insurance also predetermines action as far as possible, but, much more than McDonald's, Combined concerns itself with standardizing the personalities, attitudes, and thinking of its workers, attempting a fairly deep transformation.

This and the following chapter show how the companies' approaches to routinizing the work of those who interact with customers depend largely on the predictability of service-recipients' behavior, which in turn depends on the kinds of resources the organizations have available to channel consumer behavior. Combined's agents' routines were designed to constrain service-recipients as much as to constrain the agents. At McDonald's, where customer compliance is less of a problem, the routines sharply limit the workers' autonomy without giving them much leverage over customers.

McDONALD'S

No one ever walks into a McDonald's and asks, "So, what's good today?" except satirically. The heart of McDonald's success is its uniformity and predictability. Not only is the food supposed to taste the same every day everywhere in the world, but McDonald's promises that every meal will be served quickly, courteously, and with a smile. Delivering on that promise over 20 million times a day in 54 countries is the company's colossal challenge (*McDonald's Annual Report* for 1990: 2). Its strategy for meeting that challenge draws on scientific management's most basic tenets: find the One Best Way to do every task and see that the work is conducted accordingly.[2]

To insure that all McDonald's restaurants serve products of uniform

---

2. The 1990s may bring unprecedented changes to McDonald's. Although its overseas business continues to thrive, domestic sales have been declining. To overcome the challenges to profitability presented by the economic recession, lower-priced competitors, and changes in consumer tastes, CEO Michael Quinlan has instituted experimental changes in the menu, in pricing strategy, and even in the degree of flexibility granted to franchisees (see *Advertising Age* 1991; Berg 1991; *McDonald's Annual Report* for 1990; Therrien 1991).

quality, the company uses centralized planning, centrally designed training programs, centrally approved and supervised suppliers, automated machinery and other specially designed equipment, meticulous specifications, and systematic inspections. To provide its customers with a uniformly pleasant "McDonald's experience," the company also tries to mass-produce friendliness, deference, diligence, and good cheer through a variety of socialization and social control techniques. Despite sneers from those who equate uniformity with mediocrity, the success of McDonald's has been spectacular.

McFacts

By far the world's largest fast-food company, McDonald's has over 11,800 stores worldwide (*McDonald's Annual Report* for 1990: 1), and its 1990 international sales surpassed those of its three largest competitors combined (Berg 1991: sec. 3, 6).[3] In the United States, consumer familiarity with McDonald's is virtually universal: the company estimates that 95 percent of U.S. consumers eat at a McDonald's at least once a year (Koepp 1987a: 58). McDonald's 1990 profits were $802.3 million, the third highest profits of any retailing company in the world (*Fortune* 1991: 179). At a time when the ability of many U.S. businesses to compete on the world market is in question, McDonald's continues to expand around the globe—most recently to Morocco—everywhere remaking consumer demand in its own image.

As politicians, union leaders, and others concerned with the effects of the shift to a service economy are quick to point out, McDonald's is a major employer. McDonald's restaurants in the United States employ about half a million people (Bertagnoli 1989a: 33), including one out of fifteen first-time job seekers (Wildavsky 1989: 30). The company claims that 7 percent of all current U.S. workers have worked for McDonald's at some time (Koepp 1987a: 59). Not only has McDonald's directly influenced the lives of millions of workers, but its impact has also been extended by the efforts of many kinds of organizations, especially in the service sector, to imitate the organizational features they see as central to McDonald's success.

3. McDonald's restaurants are generally referred to as "stores" by McDonald's staff. The company's share of the domestic fast-food market has declined from 18.7 percent in 1985 to 16.6 percent in 1990 (Therrien 1991).

For a company committed to standardization, McDonald's inspires strikingly varied reactions, both as an employer and as a cultural icon. On one side, Barbara Garson (1988), for instance, presents work at McDonald's as so systematized, automated, and closely monitored that all opportunity for thought, initiative, and human contact, let alone self-development, has been removed. To other critics, the ubiquity and uniformity of McDonald's epitomize the homogenization of U.S. culture and its imperialist export. At McDonald's, they point out, local culture is invisible and irrelevant, personal interactions are flattened into standardized patterns, and individual preferences are subordinated to efficient production processes. Nutritionists scorn McDonald's menu, environmentalists its packaging.[4]

However, McDonald's has been as widely admired as reviled. To its supporters, McDonald's represents efficiency, order, familiarity, good cheer, and good value. Many business writers hold McDonald's up as an example of excellence in service management (see, e.g., Heskett, Sasser, and Hart 1990; Peters and Austin 1985; Zemke with Schaaf 1989). A pioneer in the standardization and mass-production of food and service, the company is often represented as emblematic of American capitalist know-how. It is a company whose phenomenal growth has resulted from steadfast commitment to its basic promise to customers of fast service, hot food, and clean restaurants.

The relentless standardization and infinite replication that inspire both horror and admiration are the legacy of Ray Kroc, a salesman who got into the hamburger business in 1954, when he was fifty-two years old, and created a worldwide phenomenon.[5] His inspiration was a phenomenally successful hamburger stand owned by the McDonald brothers of San Bernardino, California. He believed that their success could be reproduced consistently through carefully

4. McDonald's has responded to criticisms of its menu by introducing lower-fat menu items, including, in 1991, a 91 percent fat-free burger (Therrien 1991). Having switched from polystyrene plastic-foam packaging to coated paper and having made other well-publicized efforts to minimize solid wastes, McDonald's came in second when a national sample of consumers was asked to name the most "environmentally conscious" marketer (Chase 1991).

5. Information about McDonald's history comes primarily from Boas and Chain 1976; Kroc with Anderson 1977; Love 1986; Luxenberg 1985; and McDonald's training materials. Reiter's (1991) description of Burger King reveals numerous parallels in the operation of the two companies, although Burger King, unlike McDonald's, is a subsidiary of a multinational conglomerate.

controlled franchises, and his hamburger business succeeded on an unprecedented scale. The basic idea was to serve a very few items of strictly uniform quality at low prices. Over the years, the menu has expanded somewhat and prices have risen, but the emphasis on strict, detailed standardization has never varied.

Kroc set out to achieve the kind of tight control over work routines and product quality that centralized production in factories makes possible, although the fast-food business is necessarily highly decentralized. Not only are the stores geographically dispersed, but approximately 75 percent of McDonald's outlets are owned by individual franchisees rather than by the corporation (*McDonald's Annual Report* for 1989: i). In his autobiography, Kroc describes how he approached the problem of combining standardization with decentralization (Kroc with Anderson 1977: 86):

> Our aim, of course, was to insure repeat business based on the system's reputation rather than on the quality of a single store or operator. This would require a continuing program of educating and assisting operators and a constant review of their performance. It would also require a full-time program of research and development. I knew in my bones that the key to uniformity would be in our ability to provide techniques of preparation that operators would accept because they were superior to methods they could dream up for themselves.

McDonald's franchise owners retain control over some matters, including pay scales, but the company requires that every store's production methods and products meet McDonald's precise specifications. The company encourages and enforces compliance with its standards in a variety of ways. The franchise agreements detail the obligations of both the owners and the corporation; the corporation requires that all potential owners go through its rigorous store-management training program; the corporation provides training materials for crew people and managers that include step-by-step instructions for every task in the store; raters from the corporation regularly visit franchises to evaluate their quality, service, and cleanliness; and owners must purchase their equipment and food products from suppliers approved by the corporation. For those aspects of store operation not specifically covered by the franchise agreement, the corporation must persuade franchisees that they will maximize their profits by following the recommendations of the corporation. Given McDonald's phenomenal success, this persuasive power is considerable, as Kroc intended.

Luxenberg (1985: 77) writes that "Kroc introduced an extreme regimentation that had never been attempted in a service business." This regimentation is not limited to food-preparation techniques. McDonald's has standardized procedures for bookkeeping, purchasing, dealing with workers and customers, and virtually every other aspect of the business. But it is the assembly-line techniques used to produce and serve identical products in every McDonald's that are most salient for workers and most relevant to customers. These are the procedures designed to ensure that the food served to customers will be up to McDonald's standards and that customers will not have to wait more than a few minutes for their meal. The most comprehensive guide to corporate specifications for producing and serving "McDonald's quality" food is the "Operations and Training Manual"—McDonald's managers call it "the Bible"—which describes company procedures and standards in painstaking detail. Its 600 pages include, for instance, full-color photographs illustrating the proper placement of ketchup, mustard, and pickle slices on each type of hamburger on the menu. McDonald's stresses that these specifications are not arrived at arbitrarily, but are the accumulated fruits of years of experience and research. Franchise owners are kept up-to-date on corporate specifications by means of regularly issued bulletins.

Enforcement of McDonald's standards has been made easier over the years by the introduction of highly specialized equipment. Every company-owned store in the United States now has an "in-store processor," a computer system that calculates yields and food costs, keeps track of inventory and cash, schedules labor, and breaks down sales by time of day, product, and worker (*McDonald's Annual Report* for 1989: 29). In today's McDonald's, lights and buzzers tell workers exactly when to turn burgers or take fries out of the fat, and technologically advanced cash registers, linked to the computer system, do much of the thinking for window workers. Specially designed ketchup dispensers squirt exactly the right amount of ketchup on each burger in the approved flower pattern. The french-fry scoops let workers fill a bag and set it down in one continuous motion and help them gauge the proper serving size.

The extreme standardization of McDonald's products, and its workers, is closely tied to its marketing. The company advertises on a massive scale—in 1989, McDonald's spent $1.1 billion system-wide on advertising and promotions (*McDonald's Annual Report* for

1989: 32). In fact, McDonald's is the single most advertised brand in the world (*Advertising Age* 1990: 6).[6] The national advertising assures the public that it will find high standards of quality, service, and cleanliness at every McDonald's store. The intent of the strict quality-control standards applied to every aspect of running a McDonald's outlet, from proper cleaning of the bathrooms to making sure the hamburgers are served hot, is to help franchise owners keep the promises made in the company's advertising.[7]

The image of McDonald's outlets promoted in the company's advertising is one of fun, wholesomeness, and family orientation. Kroc was particularly concerned that his stores not become teen-age hangouts, since that would discourage families' patronage. To minimize their attractiveness to teenage loiterers, McDonald's stores do not have jukeboxes, video games, or even telephones. Kroc initially decided not to hire young women to work behind McDonald's counters for the same reason: "They attracted the wrong kind of boys" (Boas and Chain 1976: 19).

YOU DESERVE A BREAK TODAY:
CONDITIONS OF EMPLOYMENT

Although McDonald's does not want teenagers to hang out on its premises, it certainly does want them to work in the stores. Almost half of its U.S. employees are under twenty years old (Wildavsky 1989: 30). In recent years, as the McDonald's chain has grown faster than the supply of teenagers, the company has also tried to attract senior citizens and housewives as workers. What people in these groups have in common is a preference or need for part-time work, and therefore a dearth of alternative employment options. Because

---

6. In addition to paid advertising, McDonald's bolsters its public image with promotional and philanthropic activities such as an All-American High School Basketball Game, essay contests and scholarship programs for black and Hispanic students, and Ronald McDonald Houses where outpatient children and their families and the parents of hospitalized children can stay at minimal cost.

7. Conversely, details of the routines are designed with marketing in mind. The bags that hold the regular-size portions of french fries are shorter than the french fries are, so that when workers fill them with their regulation french-fry scoops, the servings seem generous, overflowing the packaging. The names of the serving sizes also are intended to give customers the impression that they are getting a lot for their money: french fries come in regular and large sizes, sodas in regular, medium, and large cups. I was quickly corrected during a work shift when I inadvertently referred to an order for a "small" drink.

of this lack of good alternatives, and because they may have other means of support for themselves and their dependents, many people in these groups are willing to accept jobs that provide less than subsistence wages.

Traditionally, McDonald's has paid most of its employees the minimum wage, although labor shortages have now forced wages up in some parts of the country, raising the average hourly pay of crew people to $4.60 by 1989 (Gibson and Johnson 1989: B1). Benefits such as health insurance and sick days are entirely lacking for crew people at most franchises. In fact, when the topic of employee benefits was introduced in a class lecture at McDonald's management training center, it turned out to refer to crew meetings, individual work-evaluation sessions, and similar programs to make McDonald's management seem accessible and fair.

The lack of more tangible benefits is linked to the organization of employment at McDonald's as part-time work. According to the manager of the franchise I studied, all McDonald's hourly employees are officially part-time workers, in that no one is guaranteed a full work week. The company's labor practices are designed to make workers bear the costs of uncertainty based on fluctuation in demand. McDonald's places great emphasis on having no more crew people at work at any time than are required by customer flow at that period, as measured in half-hour increments. Most workers therefore have fluctuating schedules, and they are expected to be flexible about working late or leaving early depending on the volume of business.

Not surprisingly, McDonald's employee-turnover rates are extremely high. Turnover averaged 153 percent in 1984, and 205 percent in 1985 (training center lecture). These high rates are partly attributable to the large percentage of teenage workers, many of whom took the job with the intention of working for only a short time. However, the limited job rewards, both financial and personal, of working at McDonald's are certainly crucial contributing factors.

Some argue that the conditions of employment at McDonald's are unproblematic to the workers who take them. If we assume that most McDonald's workers are teenagers who are in school and are not responsible for supporting themselves or others, then many of the features of McDonald's work do not seem so bad. Fringe benefits and employment security are relatively unimportant to them, and the limited and irregular hours of work may actually be attractive (see Greenberger and Steinberg 1986). These arguments are less persuasive when applied to other McDonald's employees, such as mothers of young children and retirees, although those workers might similarly appreciate the part-time hours, and access to other forms of income and benefits could make McDonald's employment conditions acceptable, if not desirable. Employment security would not be important to the many people who choose to work at McDonald's as a stopgap or for a limited period.[8] Many of the workers at the franchise I studied had taken their jobs with the intention of holding them only temporarily, and many were being supported by their parents. However, other workers there were trying to support themselves and their dependents on earnings from McDonald's, sometimes in combination with other low-paying jobs.

The average McDonald's store employs about sixty-five workers (training center lecture), most of whom are hired as "crew people" and may be trained to do more than one job. The two main jobs for crew people are grill and window (counter service). Typically, most male crew members work on the grill and most female crew members work on the window, although the corporation now encourages gender-neutral work assignment. A smaller job category is that of "host" (a polite term for workers whose main functions are to empty the trash cans and keep the lobby, windows, bathrooms, and dining areas clean). A few other crew people work primarily on equipment maintenance. People trained to work on the grill or at the window may be "cross-trained" to do the other main job or such specialized tasks as making salads, making biscuits, setting up equipment, or unloading trucks of supplies. All crew people are expected to clean and to restock supplies.

A crew member can be promoted to crew trainer and (in some restaurants) to crew chief, and eventually—if the person is over eighteen and available to work enough hours—to "swing manager." Crew trainers and crew chiefs are responsible for showing new workers their jobs, and they are also required to check the work of other crew people against the "Station Operation Checklist" provided by McDonald's for each position. They are expected to set a good example and also to report other crew people who are not

8. Some commentators fall into the trap of assuming that workers' preferences are determinative of working conditions, a mistake they do not make when discussing higher-status workers such as faculty who must rely on a string of temporary appointments.

working responsibly. Swing managers are hourly workers who are qualified to run a shift by themselves: to distribute cash-register drawers full of money, to deal with customer complaints, and to make adjustments in the number and distribution of workers.

Each McDonald's unit also employs four or five salaried managers, ranging in rank from manager trainee through second and first assistant manager to store manager. Salaried managers are treated very differently from crew people. Although they tend to work very long and somewhat unpredictable hours, they have the kinds of employment conditions associated with primary labor markets, including greater employment security, benefits, and salaries ranging from $10,000 to $36,000 as of 1988 (Parcel and Sickmeier 1988: 39). Managers may continue to advance by moving beyond store-level operations to the corporate hierarchy, perhaps moving from market-, regional-, and zone-level positions to corporate headquarters. McDonald's is proud of its promote-from-within approach. More than 50 percent of its store managers and almost 40 percent of its corporate officers started as hourly workers (Wildavsky 1989: 30).

McDonald's wants both managers and workers to dedicate themselves to the values summed up in its three-letter corporate credo, "QSC." Quality, service, and cleanliness are the ends that the company's thousands of rules and specifications are intended to achieve. Kroc promised his customers QSC,[9] and he believed firmly that if, at every level of the organization, McDonald's workers were committed to providing higher-quality food, speedier service, and cleaner surroundings than the competition, the success of the enterprise was assured. McDonald's extraordinarily elaborate training programs are designed both to teach McDonald's procedures and standards and to instill and enforce corporate values.

Kroc approached his business with a zeal and dedication that even he regarded as religious: "I've often said that I *believe in God, family, and McDonald's—and in the office that order is reversed*" (Kroc with Anderson 1977; 124 [emphasis in the original]). Throughout the organization, Kroc is still frequently quoted and held up as a

9. Actually, Kroc usually spoke of QSCV—quality, service, cleanliness, and value (see Kroc with Anderson 1977)—but QSC was the term used in most McDonald's training and motivational materials at the time of my research. The company cannot enforce "value" because antitrust restrictions prevent McDonald's from dictating prices to its franchisees (Love 1986: 145). Nevertheless, recent materials return to the original four-part pledge of QSC & V (see, e.g., *McDonald's Annual Report* for 1989: i).

model, and nowhere is his ongoing influence more apparent than at Hamburger University.

TAKING HAMBURGERS SERIOUSLY: TRAINING MANAGERS

McDonald's main management-training facility is located on eighty beautifully landscaped acres in Oak Brook, Illinois, a suburb of Chicago. Its name, Hamburger University, captures the thoroughness and intensity with which McDonald's approaches management training, and it also suggests the comic possibilities of immersion in McDonald's corporate world.[10] The company tries to produce managers "with ketchup in their veins," a common McDonald's phrase for people who love their work, take pride in it, and are extraordinarily hard-working, competitive, and loyal to McDonald's. A line I heard frequently at Hamburger U. was, "We take hamburgers very seriously here." Nothing I saw called this fixity of purpose into doubt.

Ensuring uniformity of service and products in its far-flung empire is a major challenge for McDonald's. In each McDonald's store, in regional training centers, and at Hamburger University, crew people, managers, and franchisees learn that there is a McDonald's way to handle virtually every detail of the business, and that doing things differently means doing things wrong. Training begins in the stores, where crew people are instructed using materials provided by the corporation, and where managers prepare for more advanced training. Management trainees and managers seeking promotion work with their store managers to learn materials in manuals and workbooks provided by the corporation. When they have completed the manual for the appropriate level, they are eligible for courses taught in regional training centers and at Hamburger University: the Basic Operations Course, the Intermediate Operations Course, the Applied Equipment Course, and, finally, the Advanced Operations Course, taught only at Hamburger University. Altogether, the full training program requires approximately six hundred to one thousand hours of work. It is required of everyone who wishes to

---

10. Branches of Hamburger University now operate in London, Munich, and Tokyo (*McDonald's Annual Report* for 1989: 28). Burger King University is similar in many respects (Reiter 1991).

own a McDonald's store, and it is strongly recommended for all store managers. By the time trainees get to Hamburger University for the Advanced Operations Course, they have already put in considerable time working in a McDonald's store—two to three and a half years, on average—and have acquired much detailed knowledge about McDonald's workings.

Hamburger University sometimes offers special programs and seminars in addition to the regular training courses. For example, a group of McDonald's office workers attended Hamburger University during my visit; a training manager told me that they had been brought in to get "a little shot of ketchup and mustard."[11]

The zeal and competence of franchisees and managers are of special concern to McDonald's, since they are the people responsible for daily enforcement of corporate standards. Their training therefore focuses as much on building commitment and motivation as on extending knowledge of company procedures. In teaching management skills, McDonald's also works on the personalities of its managers, encouraging both rigid adherence to routines and, somewhat paradoxically, personal flexibility. Flexibility is presented as a virtue both because the company wants to minimize resistance to adopting McDonald's ways of doing things and to frequent revision of procedures, and because managers must provide whatever responsiveness to special circumstances the system has, since crew people are allowed virtually no discretion. Hamburger University therefore provides a large dose of personal-growth cheerleading along with more prosaic skills-training.

No visitor to Hamburger University could help being impressed by the amount of resources McDonald's devotes to training and by the extraordinary attention to detail that goes into its standardization of operations. The campus itself is lovely,[12] with two custom-made lakes, Lake Ed and Lake Fred, named after Ed Rensi, chief operations officer and president of McDonald's U.S.A., and Fred

11. The effort to involve corporate employees in the central mission of the organization extends beyond such special programs. McDonald's prides itself on keeping its corporate focus firmly on store-level operations, and it wants all its employees to have a clear idea of what it takes to make a McDonald's restaurant work. Therefore, all McDonald's employees, from attorneys to data-entry clerks, spend time working in a McDonald's restaurant.

12. The language of academe is used consistently at Hamburger University. For instance, not only are the grounds called the campus, but the director is called the dean and the trainers are called professors.

Turner, former chairman of McDonald's Corporation. Students stay at The Lodge, the only Hyatt hotel that is not open to the general public, and the training building is a short walk across a bridge spanning Lake Fred. The facilities there are dazzlingly up-to-date. In addition to laboratories outfitted with all of the kinds of equipment found in McDonald's stores, there are several large classrooms, each with state-of-the-art audio-visual equipment (including nine slide projectors that can be programmed to operate simultaneously for elaborate presentations), computer keypads at each student's place so that students can enter their answers to multiple-choice questions directly into a central computer, and several rows of seats equipped with wireless headphones, through which foreign students can hear simultaneous translations of the lectures, provided by translators seated in a soundproof booth adjacent to the classroom. Training videos are produced in a television studio on the premises, and, when the trainees are back in their hotel rooms, they can get help with their studies from programs shown on closed-circuit television.

McDonald's corporate pride is visible everywhere. Much of the interior decor is bright green, reflecting Ray Kroc's pronouncement, "When you're green, you're growing; when you're ripe, you rot." The lobby and hallways of the training building and The Lodge are filled with McDonald's-related artwork. Most prominent is a bust of Ray Kroc, but many of the pieces convey a sense of humor as they celebrate McDonald's. There are holograms of a Big Mac, Speedee (McDonald's original logo), and other McDonald's items; a ceramic model of a vintage McDonald's store, complete with 1950s cars in the parking lot; a painting of a kneeling Japanese woman in full kimono, reaching into a McDonald's bag with chopsticks; a take-off on "American Gothic" in which the dour farm woman has been given a McDonald's meal, which will presumably cheer her up.

The Lodge has a gift shop that sells McDonald's memorabilia. Scores of items are for sale, including clocks, mugs, hats, totebags, shirts, aprons, and license-plate frames.[13] When I visited Hamburger University, members of the teaching staff were wearing a standard uniform of tan slacks (a skirt for the one female professor) and a blazer with a small McDonald's insignia. The professor who first

13. I limited myself to a McDonald's carpenter's cap and a tasteful necklace with a small french-fry pendant.

showed me around Hamburger U., a fourteen-year veteran of McDonald's, also had a gold McDonald's ring with a diamond (for ten years' service) and a gold watch with McDonald's Golden Arches on its face. Most of the staff people also wore at least one lapel pin. "We're very lapel pin-oriented here," I was told.

The curriculum of the Advanced Operating Course includes inculcation with pride in McDonald's. Sessions are devoted to McDonald's history and McDonald's dedication to ever-improving QSC. Lectures are sprinkled with statistics attesting to McDonald's phenomenal success. Students hear the story of Ray Kroc's rise to wealth and prominence, based on his strength of character and willingness to work hard, and are assigned his autobiography, *Grinding It Out* (Kroc with Anderson 1977). Kroc is quoted frequently in lectures, and students are encouraged to model themselves on him. They are told repeatedly that they have all proven themselves "winners" by getting as far as they have at McDonald's. The theme throughout is, "We're the best in the world, we know exactly what we're doing, but our success depends on the best efforts of every one of you."[14]

About 3,500 students from all over the world attend classes at Hamburger University each year, most of them taking the Advanced Operations Course (Rosenthal 1989). Those who complete the course receive diplomas proclaiming them Doctors of Hamburgerology. As late as 1978 or 1979, a training manager told me, most classes included only one or two women, but women now comprise 40–60 percent of the students, and women and minorities now make up 54 percent of McDonald's franchisees (Bertagnoli 1989a: 33). In my homeroom, however, the proportion of women was much smaller, and there was just a handful of minority students.

The course lasts two weeks and is extremely rigorous. Class time is about evenly divided between work in the labs and lectures on store operations and personnel management. In the labs, trainees learn the mechanics of ensuring that McDonald's food is of consistent quality and its stores in good working order. They learn to check the equipment and maintain it properly so that fries cook at

---

14. Biggart (1989: 143–47) shows that both adulation of a charismatic founder and repeated characterization of participants as winners are common in direct-sales organizations. Like McDonald's, such organizations face the problem of motivating people who are widely dispersed geographically and who are not corporate employees.

precisely the right temperature, shakes are mixed to just the right consistency, and ice cubes are uniform. "Taste of Quality" labs reinforce McDonald's standards for food quality. For instance, in a Condiments Lab, trainees are taught exactly how to store vegetables and sauces, what the shelf lives of these products are, and how they should look and taste. Samples of "McDonald's quality" Big Mac Special Sauce are contrasted with samples that have been left too long unrefrigerated and should be discarded. The importance of serving only food that meets McDonald's standards is constantly emphasized and, a trainer pointed out, "McDonald's has standards for everything, down to the width of the pickle slices."

The management classes deal with such matters as hiring and training crew people, delegating authority, building sales, managing personnel, and maintaining good community relations. Not surprisingly, the work of the professors is standardized. Most deliver their lectures in a spontaneous style with their own embellishments, but they work from scripts prepared by the curriculum-development department. If they stray too far from the script, their lectures will be out of synch with the fancy slide presentations that accompany most lectures and with the "programmed notes" that are distributed to students to help them follow along and take notes.

McDonald's strategy for teaching managers to deal effectively with people—crew members, customers, fellow managers—is to train them in transactional analysis, as popularized in *I'm OK, You're OK* (Harris 1969). Eight hours of class time are devoted to the fundamentals of transactional analysis, taught through lectures, slides and videos, and role plays. Trainees are encouraged to become more aware of their own interactive styles and more sensitive to others' "ego states" and emotional needs. McDonald's counsels managers to behave assertively rather than aggressively, teaches them to identify and straighten out "cross-communications," and advises them to give their crew people lots of recognition and positive feedback ("warm fuzzies"). In the mid-1980s, McDonald's added to the curriculum a class called "Applied Personnel Practices" that was intended to help managers make it easier for "out-group members" to be made to feel part of the team, to encourage the hiring of women and racial minorities, and to define sexual harassment clearly and prevent it. In virtually all of the classes, instructors stress the importance of treating crew people respectfully, avoiding injury to their self-esteem, and helping them to learn and develop. They emphasize that every crew person should be treated as an important member of a winning team. When managers see crew people doing tasks incorrectly or behaving badly, they should "counsel" the workers by finding the source of the problem, giving appropriate feedback, conveying a caring attitude, and reinforcing standards.

The professors emphasize that it is up to the trainees to decide whether they are willing to change the way they deal with other people, and they acknowledge that it is not easy to give up autocratic habits. To persuade the trainees that the effort is worthwhile, the staff shows them a handsomely produced videotape based on a Native American legend, in which a tribal elder points out to a young boy that trees that bend with the wind survive the worst storms, while unyielding trees are destroyed.

In addition to lectures and labs, trainees participate in competitions designed to develop team-building skills and management know-how. The first of these is "Hot Hamburgers," a week-long team competition in a game-show format. Teams are tested on their knowledge of McDonald's history and policies and on the minutiae of McDonald's standards. Trainees took this competition very seriously. I had dinner with one team just before the first round of competition, and was astonished to find that the conversation at the table consisted almost exclusively of questions and answers being fired back and forth. At what temperature do frozen apple pies thaw? What is the height of an English muffin? What is the warm-up time of a biscuit oven? What is the yield of a gallon of hotcake mix? The answers to these questions are contained in a small, green quality-standards booklet that managers are supposed to carry with them at all times. The actual competition featured a professional master of ceremonies, a panel of judges, a giant game board, and the bells and buzzers typical of television game shows.

The other team competition was intended to simulate the problems store managers face. In each round, the class was shown a videotape of a McDonald's store in trouble. The videotapes used in the classes I attended were clever take-offs on classic television shows: "The Honeyburgers," "The Customer Zone" (based on *The Twilight Zone*), "Mission McPossible," "MacNet" (*Dragnet*). Others were done in the style of Hollywood detective films, complete with mournful saxophone, 1940s decor, and trench-coat-clad leading man. Each focused on a specific type of problem, such as high employee turnover, slow service, or poor equipment maintenance.

After a videotape was shown, the trainees split up into teams of five and were given packets of information about the location and competition of the store in question and its profits, employee turn-over rate, and QSC ratings. They also received a list of steps the store's managers might take to alleviate the problems. The teams had to choose the five steps they thought would be best, a process involving much argument and negotiation. The answers were fed into a computer that was programmed to predict how the restau-rant's QSC ratings, profits, and turnover would have changed in six months if those steps had been taken. The teams' standings were calculated over four of these simulations, and winning teams were rewarded with plaques and a share of McDonald's stock for each member.

This simulation exercise provided the only reminder that social control as well as socialization constrains McDonald's managers and franchisees. Each restaurant is indeed judged by "the numbers": by sales per crew person, profits, turnover, and QSC ratings. The rat-ings are based on three-day reviews by corporate field consultants, held twice a year (Bertagnoli 1989b: 58). The corporation provides assistance to stores with disappointing ratings. Only in dire cases does it exercise sterner methods, including refusal to renew a fran-chise license. Franchisees keep their numbers up partly in the hope that they will be awarded additional franchises, and managers hope for promotions, raises, or consideration as a franchisee.

The training at Hamburger University combines a sense of fun with dead seriousness about keeping McDonald's on top in the hamburger business through relentless quality control and effective management of workers and customers. It is up to the owners and managers of individual McDonald's stores to make that happen.

ONE MCDONALD'S FRANCHISE

I was assigned to a McDonald's in the downtown area of a small city near Chicago. It was a new store, only about fifteen months old when I began my fieldwork, but an exemplary one; it had recently won a major McDonald's award. The store was far more elegant than the average McDonald's. Adjacent to an expensive hotel, the restau-rant was designed to seem "high-class," not garish or tacky. The in-terior decor included marble walls, a mahogany dining counter, black Art Deco fixtures, and mauve draperies. Outside were window boxes filled with flowers or greenery, and a relatively small Golden Arches sign, since the city council would not permit a large one.

This McDonald's differed from most in that it had neither a parking lot nor a drive-thru [*sic*] service window. It depended on pedestrian traffic for business, and its clientele included business people, college students, senior citizens, and shoppers. Fewer families came in than is typical for a McDonald's, and more people ordered just coffee or ice cream rather than a full meal; the average check size was accordingly smaller than at most McDonald's stores. At the time of my research in 1986, the store served 1,700 customers on an average day. In the course of a year, those customers collectively spent about one and a half million dollars. (The average McDonald's store brought in $1.34 million in 1985, half of it in drive-thru sales [training center lecture].[15])

The franchisee who owned the store owned three other McDonald's stores in the Chicago suburbs.[16] The business had made him wealthy, and he proudly showed off a "new toy" to me, a Corvette convertible, complete with telephone. He also had a yacht. He, his wife, and some of their grown children were closely involved in running the store, coming in several times a week, planning improvements, and overseeing the operation. Such involvement is encouraged by the corporation, which wants all of its franchisees to be "owner/operators," not just investors.

This McDonald's store had five salaried managers, all male, three white and two black. The owner's son, another white, also worked as a manager on occasion. In addition, there were as many as five hourly swing managers at a time (all female; three black, one white, one Native American). During my fieldwork, two crew people, a black woman and an Asian man, were promoted to that level of management.

The store's crew fluctuated in size between sixty-five and about one hundred people in the course of six months; the store manager believed that eighty-five was optimal. There were about equal numbers of window workers and grill workers.

Personnel policies at McDonald's franchises, including pay scales, are determined by the franchise owners, not by the corporation. Many press reports have described fast-food franchises raising wages

---

15. The current average is $1.65 million per U.S. store (*Advertising Age* 1991).
16. The average McDonald's franchisee has 3.1 stores (Bertagnoli 1989a: 33).

and offering benefits to compete for the declining number of teen-age workers, but the crew at this franchise, both grill and window workers, started work at the federal minimum wage, $3.35 in 1986, and they received no benefits such as health insurance, paid holi-days, or paid sick days. Merit raises of five or ten cents per hour were granted quarterly, when job performance reviews were made, and crew people promoted to crew trainer or crew chief received raises of five to fifteen cents per hour as well. The pay remained quite low, however. One crew trainer who had worked at the fran-chise for about a year and a half was earning $3.75.

Most, though not all, male crew members worked on the grill and most female crew members worked on the window. This pattern was usually based on managers' decisions when hiring workers. Some crew people reported having been given a choice about where they would start out, but more than half said that they had been as-signed to their job.[17] A couple of crew people reported that the first women to be cross-trained to work on the grill had to persuade managers that they should be allowed to do so. In my interview sample of window people, 75 percent of the workers were women; according to the store's manager, this proportion accurately approxi-mated the actual gender composition of the job category.

Salaried managers were expected to work forty-six to fifty hours per week. Officially, all of McDonald's crew workers are part-time, but 25 percent of my interview sample of window crew said that they usually worked thirty-five hours or more per week. The num-ber of hours worked by crew people varied greatly, since many of them were students who only wished to work a few hours per week. Those who did want longer hours were expected to compete for them, proving themselves deserving through conscientious job per-formance. In practice, a core group of about twenty steady workers was sure to get its preferred hours, but cutting back an employee's hours was a standard way the managers showed their displeasure over poor job performance or attitude. The usual strategy for getting rid of poor workers, the store manager told me, was to decrease the hours they were scheduled to work until they got the message.

Through its scheduling practices McDonald's attempted to mini-mize labor costs without sacrificing speedy service for customers. As

17. This group included three men who had been assigned to window work, so gender was not the only criterion considered.

in almost all restaurants, McDonald's business normally came in waves rather than in a steady stream, with big rushes at meal times. On the one hand, managers did not want to have to pay crew people for hours they were not needed, since crew labor productivity is one of the main criteria by which managers are judged (Garson 1988: 32). On the other hand, they wanted to be sure to have enough people to keep lines moving quickly when business was brisk. The computerized cash-register system analyzed sales by hour of the day and day of the week, and managers used these figures to schedule work crews.[18]

Since, however, computer projections are never entirely accurate, the schedules at this McDonald's were designed so that workers bore much of the burden of uncertainty. On the work schedule, posted one week in advance, a line for each crew person showed the hours she or he was scheduled to work. A solid line indicated hours the employee could count on working, and a zigzag line marked an additional hour or so. If the store was busy when a worker's guaranteed hours were finished, she or he would be required to work that extra time; if it was not busy, she or he would be asked to leave. In addition, it was quite common at unexpectedly quiet times for managers to tell workers they could leave before their scheduled hours were completed or even to pressure them to leave when they would rather have kept on working. I heard one manager say, "Come on, can't I make a profit today?" when a crew person resisted being sent home fifteen minutes early. Conversely, when the store was busy, managers were reluctant to let workers go when their scheduled hours, including the optional time, were done. When lines of people were waiting to be served, workers—I was one of them—would often have to ask repeatedly to be "punched out" (off the time clock) at the end of their shift.

Workers' preferences for longer or shorter hours varied; some wanted to earn as much as possible, others preferred to have more time for other activities. Whatever their preferences, the scheduling practices made it difficult for workers to plan ahead. Arrangements for transportation, social activities, child care, and so on could be disrupted by unexpected changes in the schedule, and workers

---

18. Burger King has similar procedures, of course; an executive showed me how managers are taught to chart labor needs down to the half-hour. *McDonald's Annual Report* for 1989 states that the "in-store processor" now schedules labor in each store (29).

could not accurately predict how much money they would earn in a given week. Furthermore, one of the most common complaints among the workers was that they had been scheduled to work at times they had said they were not available. Once on the schedule, they were held responsible for finding a replacement (see Garson 1988: 32–33). Since the McDonald's schedule was made up of such small units of time, however, it was usually relatively easy for workers to arrange hours for their convenience, an advantage McDonald's emphasized in recruitment. For example, workers who played on a high school team could cut down their hours during the sports season, and workers who needed to take a particular day off could usually arrange it if they gave sufficient notice.

The Interview Sample

Thirty-five percent of my sample was of high school age. (It is possible that I undersampled high school students simply because, since they were less likely to work many hours, I had less opportunity to meet them.) Although the majority of my sample (65 percent) were eighteen years old or over, 60 percent of the crew people told me that this was their first job.

The great majority of the crew people in the store were black, although blacks are a minority, albeit a large one, of the city's population. In my interview sample, 80 percent were black (including three Caribbean immigrants), one person was Hispanic-American, one was an Asian immigrant, and the rest were American-born white. A sizable minority of the workers commuted long distances, from the South Side and the West Side of Chicago. A full 25 percent of my sample had one-way commutes that took at least an hour and required at least one change of train, and I knew of several other workers with commutes at least that long. Given that the crew people started work at McDonald's at minimum wage, this pattern strongly suggests that these workers had been unable to find work near their homes or better-paying jobs elsewhere.

About two-thirds of the store's crew people were trained to work at the window. My sample of twenty-six window workers was not completely representative of all of the employees who worked behind the counter during the months I was there. Since my sampling method depended on my meeting the worker in the crew room, I probably oversampled those who worked relatively long or relatively steady hours and missed both those who worked only a few hours per week and those who worked for only a short time before quitting. I oversampled crew trainers and crew chiefs—30 percent of my sample had been promoted to one of these jobs. However, according to the store's manager, my sample was fairly representative of the store's population of customer-service workers in its gender, race, and age distributions.

Learning the Job

As a manager at Hamburger University explained to me, the crew training process is how McDonald's standardization is maintained, how the company ensures that Big Macs are the same everywhere in the world. The McDonald's central administration supplies franchisees with videotapes and other materials for use in training workers to meet the company's exacting specifications. The company produces a separate videotape for each job in the store, and it encourages franchisees to keep their tape libraries up-to-date as product specifications change. The Hamburger University professor who taught the Advanced Operating Course session on training said that, to keep current, franchisees should be buying ten or twelve tapes a year. For each work station in the store McDonald's also has a "Station Operation Checklist" (SOC), a short but highly detailed job description that lays out exactly how the job should be done: how much ketchup and mustard go on each kind of hamburger, in what sequence the products customers order are to be gathered, what arm motion is to be used in salting a batch of fries, and so on.

At the store level, it is the responsibility of the first assistant manager, the person directly below the store manager in the store hierarchy, to oversee training, but other managers, crew chiefs, and crew trainers all participate in training new workers.[19] McDonald's recommends that its managers use a four-step process to train crew people: prepare, present, try out, follow up. In this method trainees first watch the videotape and then watch an experienced worker, a crew trainer, do the job and ask questions of the trainer. Next, trainees try the job while the trainer watches and makes corrections. In

---

19. The store manager is responsible for overseeing the training of other managers, working with them as they go through the series of manuals issued by the corporation and helping them prepare for intensive courses at the regional training centers and Hamburger University.

the follow-up stage, trainees build speed and competence and the trainer checks on performance, using a Station Operations Checklist as a guide.

Before this task-oriented training begins, newly hired employees attend an orientation session at which they see a videotape about McDonald's, fill out employment forms, and learn the store's rules and regulations. New employees at the store I worked at were told to show up for this session wearing a white shirt or blouse and dark blue or black slacks. Since the orientation session was held in the basement crew room, out of sight of customers, the requirement about dress was apparently intended primarily to see whether the new workers could follow directions. My orientation session was attended by three new workers, including myself, and was run by Jim, the first assistant manager.

The videotape we saw featured ostentatiously smiling managers who welcomed their recruits and put them at ease. Jim's manner contrasted markedly with theirs. Rather than fulsomely reassuring the new workers that we would soon be important members of McDonald's winning team, he greeted one recruit, a young woman wearing a dangling earring, by saying gruffly, "The first thing [is], get rid of that earring."[20] I was startled by the brusque, no-nonsense tone Jim used throughout the orientation, since I had seen him behave very differently at a crew trainers' meeting and when talking with me. Moreover, his attitude was hardly one of trust and respect: when one woman said she would not be available for work on Sundays because "Sunday's church," he muttered skeptically, "I've met more religious people here . . ." My field notes record: "I'm already resenting him."[21] The "one big happy family" motif of the orientation videotape was further undercut by the requirement that new employees sign a Polygraph Consent Form.

Much of the orientation session was spent reviewing the rules crew people were expected to follow. Jim started with the dress code and other rules about personal appearance. Some of these rules reflected concerns about safety and hygiene; others were intended to promote a uniform image of neatness and wholesomeness.[22] All

20. For safety reasons, dangling earrings are forbidden.
21. Jim had not yet received "I'm OK, You're OK" training at Hamburger University, and no doubt the trainers there would have recommended that he try to establish "adult-adult" interactions with workers rather than "parent-child" ones.
22. I assumed for weeks that one window worker who always had a piece of adhesive tape on his ear must have some sort of injury, and was amused to learn

workers had to wear a clean uniform complete with hat and name tag. Women had to wear white nonskid shoes, had to tuck their hair up under their hat, and could not wear heavy makeup, brightly colored nail polish, more than two rings, or dangling jewelry. Men had to wear black shinable shoes and could not have long sideburns, beards, or hair touching their collars.

Jim next went over "easy ways to get fired." These included arguing on the work floor, fighting, stealing (including giving away food), failing to show up for work, or coming to work drunk or on drugs. He explained the store's procedures for finding out one's work schedule, calling in sick, arranging for days off, and picking up paychecks, and he told us what benefits workers received: a fifteen-minute paid break for four hours of work (with an additional five minutes for every additional hour), and meals at half-price.

Finally, Jim scheduled job-training sessions for each of the new workers. The window crew, of which I was to be a member, was responsible for cooking french fries, so I was scheduled to be "trained on fries" and to work one shift at the french-fry station before attending a window training session where I would learn to work the cash register and deal with customers.

My french-fry training was not what I had been led to expect. I was sent down to the crew room to watch the videotape, which presented very detailed instructions on loading fries into their baskets, using the cooking equipment, salting and bagging the cooked fries, and making sure that only fresh, hot fries are served. My field notes record what happened when the video ended:

> I go back upstairs and find [the manager], who says, "OK, now you're on fries, go ahead." I say, "Are you serious? That's it for training?" She says, "Oh, no," but I'm not sure that she wouldn't have put me right on if I hadn't said anything.

I was very relieved to have a crew trainer assigned to show me the job, since I did not feel at all prepared to handle it myself based on one viewing of the training tape. Diana did not follow the procedures recommended for training—her tendency was to do things herself rather than let me try—but she explained what she was doing as

---

that the tape hid a small, gold pierced earring. The tape was much more noticeable than the earring (the worker was black, the tape white), but apparently the managers considered it less offensive.

she went along, and she answered my questions. I found that the job was harder than it had looked in the videotape, but by the end of the shift I was able to handle the french-fry station myself.

The training to work on the window was more formal. "Window class" was run by a swing manager, Charlene, and lasted a whole morning. My training group included two other newly hired window workers and a grill worker who was being cross-trained to work window. The training began, as usual, with a videotape. It emphasized the importance of the window crew's work, telling us that to guests (McDonald's word for customers), "You ARE McDonald's." Interactive work is only part of the window crew's job, though. In addition to learning about dealing with people, we had many details to learn about dealing with things. The videotape provided instructions on what the various-sized cups and bags were used for, how to stock the counter area, how to work the soda and shake machines, and how to load a bag and set up a tray properly.

Interactions with customers, we were taught, are governed by the Six Steps of Window Service: (1) greet the customer, (2) take the order, (3) assemble the order, (4) present the order, (5) receive payment, and (6) thank the customer and ask for repeat business.[23] The videotape provided sample sentences for greeting the customers and asking for repeat business, but it encouraged the window crew to vary these phrases. According to a trainer at Hamburger University, management permits this discretion not to make the window crew's work less constraining but to minimize the customers' sense of depersonalization:

> "We don't want to create the atmosphere of an assembly line," Jack says. They want the crew people to provide a varied, personable greeting—"the thing that's standard is the smile." They prefer the greetings to be varied so that, for instance, the third person in line won't get the exact same greeting that he's just heard the two people in front of him receive.

At the franchise where I worked, Charlene set limits on the variations permitted. She would not allow window workers to say "Next!" or "Is that all?" because she considered both phrases brusque and

---

23. The six steps were performed in this order at the McDonald's I studied, but elsewhere the money is collected earlier in the interaction. The sequence we followed made it easier to deal with customers who changed their minds about what they wanted.

impolite. She also thought that "Can I help someone?" sounded disrespectful and insisted that workers ask, "May I help you, sir?" or "May I help you, ma'am?" She advised, "If you can't tell *what* a person is, then say, 'May I help you, please?'"

In the training session Charlene expanded on the material the videotape had presented, using hand-outs that listed the rules for service, cash-register policies, and performance standards. She provided further information about procedures in this store and made it clear that she took the standards very seriously. Charlene stressed smiling, speed, and professionalism as crucial components of the job. "Professionalism," not a concept usually associated with fast-food work, meant in this context that workers should know what they were doing and take the trouble to do things right. For instance:

> Charlene says that all bags must be double-folded neatly before being presented to customers. "I mean folded. Don't let me catch you balling up the top of the bags. You should fold it neatly twice so you look like a professional."

To instill this professionalism, Charlene made the trainees active participants in the class, frequently quizzing us individually and asking us to explain the rules in our own words, to make sure we were getting the ideas. The trainees all took the work of learning these rules and regulations seriously, though their "own words" did not always have that cheerful McDonald's ring to them:

> Charlene asks Earl to read and explain the Six Steps on the sheet. He explains the instruction "Be enthusiastic and smile. You never get a second chance to make a first impression" by saying something like, "You don't want people to think, 'Shit, what the fuck is this?'"

Much of the class time was devoted to instructions on how to use the store's complicated cash registers. Though crucial, this training was the least adequate part of the curriculum. It was not very systematic, and I was left confused about how to "punch in grills" (take special orders), how to store orders in the machine's memory and then recall them, and even where to find the right key for each product. Moreover, as I noted:

> Charlene doesn't tell us how to make corrections if we enter something wrong, which turns out to be the information I need most.

There was one other major omission. McDonald's stresses that no hamburgers or other sandwiches are to be served if they have been sitting in the food bin for more than ten minutes. At this store, the person who wrapped the burgers put a little sticker on each one bearing a number that indicated the time it was prepared. Charlene did not tell us how to interpret the numbers, and I never did find out how we were supposed to know whether a sandwich was too old to serve.

The trainees were given a short written test on the material covered in class and were then shown how to stock the counter area, where to find the things we would need, and how to make coffee and ice cream cones. Then we were set right to work on the cash registers. Although Charlene hovered nearby to help us out, I was petrified.

> I do *very* badly at first. I hit the wrong keys and don't know how to undo the errors. At first I don't even realize that I should be entering the items as people say them—I listen until they're through and then try to enter the order. I have to explain to many people that it's my first day, and I'm constantly calling Charlene for help. I do things in the wrong order, forgetting my lessons from Charlene and the videotape.

The cash register was my biggest problem. Lights kept flashing for reasons I did not understand, it took me forever to find the right keys, and I kept botching up special orders. (In fact, Charlene had given us incorrect instructions on which keys to hit in what sequence for special orders.) Nonetheless:

> I start to get the hang of it fairly soon. The other crew people are quite nice and helpful, and the customers are all polite, too—I don't serve any nasty guests. One customer startles me by saying, "Thank you, Robin." It takes me a moment to realize that I'm clearly labeled. When I mess up, I send the customers off with, "Come back soon—I'll do better."

Unlike this relatively thorough and successful training, my preparation to work the window at breakfast time was completely inadequate and left me frustrated and angry as well as incompetent. No videotape was shown, and the four-step training procedure was also abandoned. Diana was my crew trainer again, but this time she did not explain procedures to me carefully. At the beginning of the shift, she had me take a few orders on her cash register, but soon I was given my own register:

> I start working, with Diana by my side, without being given any training. For a while she just points to the keys as people order things,

since I don't know where they are, and can't figure out the abbreviations. Most of the time I take the orders and money and Diana goes to get the products—a good thing, since I still don't know what goes with what. . . . I am finding this extremely frustrating—I feel very unprepared and don't like having to do the job without being competent to do it.

Eventually Diana goes through the keyboard with me, reciting what each key does. After reciting them, she names a few items and has me point to the keys. When a customer comes in after we've gone through only a few keys, my "training" is abandoned. I find the keys confusing—there's an Egg McMuffin key and a Muffin and Egg key; a biscuit with sausage and egg, biscuit with sausage and no egg, muffin with sausage and egg, etc. Some of the biscuit sandwiches have cheese on them, some don't. Often I can't tell whether someone is ordering a special grill or a regular sandwich, because I don't know what's on those things.

I had to ask for directions continually from Diana or another worker. This dependence was frustrating, and since their way of helping me was to punch the orders in themselves without explaining how to do it, I had to keep on asking. When business picked up, Diana's "help" was even more confounding:

I go on taking orders. Practically every time I start to go get the items, Diana says, "I'll get it; take your money." Worse, when it gets more crowded she takes new orders before I've finished taking the money for the last one. Often while I'm busy making change or something, she's shouting, "Can I help you?" and keeping the new order in her head. She then expects me to hear the second order, remember it, and key it in after I finish with the first order. (At least I guess that's what she expects.) I often have to ask her what she's gotten or ask the customers to repeat to me what they've just told Diana. On top of this, Diana sometimes reaches over and keys an order in on my register. This is tolerable while I'm standing there, but sometimes when I do go to get food items, I come back to find that there's some new order on my register and Diana is shouting, "Take the money." When there are several parties at the counter, I don't even know who ordered what or whose money I should be taking.

Whereas my field notes for the day I was trained to work on window ended, "I leave in a good mood—it was fun," I went through this breakfast shift in a state of suppressed rage. This object lesson in what happens when McDonald's training procedures are not followed made me appreciate the company's ceaseless efforts to see that its standards are enforced. It was also a good lesson in why workers do not necessarily resent routinization—clear, well-planned routines make them feel they can do at least an adequate job. But what is left of the job?

The Routine

McDonald's had routinized the work of its crews so thoroughly that decision making had practically been eliminated from the jobs. As one window worker told me, "They've tried to break it down so that it's almost idiot-proof." Most of the workers agreed that there was little call for them to use their own judgment on the job, since there were rules about everything. If an unusual problem arose, the workers were supposed to turn it over to a manager.

Many of the noninteractive parts of the window workers' job had been made idiot-proof through automation.[24] The soda machines, for example, automatically dispensed the proper amount of beverage for regular, medium, and large cups. Computerized cash registers performed a variety of functions handled elsewhere by human waitresses, waiters, and cashiers, making some kinds of skill and knowledge unnecessary. As a customer gave an order, the window worker simply pressed the cash register button labeled with the name of the selected product. There was no need to write the orders down, because the buttons lit up to indicate which products had been selected. Nor was there any need to remember prices, because the prices were programmed into the machines. Like most new cash registers, these added the tax automatically and told workers how much change customers were owed, so the window crew did not need to know how to do those calculations. The cash registers also helped regulate some of the crew's interactive work by reminding them to try to increase the size of each sale. For example, when a customer ordered a Big Mac, large fries, and a regular Coke, the cash register buttons for cookies, hot apple pies, ice cream cones, and ice cream sundaes would light up, prompting the worker to suggest dessert. It took some skill to operate the relatively complicated cash register, as my difficulties during my first work shift made clear, but this organizationally specific skill could soon be acquired on the job.

24. The in-store processors similarly affected managers' work. A disaffected McDonald's manager told Garson, "There is no such thing as a McDonald's manager. The computer manages the store" (Garson 1988: 39).

In addition to doing much of the workers' thinking for them, the computerized cash registers made it possible for managers to monitor the crew members' work and the store's inventory very closely.[25] For example, if the number of Quarter Pounder with Cheese boxes gone did not match the number of Quarter Pounders with Cheese sold or accounted for as waste, managers might suspect that workers were giving away or taking food. Managers could easily tell which workers had brought in the most money during a given interval and who was doing the best job of persuading customers to buy a particular item. The computerized system could also complicate what would otherwise have been simple customer requests, however. For example, when a man who had not realized the benefit of ordering his son's food as a Happy Meal came back to the counter to ask whether his little boy could have one of the plastic beach pails the Happy Meals were served in, I had to ask a manager what to do, since fulfilling the request would produce a discrepancy between the inventory and the receipts.[26] Sometimes the extreme systematization can induce rather than prevent idiocy, as when a window worker says she cannot serve a cup of coffee that is half decaffeinated and half regular because she would not know how to ring up the sale.[27]

The interactive part of window work is routinized through the Six Steps of Window Service and also through rules aimed at standardizing attitudes and demeanors as well as words and actions. The window workers were taught that they represented McDonald's to the public and that their attitudes were therefore an important component of service quality. Crew people could be reprimanded for not smiling, and often were. The window workers were supposed to be cheerful and polite at all times, but they were also told to be themselves while on the job. McDonald's does not want its workers to seem like robots, so part of the emotion work asked of the window crew is that they act naturally. "Being yourself" in this situation meant behaving in a way that did not seem stilted. Although workers had some latitude to go beyond the script, the short, highly schematic routine obviously did not allow much room for genuine self-expression.

25. Garson (1988) provides an extended discussion of this point.
26. The manager gave him the pail but had to ring it up on the machine as if he had given away a whole Happy Meal.
27. Thanks to Charles Bosk for this story.

Workers were not the only ones constrained by McDonald's routines, of course. The cooperation of service-recipients was crucial to the smooth functioning of the operation. In many kinds of interactive service work, including the insurance sales discussed in Chapter 4, constructing the compliance of service-recipients is an important part of the service worker's job. The routines such workers use may be designed to maximize the control each worker has over customers. McDonald's window workers' routines were not intended to give them much leverage over customers' behavior, however. The window workers interacted only with people who had already decided to do business with McDonald's and who therefore did not need to be persuaded to take part in the service interaction. Furthermore, almost all customers were familiar enough with McDonald's routines to know how they were expected to behave. For instance, I never saw a customer who did not know that she or he was supposed to come up to the counter rather than sit down and wait to be served. This customer training was accomplished through advertising, spatial design, customer experience, and the example of other customers, making it unnecessary for the window crew to put much effort into getting customers to fit into their work routines.[28]

McDonald's ubiquitous advertising trains consumers at the same time that it tries to attract them to McDonald's. Television commercials demonstrate how the service system is supposed to work and familiarize customers with new products. Additional cues about expected customer behavior are provided by the design of the restaurants. For example, the entrances usually lead to the service counter, not to the dining area, making it unlikely that customers will fail to realize that they should get in line, and the placement of waste cans makes clear that customers are expected to throw out their own trash. Most important, the majority of customers have had years of experience with McDonald's, as well as with other fast-food restaurants that have similar arrangements. The company estimates that the average customer visits a McDonald's twenty times a year (Koepp 1987a: 58), and it is not uncommon for a customer to come in several times per week. For many customers, then, ordering at McDonald's is as routine an interaction as it is for the window worker.

28. Mills (1986) elaborates on "customer socialization." Environmental design as a factor in service provision is discussed by Wener (1985) and Normann (1984).

Indeed, because employee turnover is so high, steady customers may be more familiar with the work routines than the workers serving them are. Customers who are new to McDonald's can take their cue from more experienced customers.[29]

Not surprisingly, then, most customers at the McDonald's I studied knew what was expected of them and tried to play their part well. They sorted themselves into lines and gazed up at the menu boards while waiting to be served. They usually gave their orders in the conventional sequence: burgers or other entrees, french fries or other side orders, drinks, and desserts. Hurried customers with savvy might order an item "only if it's in the bin," that is, ready to be served. Many customers prepared carefully so that they could give their orders promptly when they got to the counter. This preparation sometimes became apparent when a worker interrupted to ask, "What kind of dressing?" or "Cream and sugar?", flustering customers who could not deliver their orders as planned.

McDonald's routines, like those of other interactive service businesses, depend on the predictability of customers, but these businesses must not grind to a halt if customers are not completely cooperative. Some types of deviations from standard customer behavior are so common that they become routine themselves, and these can be handled through subroutines (Stinchcombe 1990b: 39). McDonald's routines work most efficiently when all customers accept their products exactly as they are usually prepared; indeed, the whole business is based on this premise. Since, however, some people give special instructions for customized products, such as "no onions," the routine allows for these exceptions.[30] At the franchise I studied, workers could key the special requests into their cash registers, which automatically printed out "grill slips" with the instructions for the grill workers to follow. Under this system, the customer making the special order had to wait for it to be prepared, but the smooth flow of service for other customers was not interrupted. Another type of routine difficulty was customer dissatisfaction with

29. The importance of customer socialization becomes apparent when people with very different consumer experiences are introduced to a service system. When the first McDonald's opened in the Soviet Union in 1990, Moscow's citizens did not find the system immediately comprehensible. They had to be persuaded to get on the shortest lines at the counter, since they had learned from experience that desirable goods were available only where there are long lines (Goldman 1990).

30. Burger King's "Have it your way" campaign virtually forced McDonald's to allow such customized service.

food quality. Whenever a customer had a complaint about the food—cold fries, dried-out burger—window workers were authorized to supply a new product immediately without consulting a supervisor.[31]

These two kinds of difficulties—special orders and complaints about food—were the only irregularities window workers were authorized to handle. The subroutines increased the flexibility of the service system, but they did not increase the workers' discretion, since procedures were in place for dealing with both situations. All other kinds of demands fell outside the window crew's purview. If they were faced with a dispute about money, an extraordinary request, or a furious customer, workers were instructed to call a manager; the crew had no authority to handle such problems.

Given the almost complete regimentation of tasks and preemption of decision making, does McDonald's need the flexibility and thoughtfulness of human workers? As the declining supply of teenagers and legislated increases in the minimum wage drive up labor costs, it is not surprising that McDonald's is experimenting with electronic replacements. So far, the only robot in use handles behind-the-scenes work rather than customer interactions. ARCH (Automated Restaurant Crew Helper) works in a Minnesota McDonald's where it does all the frying and lets workers know when to prepare sandwich buns, when supplies are running low, and when fries are no longer fresh enough to sell. Other McDonald's stores (along with Arby's and Burger King units) are experimenting with a touchscreen computer system that lets customers order their meals themselves, further curtailing the role of the window worker. Although it requires increased customer socialization and cooperation, early reports are that the system cuts service time by thirty seconds and increases sales per window worker 10–20 percent (Chaudhry 1989: F61).

Getting Workers to Work

The extreme routinization does not mean that McDonald's work is undemanding. I found that the company asked a lot of its workers, and the stresses of the job could be considerable. Especially when

31. The defective food or its container was put into a special waste bin. Each shift, one worker or manager had the unenviable task of counting the items in the waste bin so that the inventory could be reconciled with the cash intake.

the store was busy, window work was extraordinarily hectic. From the grill area came the sounds of buzzers buzzing and people shouting instructions. Workers dashed from side to side behind the counter to pick up the various products they needed. Just getting around was extremely difficult. There might be six window workers, a manager or two overseeing the flow of food from the grill and backing up window workers, and another worker in charge of french fries, all trying to maneuver in a very small area, all hurrying, often carrying drinks, ice cream cones, stacks of burgers. Workers with pails of soapy water would frequently come to mop up the greasy floor, leaving it slippery and treacherous even for workers in the regulation nonskid shoes. Traffic jams formed around the soda machines and the salad cases. In the course of a shift various supplies would run out, and there would be no lids for the large cups, no clean trays, no Italian dressing, no ice, until someone found a moment to replenish the stock. Food products were frequently not ready when needed, frustrating window workers' efforts to gather their orders speedily—the supply of Big Macs in the food bin could be wiped out at any moment by a worker with an order for four of them, forcing several other workers to explain to their customers that they would have to wait for their food. The customers, of course, could be a major source of stress themselves. All in all, McDonald's work may be regarded as unskilled, but it was by no means easy to do well. Window workers had to be able to keep many things in mind at once, to keep calm under fire, and to exhibit considerable physical and emotional stamina.

Even when the store was not crowded, workers were expected to keep busy, in accordance with the McDonald's slogan "If there's time to lean, there's time to clean." I was struck by how hard-working most of the crew people were:

> Matthew moves very fast, sweeps up whenever he has a spare moment. In fact, all of the crew people work like beavers—backing each other up, cleaning, etc.

Considering workers' low wages and limited stake in the success of the enterprise, why did they work so hard? Their intensity of effort was produced by several kinds of pressures. First, it seemed to me that most workers did conceive of the work as a team effort and were loath to be seen by their peers as making extra work for other people by not doing their share. Even workers who had what managers would define as a "bad attitude"—resentment about low wages, disrespectful treatment, or any other issue—might work hard in order to keep the respect of their peers.

Naturally, managers played a major role in keeping crew people hard at work. At this store, managers were virtually always present behind the counter and in the grill area. During busy periods several managers would be there at once, working side by side with the crew as well as issuing instructions. Any slacking off by a worker was thus very likely to be noticed. Managers insisted on constant effort; they clearly did not want to pay workers for a moment of nonproductive time. For instance, I heard a manager reprimand a grill worker for looking at the work schedule: "Are you off work? No? You look at the schedule on your time, not on my time." A hand-written sign was posted recommending that window workers come in fifteen minutes early to count out the money in their cash-register drawers on their own time so that, if the amount was wrong, they would not later be held responsible for a shortage. Crew trainers and crew chiefs were encouraged to let managers know about any workers who were shirking or causing problems.

The presence of customers on the scene was another major factor in intensifying workers' efforts. When long lines of people were waiting to be served, few workers had to be told to work as swiftly as possible. The sea of expectant faces provided a great deal of pressure to keep moving. Window workers in particular were anxious to avoid antagonizing customers, who were likely to take out any dissatisfactions on them. The surest way to keep people happy was to keep the lines moving quickly. The arrangement of the workplace, which made window workers clearly visible to the waiting customers as they went about their duties, and customers clearly visible to workers, was important in keeping crew people hard at work. This pressure could have an effect even if customers did not complain. For example, on the day I was to be trained to work window during breakfast, I spent quite a while standing behind the counter, in uniform, waiting to be given instructions and put to work. I was acutely aware that customers were likely to wonder why I did not take their orders, and I tried to adopt an air of attentive expectancy rather than one of casual loitering, in the hope that the customers would assume there was a good reason for my idleness.

These sorts of pressures were not the only reasons crew people worked hard and enthusiastically, however. Managers also tried to motivate them to strenuous efforts through positive means. The managers' constant presence meant that good work would not go unnoticed. McDonald's Corporation stresses the importance of acknowledging workers' efforts, and several workers mentioned that they appreciated such recognition. Indeed, I was surprised at how much it cheered me when a manager complimented me on my "good eye contact" with customers. Various incentive systems were in place as well, to make workers feel that it was in their individual interest to work hard. Free McDonald's meals (instead of the usual half-priced ones) and free record albums were some of the rewards available to good workers. Contests for the highest sales totals or most special raspberry milk shakes sold in a given hour encouraged window workers to compete in speed and pushiness. The possibility of promotion to crew trainer, crew chief, or swing manager also motivated some workers to work as hard as possible.

Group incentives seemed to be especially effective in motivating the crew. As part of a national advertising effort stressing service, all of the stores in McDonald's Chicago region competed to improve their speed. The owner of the store where I worked promised that if one of his stores came out near the top in this competition, the entire crew would be treated to a day at a large amusement park and the crew trainers would be invited for a day's outing on his yacht. The crew trainers and many other workers were very excited about this possibility and were willing to try to achieve unprecedented standards of speed. (They did not win the prize, but the crew of one of the owner's other stores did.) Some workers, though, especially the more disaffected ones, had no desire for either promotions or the low-cost rewards available and spoke derisively of them.

Managers also tried to make workers identify with the interests of the store, even when it clearly resulted in harder work for the same pay. At a monthly meeting for crew trainers, a manager acknowledged that workers were always asking why the store would not pay someone for an extra fifteen minutes to sweep up or do other such tasks not directly related to production, instead of making workers squeeze these tasks in around their main duties. He explained the importance to management of keeping labor costs down:

> "Say we use four extra hours a day—we keep extra people to [wash] the brown trays" or some other tasks. He reels off some calculations—"that's 120 hours a month, times—let's pay them the minimum wage—times twelve months. So that's 1,440 hours times $3.35,

equals $4,825." There are oohs and ahs from the trainers—this sounds like a lot of money to them. I don't think it sounds like that much out of $1.5 million (which he had just said the store brought in annually). The manager went on, "So how do we get extra labor? By watching how we schedule. A $200 hour [an hour with $200 in sales], for instance, will go smoother with four window people, but three good people could do it. We save money, and then we can use it on other things, like training, for instance."

The crew trainers were willing to agree that it was only reasonable for the store to extract as much labor from them as possible, though resentments about overwork certainly did not disappear. The manager was also successful enough in getting the crew trainers to identify with management that they were willing to give the names of crew people who were uncooperative.

When I thought about the crew trainers' meeting after it was over, the manipulative and exploitative aspects of management's relations with workers seemed dominant, but that was not the impression I had during the meeting. What struck me most then was the manager's skill in turning the group of young people, who had seemed listless and vaguely sullen at first, into an enthusiastic, energized group eager to work together to improve the store. He got each of the crew trainers to contribute ideas, defused discontent by soliciting complaints and apparently taking them seriously, and built the crew trainers' commitment to the store by emphasizing their elite status and their importance in keeping the operation running smoothly. The manager obviously knew the crew trainers as individuals, and considerable joking was mingled with the discussion of business. All in all, the meeting seemed a good demonstration of the company's favored management techniques of establishing an atmosphere of teamwork and fun, providing plenty of recognition to individual workers, and avoiding authoritarianism.

The atmosphere in the store was not always equally harmonious—the crew trainers were, after all, chosen in part for their good attitudes—but, despite the strict discipline, it was usually pleasant enough. Most of the managers treated workers respectfully most of the time, and many were on terms of affectionate teasing. There were a lot of rules, though, and managers were strict about insisting that jobs be done exactly according to McDonald's specifications, so workers were used to being given frequent orders and corrections as they went about their work.

Not all of the workers I interviewed felt that they were treated well by managers, and I heard about some instances of disrespectful or unfair treatment, reflecting the corporation's incomplete success in standardizing managerial work. One worker had heard a manager call a window worker "a stupid broad," and she felt that in general the managers did not show enough concern or respect for workers. Another described how embarrassed and upset she felt when managers yelled at her in front of customers. Others said that they had been misled about how much they would be paid or what their hours would be. I myself heard one manager speak sharply or sarcastically to workers quite routinely. In answer to my question about whether they were treated well by managers, though, almost three-quarters of my sample gave unequivocally positive replies.

Respectful treatment was only one of the criteria by which workers judged managers. Competence was another central criterion: everyone resented managers who were bad at figuring out how much food to order from the grill workers, for example, letting products run out and then expecting the crew to be able to replenish everything at once. Predictability was another important attribute: workers wanted to know that managers would treat everyone fairly and would not be friendly and relaxed one shift and humorless and tyrannical another. The workers understandably disliked managers to whom "the customer is always right" meant that workers had to put up with abusive behavior, and the crew was especially fond of one manager who was known to have backed up window workers on some occasions of conflict with customers. For instance, a swing manager told me that when she had been a crew person, she had once reached over the counter and grabbed a customer who had called her a "stupid bitch"; this manager backed her up and told the customer to leave.

All of these factors affected store morale and presumably had an impact on crew efficiency, turnover rates, and customer satisfaction, just as Hamburger University preaches. For the most part, it seemed that sticking to corporate directives on proper management produced good results, while, predictably, more authoritarian and arbitrary interactions with staff produced resentment. The apparently respectful, even-handed, psychologistic management style that McDonald's encourages helped make the repetitive, fast-paced, low-autonomy, low-paid jobs tolerable to workers.[32] Workers learned

32. On the use of "human relations" managerial techniques to accommodate workers to Taylorist work regimes, see Braverman (1974: 139–51) and Howard (1985).

to accept even rules that were quite disadvantageous to them when they perceived those rules to be fairly administered by people who regarded them as human beings. The official McDonald's stance was likely to anger workers, however, when, faced with customers who did not treat the crew as human beings, managers felt it was more important to satisfy the paying public than to defend the workers' dignity.

OVERVIEW

McDonald's pioneered the routinization of interactive service work and remains an exemplar of extreme standardization. Innovation is not discouraged at McDonald's; the company favors experimentation, at least among managers and franchisees. Ironically, though, "the object is to look for new, innovative ways to create an experience that is exactly the same no matter what McDonald's you walk into, no matter where it is in the world" (Rosenthal 1989: 12). Thus, when someone in the field comes up with a good idea—and such McDonald's success stories as the Egg McMuffin and the Big Mac were store-level inspirations (Koepp 1987a: 60)—the corporation experiments, tests, and refines the idea and finally implements it in a uniform way systemwide. One distinctive feature of McDonald's-style routinization is that there, to a great extent, uniformity is a goal in itself.

The company described in Chapter 4, Combined Insurance, provides a contrast. Combined's managers encouraged strict adherence to detailed routines because they believed that those routines incorporated effective selling techniques, not because they wanted to guarantee every prospective customer a particular kind of "Combined experience."

McDonald's, however, does promise uniform products and consistent service, and to provide them the company has broken down virtually every task required to run a store into detailed routines with clear instructions and standards. For those routines to run smoothly, conditions must be relatively predictable, so McDonald's tries to control as many contingencies as possible, including the attitudes and behavior of workers, managers, and customers. The company uses a wide array of socialization and control techniques to ensure that these people are familiar with McDonald's procedures and willing to comply with them.

Most McDonald's work is organized as low-paying, low-status, part-time jobs that give workers little autonomy. Almost every decision about how to do crew people's tasks has been made in advance by the corporation, and many of the decisions have been built into the stores' technology. Why use human workers at all, if not to take advantage of the human capacity to respond to circumstances flexibly? McDonald's does want to provide at least a simulacrum of the human attributes of warmth, friendliness, and recognition. For that reason, not only workers' movements but also their words, demeanor, and attitudes are subject to managerial control.

Although predictability is McDonald's hallmark, not all factors can be controlled by management. One of the most serious irregularities that store management must deal with is fluctuation in the flow of customers, both expected and unexpected. Since personnel costs are the most manipulable variable affecting a store's profitability, managers want to match labor power to consumer demand as exactly as possible. They do so by paying all crew people by the hour, giving them highly irregular hours based on expected sales—sometimes including split shifts—and sending workers home early or keeping them late as conditions require. In other words, the costs of uneven demand are shifted to workers whenever possible. Since most McDonald's crew people cannot count on working a particular number of hours at precisely scheduled times, it is hard for them to make plans based on how much money they will earn or exactly what times they will be free. Workers are pressured to be flexible in order to maximize the organization's own flexibility in staffing levels. In contrast, of course, flexibility in the work process itself is minimized.

Routinization has not made the crew people's work easy. Their jobs, although highly structured and repetitive, are often demanding and stressful. Under these working conditions, the organization's limited commitment to workers, as reflected in job security, wages, and benefits, makes the task of maintaining worker motivation and discipline even more challenging. A variety of factors, many orchestrated by the corporation, keeps McDonald's crew people hard at work despite the limited rewards. Socialization into McDonald's norms, extremely close supervision (both human and electronic), individual and group incentives, peer pressure, and pressure from customers all play their part in getting workers to do things the McDonald's way.

Because franchisees and store-level managers are responsible for enforcing standardization throughout the McDonald's system, their socialization includes a more intensive focus on building commitment to and pride in the organization than does crew training. In fact, it is the corporate attempt at transforming these higher-level McDonald's people by making them more loyal, confident, flexible, and sensitive to others, as well as more knowledgeable about company procedures, that makes the extreme rigidity of the crew training workable. The crew people do not have to be trusted with decision-making authority, because all unusual problems are referred to managers. Their more extensive training gives them the knowledge and attitudes to make the kinds of decisions the corporation would approve. (Combined Insurance, as we will see, takes routinization by transformation even further.) In addition to thorough socialization, McDonald's managers and franchisees are subjected to close corporate oversight. Every aspect of their stores' operations is rated by corporate staff, and they are sanctioned accordingly.

Despite elaborate socialization and social controls, McDonald's stores do not, of course, carry out every corporate directive exactly as recommended. In the store I studied, managers did not always provide their workers with the mandated support and encouragement, crew trainers did not always follow the four-step training system, and window workers did not always carry out the Six Steps of Window Service with the required eye contact and smile. There were many kinds of pressures to deviate from corporate standards. Nonetheless, the benefits of standardization should not be underestimated. As every Durkheimian knows, clear rules and shared standards provide support and coherence as well as constraint. Although some aspects of the routines did strike the participants as overly constraining, undignified, or silly, the approved routines largely worked. In all of these examples of deviation, the routines would have produced more efficient and pleasant service, and those that apply to management and training would have benefited workers as well as customers.

Obtaining the cooperation of workers and managers is not enough to ensure the smooth functioning of McDonald's relatively inflexible routines. Customers must be routinized as well. Not only do customers have to understand the service routine and accept the limited range of choices the company offers, they also must be willing to do some kinds of work that are done for them in conventional restaurants, including carrying food to the table and throwing out their trash. Experience, advertising, the example set by other customers, and clear environmental cues familiarize customers with McDonald's routines, and most want to cooperate in order to speed service. For these reasons, McDonald's interactive service workers do not have to direct most customers, and window workers' routines are therefore not designed to give them power over customers. Combined Insurance takes a very different approach to routinizing service interactions and to shaping the balance of power between workers and service-recipients.

4

Orchestrating Optimism
Combined Insurance

The McDonald's approach to routinization closely follows the logic of Taylorism: to maximize managerial control of the work process, break work down into its constituent tasks and predetermine how those tasks are to be done. McDonald's demonstrates that even when human beings are important raw materials and human interactions are a major part of the work process or product, routinization is possible if the work specifications can be made relatively predictable. The company has designed customer encounters that are short, schematic, and simple, and its customers have been well prepared to play their part smoothly. Moreover, these customers are generally motivated to fill their roles as expected in order to expedite service. Although nonroutine problems do still arise, the presence of managers with more elaborate training makes it possible to handle these problems without expanding window workers' decision-making scope.

Not all service organizations are blessed with, or can engineer, conditions so admirably suited to routinization. Many kinds of service work involve lengthier, more complex, and more varied interactions. Service-recipients' behavior is often considerably harder to predict than is that of McDonald's guests, either because the problems they bring to the service encounter are idiosyncratic or complicated or because, believing that the standard service routine will not adequately serve their interests, they resist it. Under these conditions, workers need discretion to customize their work in response to varied customer behavior and requirements. Can the logic of routinization be adapted to circumstances that demand significant worker decision-making?

Combined Insurance Company faces this dilemma. It is common industry practice to deal with varied and unpredictable work specifications by using agents who are broadly knowledgeable about

86

insurance and other investments, but such professionalization has not been Combined Insurance's approach. Instead, it has followed a strategy of routinization, although with mixed success. As in other organizations, routinization at Combined Insurance does enhance managerial control over workers. In this business, however, customer compliance is as significant a problem for management as worker compliance is. Thus the agents' routines are designed not simply to limit their decision-making scope but also to enhance their power, vis-à-vis prospective customers if not vis-à-vis management. To acquire this enhanced power over customers, and hence over the work, agents are asked to cede to the company the right to reshape many aspects of their selves, including their emotions, values, and ways of thinking. Such routinization through transformation need not be experienced by agents as corporate control at all, however, because it is presented as the agents' choice to exercise control over themselves (see Biggart 1989: 135–59). If this transformative process works correctly, the company should be able to count on agents themselves to make the same decisions that the company would have chosen.

Several differences between the work of the Combined Insurance agents and the McDonald's crew explain why Combined Insurance tried to appropriate more of the self of each new worker than McDonald's does. One clear difference is that customers come to McDonald's having already decided that they want to do business there, while Combined Insurance relied on its workers to find prospects and persuade them to become customers. In addition, since the agents were usually free of immediate supervision, the company's success was dependent on the self-motivation and self-discipline of its agents. Furthermore, since the agents were sure to face considerable opposition as they tried to carry out their routines, they needed to be both more determined and more flexible in dealing with customers than do McDonald's workers. Faced with the inescapable element of discretion in the agents' work, Combined Insurance tried to exert control by shaping their characters and habits of thought.

COMBINED INSURANCE

While McDonald's has become an exemplar for standardizing service work, Combined Insurance's extensive routinization of the work of insurance agents makes it unusual among insurance companies.

Few have gone as far as Combined Insurance has in scripting agents' presentations or in trying to standardize agents' attitudes and ways of thinking. Like McDonald's, Combined Insurance was built by one man whose ongoing influence is pervasive. The company was founded in 1922 by W. Clement Stone, then twenty years old, and his Positive Mental Attitude philosophy, PMA, still permeates the company.

For most of its history, Combined Insurance was the kind of monolithic organization that McDonald's is, a company that prospered by carving out a distinct business approach and sticking to what it knew best. During its first sixty years, although the company expanded the types of insurance it sold, it did not abandon its traditional market segment, distribution system, sales approach, or philosophy. Its agents called on homes and businesses door to door, using a tightly scripted sales pitch to sell small, low-priced individual policies to lower-middle-class and working-class people. The company's culture, based on PMA, was strong and unified.

Combined Insurance changed considerably during the 1980s and continues to change. In 1980, Combined International Corporation was formed as a holding company for Combined Insurance Company of America. Business was stagnating, so in 1982, seeking both a renewal of the company's profitability and a successor for the eighty-year-old Stone, Combined International merged with the much smaller Ryan Insurance Group. Pat Ryan became president and chief executive officer of Combined International, as well as its largest shareholder (Simon 1986). Ryan immediately began an ambitious program of acquisitions that gradually transformed what had been a single business into a diversified financial conglomerate. Combined International bought several insurance companies and brokerage houses during the 1980s, thereby expanding the types of insurance it sold, its target markets, and its range of distribution systems.

In 1987, Combined International's name was changed to avoid confusion between the holding company and its main operating subsidiary, Combined Insurance. The new name, Aon Corporation, was taken from a Gaelic word suggesting oneness or unity (*Combined International Annual Report* for 1986). Since Combined International had become a conglomerate of companies with cultures and business approaches quite unlike those Stone had created, the name change apparently reflected the aspiration toward rather than the reality of a spirit of cohesion.

W. Clement Stone stepped down as chairman of Aon Corporation in 1990, but he remains chairman of Combined Insurance. Aon Corporation by then encompassed nearly forty product lines (Byrne 1990), and its assets put it among the two hundred largest American corporations (*Forbes* 1990: 247). Among diversified financial companies, it ranked twenty-fourth in profits and twelfth in profit margins (profits as a percentage of revenues) (*Fortune* 1990: 316–17).

Combined Insurance's Superior Policy Division, which handles direct sales of accident, health, and life insurance, is still the biggest contributor to corporate revenues (*Aon Corporation Annual Report* for 1989). Although it provided the cash for the corporation's acquisition program, its growth rates have been slower than those of other Aon subsidiaries (Simon 1986). The bulk of Combined's earnings derive from its accident division, the part of the business that follows Stone's original plan most closely. Most of Aon Corporation's profits from life insurance, by contrast, come not from Combined Insurance but from another subsidiary, Life Insurance Company of Virginia (Byrne 1990).

At the time of my fieldwork in 1987, Combined's life insurance division was still using the highly routinized sales and training techniques Stone had developed. This chapter presents the practices that were then in place in the life division. In response to a variety of kinds of problems that undermined profitability, that division was then about to introduce major changes in the way it structured its policies, hired and compensated agents, and sold to the public.[1] Combined's accident division, its largest and most profitable, has not undergone similar changes, however, so most of the analysis in the present chapter still applies to much of the company.[2]

Stone founded Combined Insurance with the idea of selling policies that could be purchased on impulse, with pocket change. The first policies, for accident insurance, cost fifty cents for six months of coverage. The agents in Combined's accident division still use a "pennies a day" approach in selling, and the policies available in

1. Appendix 2 describes the pressures for change and the kinds of procedures that were about to be implemented.

2. As is described in Appendix 1, I studied agents who sold life insurance rather than accident insurance because the contacts I had at Combined Insurance were in the life division. There were advantages to being placed in the division where difficulties were prompting changes, since it allowed me to see the drawbacks as well as the strengths of Combined's routinization approach and to consider which circumstances made that approach problematic.

the life and health divisions at the time of my fieldwork were also intended to be impulse buys. The routines Stone developed reflected this business strategy. Agents did not normally spend a lot of time with each potential customer; they quickly delivered a short, very enthusiastic sales pitch, designed to sweep customers up so that they would make an immediate decision. As one Combined Insurance employee told me, the company's basic strategy has been "to sell products the way you'd sell Fuller Brushes," relying on a quick pitch and high volume. Stone systematized his sales methods, reducing them to formulas presented in Sales Manuals 1 through 5. The sales routine used by Combined's accident insurance agents now differs very little from the one Stone first developed. By 1987, the routines used to sell life insurance, which is more expensive, were somewhat longer and a bit more interactive, but they continued to follow Stone's principles for encouraging impulse buying.

Combined Insurance is highly specialized in its marketing. It focuses on lower-middle-class and working-class families in small towns and rural areas, ignoring the "upscale demographics" preferred by most of its competitors. These types of families are assumed to have little need for sophisticated financial services, so at the time of my fieldwork Combined Insurance did not offer a broad range of insurance policies or any other kinds of investments. The company's agents were even more highly specialized. Assigned to either the life, the accident, or the health division, they sold only one type of insurance. Their job was to find people who could be persuaded to buy one of the few policies they had to offer, not to help clients choose from a broad range of insurance and investment options to meet their particular needs. They carried out their work by following highly detailed scripts.

The accident division, on which the company was founded, is still its mainstay. The company had approximately 4,000 agents in 1987, and about six times as many sold accident insurance as sold life insurance. The life division was founded in 1966, and its first product, the Little Giant Life policy, was extraordinarily successful, breaking industry sales records. The division sold one billion dollars' worth of face value in only four and a half years (seven years had been the previous record for selling that much life insurance), a feat that is especially remarkable because the face value of each policy was very small. The first Little Giant Life policies provided $2,400 in whole life insurance,[3] which a customer could, if eligible, increase to $9,600 over a four-year period. Since that time, the division has made larger and larger policies available. When I was trained, however, the highest face value available was only $15,000 at the time of sale, which eligible customers could eventually increase to $25,000 (in whole and term life insurance). Such policies are not sufficient to cover the life insurance needs of most people. They were designed to supplement other kinds of insurance and investments by covering policyholders' "final expenses"; the smaller policies were basically intended to cover only burial costs. Because the policies were inexpensive compared to more substantial investments, the agents tried to present the decision to buy as a relatively trivial one that could reasonably be made on the spur of the moment.

Working for Combined Insurance

Combined's agents moved from town to town within their sales areas, calling on prospective customers door to door. The team I was eventually assigned to study worked in northern Illinois. The team had four regular members, including the sales manager, plus one agent who was in the process of switching to this team from another one nearby. All of the agents on the team were white men in their early twenties, and most were new to the company. The sales manager had been with the company a year and a half, and one agent had been working for six months, but the other three, who had been in the same training class, had been with Combined Insurance for only three months.

The sales team was apparently typical for Combined Insurance in having only male, relatively inexperienced agents, most of whom came from a small town or a farm and had a working-class or a lower-middle-class background. The team was not typical in its productivity, though: two of the newest agents were the region's top two salesmen. It is possible that the team was also unusual in its ethical standards. I learned from one of the agents that I had not

---

3. Whole life insurance differs from term life insurance in two important ways. First, its contract provisions remain in effect for the life of the policyholder, rather than for a specified period of time. Second, the policyholder builds equity in the policy. The cash value of the policy can be borrowed while the policy is in effect or redeemed if it is canceled.

been assigned to the sales team most convenient for me to study. The agent surmised that I had been placed with his own team because of its "greater work ethics" as well as higher sales, and in the course of the fieldwork I heard a few more references to the other team's use of misleading tactics, which of course were contrary to company policy.

In their door-to-door sales, Combined's agents called, without appointments, on homes and businesses. Accident insurance agents, then as now, followed a plan developed by Stone for systematically canvassing a town by making cold calls ("Gold Calls," he termed them). Life insurance agents were also supposed to make some cold calls, but most of their time was spent calling on people who already had Combined Insurance accident policies.

The company's agents did not work out of local offices; instead, they moved from place to place in accordance with Combined's "route/month system." Each sales team covered a given sales territory over a six-month period, then started at the beginning again. Sales teams from each of the company's three divisions covered the same territory on a synchronized schedule, so that a given household might expect to be visited by a Combined Insurance life insurance agent in January and July, by a health insurance agent in March and September, and by an accident insurance agent in May and November. On these calls the agents tried to sell new policies (perhaps to people who had said no six months earlier), to renew existing policies, and to persuade customers to increase their coverage. For most types of policies, Combined Insurance had its agents pick up the premium payments in the field every six months, rather than having customers mail their payments to the company.

This system required the agents to spend a lot of time away from home. In sparsely populated parts of the country, some agents were on the road all week, spending only weekends at home. According to one of the agents on the sales team I worked with, that team spent about 40 percent of its time away from home.

The organization of the work also meant that Combined's agents were unlikely to develop longstanding relationships with their customers or to develop a sense of having their own clientele. Although the last line of the agents' script was "I'll see you again in six months," there was no guarantee that the agent who sold a policy to a customer would be the one who would be back six months later to collect the premium and try to increase the coverage. First, because of the extremely high job turnover among Combined's agents, the agent who sold the original policy might well have left the company six months later. Furthermore, the company apparently did not have a consistent policy on the desirability of having an agent call on the same people repeatedly. One agent told me that this practice was being encouraged but that it had formerly been discouraged on the grounds that an agent who had been turned down on a sales call would be less likely to approach that household with a positive attitude on subsequent calls.

Although Combined's sales system did not foster ties between customers and agents, the company was of course concerned with developing a loyal customer base:

> Bill, the director of market research, says that the sales approach is . . . not designed around building a personal relationship between the customer and an agent. He says that they definitely do try to build a relationship between the customers and the company, however. I say (having previously mentioned my research at McDonald's), "Like McDonald's, actually." He seems struck by this and says that it's true. There are some restaurants you go to because you like the waitress or you know the owner, but you go to a McDonald's because you know exactly what you're going to get. "And there's nothing wrong with that," he says.

Unlike McDonald's, Combined's Superior Policy Division does not use advertising to build this bond between the company and current or potential policyholders. It does not advertise at all. Nonetheless, it was true that many of the people I met while accompanying agents on sales calls seemed to have strong positive feelings about the company, often based on their satisfaction with how Combined Insurance had handled claims filed under their accident policies. Most of my city-dwelling acquaintances had never heard of Combined Insurance, but almost all of the small-town and rural people we called on recognized the company as one that had done business in their area for years.

Some policyholders were baffled by Combined's ever-changing personnel, though. Several asked the agents I was with, "How come they always send a different person?" The question was common enough to be covered in the training manual, which suggested the response, "You've finally got the best." In the field, Tom was ready with the answer, "Well, we have 8,000 employees, and they all heard what nice folks you are and want to meet you," which got a big laugh.

Because of Combined's selling system and its limited array of products, its insurance agents had different sorts of satisfactions and different career paths than are typical of the industry. Unlike most insurance agents, who are expected to build up their own clientele and who can derive satisfaction from establishing ongoing relationships with clients, working with them to alter their coverage as family and financial situations change, Combined's agents' relations with customers were generally brief, single encounters. Both agents who work for companies that allow them to handle various kinds of insurance policies and a wide variety of plans and agents who sell policies for several different companies usually develop enough knowledge about insurance to be able to choose from among many options the policies that best meet their clients' needs. These agents typically develop their careers by expanding their clientele to include people whose larger incomes and greater assets lead them to use a broader variety of insurance products and investment plans. Accordingly, the agents expand their expertise. Combined's agents received very little training in insurance and had no occasion to broaden their understanding of the business or to learn about other kinds of investments, because the company offered very few options. Since their sales presentation was closely scripted, once they had attained a certain level of proficiency Combined's agents were not even expected to continue to improve significantly at their work.

Combined's agents were expected to advance their careers not by expanding their clientele or their expertise but by becoming managers. Combined Insurance promoted agents to sales managers very quickly, in part because high turnover meant that new managers were needed frequently. An executive told me, with only slight exaggeration, "Here, if an agent isn't a manager within six months, he's practically considered a failure."[4] The most successful agents on the team I studied, both of whom had been working only three months, expected to become sales managers within a couple of months. Combined's sales managers continue to sell insurance, but they are also responsible for hiring new agents and training them in the field, for conducting ongoing training, and for a good deal of paperwork. In addition to their own higher commissions, they receive a share of the commissions of the members of their sales team.

4. This expectation is one of the many features of the agents' work and career that has since been changed. See Appendix 2.

In fact, though, one regional manager estimated that before the changes were made in the life division about one-third of the sales managers had no sales team. For them, promotion to manager simply meant higher earnings per sale. The average size of a sales team was only 2.9, including the manager, he said.

By all accounts, Combined Insurance had a serious problem keeping agents. Andrew, an executive who had recently joined the company after many years' experience in the business, told me that his former employer had a 38 percent retention rate for agents after five years, compared to an industry average of 18 percent. Combined's five-year retention rate, he said, was only 5–7 percent, and the company had to recruit approximately 150 percent of its total sales force annually. Another manager said of my training class, which was held in January and had ten members (excluding me), "If one lasts through June, it'll be a lot."[5] The manager of the sales team I studied had been trained eighteen months earlier in a class with eighteen people from Illinois and Wisconsin, of whom only two were still with Combined Insurance.

The high turnover among life agents was a matter of serious concern to the company and was one reason that the division was planning major changes in its hiring practices, compensation system, and sales approach. It seemed clear to the sales manager of the team I observed that the difficulty of earning a good living was the main cause of employee turnover: "People only stick around if they're making consistent money." The regional manager expanded on this issue, explaining that the combination of highly stressful work with uncertain earnings led to high turnover. He saw the job as making extraordinary emotional demands on agents, who had to be able to tolerate considerable frustration and even abuse in the course of their work and nonetheless to throw themselves into their selling efforts wholeheartedly. He spoke of their "going through hell" and "leaving their blood on the sidewalk" after some encounters with customers. In his opinion, the likelihood that even many of these heroic efforts would fail and that the agents could lose money if they were not selling consistently was what cost the company employees.

Marty tells me that agents go through really hard times. He says that people (prospects) can really be crude, crass, and mean—"'I

---

5. When I conducted follow-up interviews at Combined Insurance two and a half years later, I learned that not one member of my ten-person training class was still with the company.

didn't ask to be sold insurance.'" He says that "Combined is for the tough." . . . Selling is not as simple as giving the sales presentation and rattling off rebuttals. You can do that all week [and never get anywhere]. You can spend $90 on a hotel, $75 on gas, $80 a week on keeping your car in shape, because you're putting on two thousand miles per week—"that's why there's t.o. [turnover]," he says. That's why any kind of commission sales job is "gonna spit people out."

The stressfulness of the job and the difficulty of earning a living would not explain why Combined's turnover rates were so much higher than those of other insurance companies. (Some companies, it is true, do guarantee a minimum salary for agents in their first year, making it less likely that they will quit in discouragement right away. At Combined Insurance, additional income was provided if the agent did not earn a minimum amount in the first thirteen weeks. The difference between the agent's commissions and the minimum was made up by the sales manager, who presumably was therefore motivated to provide good field training and support.) Combined's director of market research told me that he had learned from his colleagues in other companies that to reduce turnover it was important to establish solid relationships between salespeople and clients. Another company executive believed that the company's highly routinized selling system and limited array of products were important contributors to Combined's problem with retaining agents:

> Those people the company hires who really want to expand and get into the life insurance business end up leaving, because you can't really do that with Combined. Andrew feels that he has twenty-six years' experience in life insurance; if he'd spent all that time with Combined, he'd have one year's experience twenty-six times.[6]

High turnover rates meant that the company had to hire new agents continually. At the time of my research, Combined Insurance used one interview, a multiple-choice test, and a field demonstration to select life agents from applicants who answered newspaper ads placed by sales managers. Andrew said that this method was "OK for just hiring bodies" but not so good for hiring people who were likely to be successful. In contrast, his former company put its recruits through six interviews and hired only about one in fifteen

---

6. Appendix 2 describes the changes the company instituted to try to ameliorate excessive agent turnover, as well as declining sales and poor renewal rates, two other serious problems.

applicants. The multiple-choice test used by Combined, which was created by the Life Insurance Marketing Research Association (LIMRA) and graded by that organization, asked questions about how applicants saw other people, about their job preferences, and about their own personalities and characters (Did they feel happy and lucky most of the time? Did tears come to their eyes easily? Did they talk a lot, even around strangers?). Bill, the director of market research, said that he did not know what sorts of traits they were looking for. If the companies knew how to grade the test, he said, LIMRA could not charge them for doing the grading.[7] Andrew felt that the test was of little use.

Marty, the regional sales manager, had quite specific ideas about what kind of people the company should be hiring. Although he felt that "anyone with the courage to stick it out for a year, regardless of their talent, will learn enough to be a success," he said that they looked for people who were:

> independent, outgoing, goal-oriented, and competitive. "They are people who GOTTA win. We want people who, if they were in a war and found themselves face to face with an enemy soldier with a machine gun, wouldn't run. Instead, they'd rip the machine gun out of the enemy's hands." . . . Agents should be stubborn, independent, and cocky. "The successful types are the ones who are willing to fight. They are the ones who don't let what others say and do affect what they will do. Otherwise, if three customers tell you how terrible life insurance is, you'll stop selling. You have to ignore that sort of thing." . . . Marty also says that they want people who will be able to talk to anyone. Those people who have to be in a structured, organized environment wouldn't be good for this job. They need "freewheeling people—the best people may be the hardest to control."

This gladiatorial image of sales work may explain why Combined Insurance had only a handful of women agents.[8] The description is also notable for highlighting a paradox of the Combined Insurance agents' job. The job demanded independence and cockiness, yet, as we will see, it also demanded that workers both closely follow a prescribed routine and be sufficiently empathic and sensitive to adapt their behavior in response to their customers.

---

7. My reaction upon seeing the test was that I would never have been hired to sell life insurance based upon it, since, had I answered honestly, it would have revealed me to be both pessimistic and thin-skinned.

8. Chapter 6 provides an analysis of the gender meanings of the agents' work.

Combined Insurance did not rely exclusively on newspaper advertising to recruit employees. It also encouraged its agents to refer people they knew to the company. Andrew believed that this method of recruitment had a much higher likelihood of success than newspaper advertising. In training class, the new trainees received forms on which to list names of people they would like to sponsor, as well as brochures to hand to potential recruits. The brochure's list of questions to ask prospects provides insight into both what Combined Insurance sees as the advantages of the job and what it wants of agents:

1. Do you like what you're doing?
2. Are you making enough money?
3. Is your job going anywhere?
4. Do you believe you are lucky?
5. Do you like sports and competition?

These dissatisfied, ambitious, optimistic, and competitive people would be taught in training class that it was up to them to create their own luck and to maintain their optimistic self-image at all costs.

Learning to Sell Insurance

Once agents were hired and had accompanied a sales manager on some calls to see what the job was like, they went to one of nine regional training centers for two weeks of classes. The classes I attended in Chicago were held in the new skyscraper where Combined's corporate offices are located. The training facilities were not nearly as elaborate, slick, or capital-intensive as McDonald's, but the program was carefully designed to give completely inexperienced trainees both the skills and the confidence they would need to face prospective customers. Unlike Hamburger University, where large cohorts of trainees attend lectures and laboratory classes taught by many different instructors, Combined's training was carried out in relatively small classes taught almost entirely by one trainer for each group. The company covered the trainees' expenses but did not pay them for the training period.

The training class I joined had ten other members, eight men and two women. Most of the trainees were from a small town or a rural area. Three lived in Texas, and the rest in Illinois, Iowa, or Wisconsin.

All of the trainees were white, and six were men in their early twenties. These six had varied work experience, including plumbing, hotel management, biological research, rock and roll, supermarket work, and office work. Three were about to get married and, presumably, hoped that insurance sales would be a lucrative career for them, and three had at least some college. The two women were both middle-aged and had grown children. Both had considerable and varied sales experience, and one had sold Combined Insurance accident policies for a brief time. The two middle-aged men also had grown families, and both had sold insurance in other Combined Insurance divisions—one for twenty-one years—and were switching to life in the hope of increasing their earnings.

The training course was quite intensive. We were instructed to arrive by 8 A.M., and classes never ended before 5 P.M. Trainees were expected to spend four hours every night on homework and to devote much of the weekend to study.

The walls of our classroom were decorated with photographs of W. Clement Stone and Pat Ryan and with many inspirational slogans, hallmarks of Stone's Positive Mental Attitude philosophy. These included: "Whatever the mind of man can conceive and believe, the mind of man can achieve for those . . . who have PMA"; "If it is to be, it is up to me"; and "We are quality in motion . . . do it now!" (ellipses in originals). In the central position hung a large medieval-style shield with crossed swords, inscribed with the words "W. Clement Stone, Royal Knight." (Later in the week, we learned that agents could be similarly knighted if they sold one million dollars' worth of life insurance in three months.) The classroom was outfitted with a video cassette player and television, felt-tip-marker boards, and an overhead projector.

On the first day of class, the trainer, Mark, had us write down the objectives of the training course. He intended to:

1. Teach us the PMA philosophy.
2. Teach us the standard sales talks and rebuttals ("Give that an asterisk.").
3. Teach us the principles and techniques of Combined's sales system.
4. Help us set and strive for meaningful goals.

This list accurately reflected Combined's emphasis on teaching proper attitudes and selling techniques and its relative lack of attention to teaching agents about life insurance. The company conceived its task as that of turning recruits into sales professionals, not into insurance professionals, and trainees were taught just enough about the business to be able to talk about their products. That, it seemed to me, might not be enough to allow agents to answer prospects' questions intelligently, if the prospects were at all knowledgeable. Just how little we had learned about life insurance was brought home to me shortly after I completed the training course, when a friend told me that she and her husband had recently bought universal life policies. I did not know what they were.

Point number 2 on the list of objectives certainly deserved its asterisk. The trainees spent much of their time memorizing and rehearsing sales routines. Not only were they taught to recite the words of the sales scripts, they were instructed in proper gestures, intonation, eye contact, and other physical and emotional aspects of the routine. Considerable class time was devoted to chanting aloud in unison, as the trainees struggled to get the words of the scripts exactly right and to synchronize their hand and eye motions properly:

> We do the sales presentation as a group, chanting in unison, pointing to the words in the presentation books as we would with customers, and turning the pages at the right times. Mark has a cowbell, which he says he will ring if he sees anyone look up from the floppy [the presentation book] at the wrong time. No one gets caught.

In addition, the trainees rehearsed knocking on doors, getting inside, and leaving properly.

Even though much of the training course involved this sort of rote work, Combined's message was not that a robot could do the agent's job. On the contrary, the trainer constantly emphasized that personal character was a crucial aspect of success, and the most important quality of all was what W. Clement Stone called PMA, Positive Mental Attitude. The first day of class began with warm-up chants, which were to become extremely familiar:

> Mark has us all stand up and teaches us to yell, "I FEEL HEALTHY, I FEEL HAPPY, I FEEL TERRIFIC!"[9] We are to use appropriate arm

---

9. By the end of the training period, this chant had become comically inappropriate, since almost every member of the class, plus the trainer, had a cold or some other illness. (The group chose "The Germs of Life" as its class name.) Those feeling sick nevertheless chanted that they felt healthy.

movements while yelling, which simulate throwing "the winning punch" or "the winning pitch." He then asks, "How's your PMA?" and we all yell, "TERRIFIC!" He leads applause.

We repeated these cheers and similar optimistic slogans several times every day. I was surprised at how effective they were.

> That night, telling a friend about my first day of training, I note that I do sound enthusiastic as I talk about the exercises—PMA seems to work. I point out that even if you feel ridiculous while shouting out the HHT (happy, healthy, terrific) cheer, you can't sulk while you're doing it.

I learned that the PMA philosophy and exercises suffused the company and that even home office managers and workers did the HHT cheer on occasion, although such practices were less prevalent than they had been when Stone maintained day-to-day control of the organization. In class, we spent time every day talking about PMA, but there too, according to a veteran Combined Insurance manager involved with training, the emphasis on PMA had diminished in recent years.

> In the past there might be a thirty- or forty-five-minute warm-up before you'd even get started. . . . Training sometimes seemed like a circus, rather than a serious business. . . . There were banners and whistles.

The manager told me that although Pat Ryan, the new corporate president, did believe in the PMA philosophy, the word had gotten around that he thought that "Enough is enough."

When I took the course, plenty of time was spent on "serious business." The curriculum included, in addition to sales techniques, information about Combined's history, basic information about life insurance, explanations of the policies the agents would sell and renew, work on setting goals, and discussions of business ethics. Lectures and group chanting were varied with other instructional methods. The trainees did a lot of role-playing in order to learn how to deal with various kinds of selling situations and to respond to customer objections. During the first week each trainee was video-taped giving the sales presentation, and Mark watched each trainee's tape with the performer and gave feedback (almost all positive) on his or her performance. A couple of written tests on policy features and on underwriting rules were given. Videotapes were used to teach proper sales techniques, and many classes began or ended with inspirational videotapes, including tapes of W. Clement Stone lectures and interviews.

Mark worked hard to motivate the trainees to master the course materials. He had us write down such thoughts to ponder as "I will be in front of real customers very soon. My income depends on my knowledge," and "If I had a loved one who was very ill and on the operating table, would I want the doctor to know his job as well as I know my own?" The trainees varied in their diligence. Some of the young men, not wanting to spend all of this rare visit to a big city studying, devoted their evenings and weekends to bar-hopping instead. But others took the training very seriously indeed, as I found when I visited the trainees' hotel for a weekend study session:

> Virgil is sleeping when Mike and I come into the room, but he wakes up right away. He is feeling sick, but he sits up and immediately quizzes me on a rebuttal.

Transforming Character

Positive Mental Attitude training was not just a matter of motivating trainees. It was intended to transform them, to make them more optimistic, confident, enthusiastic, determined, and persevering. Like a military boot camp, Combined's training course was designed not only to teach raw recruits new skills but also to prepare them for the tough road ahead.

> Bill says that a central part of building this company was, and is, building individuals' characters so that they are prepared to deal with emotional challenges. He says that door-to-door sales is not easy, and it's important to build people up so that they're ready for it.

Stone based his PMA techniques on the mind-over-matter principles developed by, among others, Emile Coué, who recommended that people chant, "Day by day, in every way, I'm getting better and better" (see Hill and Stone 1960). Similarly, the "I feel healthy, I feel happy, I feel terrific" chant was designed to imprint on the subconscious mind positive thoughts that would overcome habits of negativity. The Combined Insurance sales manual instructed agents to "DIRECT YOUR THOUGHTS . . . CONTROL YOUR EMOTIONS . . . ORDAIN YOUR DESTINY" (ellipses and emphasis in original).

PMA does not simply promote wishful thinking. Its whole point is to spur people on to work toward their goals without being held back by what Stone refers to as "t and f," timidity and fear. PMA is oriented toward action. Stone recommends repeating the phrase "Do it now!" fifty to one hundred times, morning and evening. Other favorite "self-motivators" of Stone's, frequently chanted in class, are "Success is achieved and maintained by those who try and keep trying with PMA," and "Where there is nothing to lose by trying, and a great deal to gain if successful, by all means try." The trainees were taught that through proper self-conditioning they could learn to suppress negative thinking altogether (training manual). Just as the Little Engine That Could succeeded in pulling its heavy load by chanting "I think I can, I think I can" (Piper 1930), Combined's agents were trained to believe that any task they faced was within their power.[10]

Actually, the Little Engine's chant would not be positive enough for Combined Insurance. Modifiers such as "I think" or "I'll try" are not permitted in the PMA philosophy, as I learned on my first day of class.

> Before class, Mark asks me how fully I will participate in training: "Are you going to learn the presentations?" I reply, "I'm certainly going to try," and he says, "That's not what I asked." He gives a little canned spiel about the difference between saying you're going to do something and saying you're going to try. He points to a videocassette box on his desk and says, "Try to move that box." When I move it, he says, "No, I didn't say to move the box, I said to try to move it." I find this little lesson rather irritating, but I commit myself to learning the presentations, and he says he thinks that's great.

This was not the only time the PMA philosophy evoked a somewhat jaundiced response in me:

> When I come in in the morning, the video machine is running a tape that plays peppy music and flashes motivational slogans; they aggravate my headache. The slogans include: "Awaken the sleeping child within you," "Do it now!" "To be happy, make others happy," "Every adversity carries within it the seeds of an equivalent or greater

10. Martin Seligman has demonstrated that, among insurance agents, an optimistic explanatory style is in fact associated with greater persistence on the job and higher sales. (His research measures agents' ways of explaining events, not their predictions of future success.) Metropolitan Life Insurance Company now hires agents based in part on a test of their "attributional style." See Seligman (1990) and Seligman and Schulman (1986).

benefit," "Get ready to succeed," and "I dare you to develop a winning personality."

As that last slogan makes clear, trainees were encouraged to regard their personalities as something to be worked on and adjusted to promote success. All aspects of an agent's life were considered relevant to business success. In one exercise, Mark asked the trainees to imagine the most successful salesperson they could, encouraging them to develop as concrete and detailed an image as possible. "What is that person's attitude like? How do they dress? How do they look? What is their home life like?" After discussing the images the trainees imagined, Mark asked, "Do you see it as desirable to be that person? How closely do you fit the image? In what areas do you need to professionalize your image?" One of my classmates declared, "I will *be* that image"; another said, more prosaically, "It's only a haircut and a pick-up away." The process was exactly as C. Wright Mills described it in *White Collar* (1951: 182, 186): "The Successful Person thus makes an instrument of his own appearance and personality" as "the business with a personality market becomes a training place for people with more effective personalities."

The emphasis on self-development and control over one's own destiny through PMA had an odd relation to the parallel track of the training, which involved strict standardization. The apparent paradox was bridged by stressing that the sales system worked. It could be thought of, not as an imposed routine, but as a framework for success, which the trainees would choose freely if they had perfect information. Thus the PMA system involved promoting belief in the Combined Insurance system and in PMA itself at the same time that it promoted belief in one's own capacities. Stone titled one of his self-help books *The Success System That Never Fails* (Stone 1962). The guarantee of success was possible because an explanation for failure was built in: insufficient belief or effort on the part of those who fail. For instance, my class was shown a videotape of a W. Clement Stone lecture that included the nonfalsifiable claim that audiences had never failed to be changed by hearing him talk, "among those of you who are ready." Similarly, Mark told us that Stone used to have a check for $50,000 on his desk, which he vowed to give to anyone "who used the system faithfully and failed. He never paid." Under the Combined Insurance system, then, all failure was personal, and doubt in the system was evidence of insufficient commitment and of negativity.[11]

Trainees were encouraged to model themselves on Stone himself, who, as he tells it, started out as a poor boy and built a successful corporation and a huge personal fortune through PMA, hard work, and a sales system that worked. He codified his philosophy and his sales system into routines available to the trainees. The message was that agents did not have to be as ingenious or as intelligent as Stone in order to succeed, so long as they were as hard-working and determined. The contradiction between self-development and autonomy and strict regimentation was thus resolved.

This corporate mythology parallels McDonald's almost exactly. There, too, managers were encouraged to model themselves on the charismatic founder who had built an astonishingly successful business from scratch and who provided a highly detailed blueprint by which his success could be replicated. The obvious irony is that the organizations built by W. Clement Stone and Ray Kroc, both highly creative and innovative entrepreneurs, depend on the willingness of employees to follow detailed routines precisely.

THE ROUTINE

The basic routine of Combined's life insurance agents was a good deal longer, more flexible, and more complex than that of the workers at McDonald's. Several features of the agents' job account for these differences. Unlike the window workers, the life insurance agents met with potential customers one-to-one on the customers' own turf. The agents worked without supervision, but also without any of the environmental supports that can be built into a central workplace to guide or control customers. Because the agents did not deal with people who had sought out their services, they encountered much resistance as they tried to carry out their routines. McDonald's workers interacted with "guests" who had chosen to patronize McDonald's, but the agents called on "prospects" who had to be turned into customers. The transformation of prospects into customers was in fact the agents' basic task. Most prospects,

11. Biggart (1989: 122) shows that "failure is privatized" similarly in direct-sales organizations.

however, did their best to prevent this outcome by cutting the interaction short.[12] The agents, of course, were strongly motivated to overcome the opposition they faced, since their income depended entirely on their success in doing so. Their routine was designed to help them succeed.[13]

The interactive routine, if completed, had six distinct stages. Progress from one stage to the next could not be taken for granted; each step was a challenge for the agents. The routine was meant to make it as difficult as possible for the prospect to refuse to listen to the agent, to interrupt him, to sustain objections to the policies, or to decline to buy. The first stage of the routine was to find a prospect at home or at work, introduce oneself, and get inside. "Warming up the prospect" was the next stage, three to five minutes of informal chat during which the agent tried to establish rapport and to pick up information that could help him tailor the sales presentation to the prospect's circumstances and attitudes. During this period, the agent also tried to "get into a selling situation," that is, to find an advantageous setting for the sales presentation and position himself and the prospect to maximize his chances for success. In the third stage, after "verifying some information" on the prospect's lead card,[14] the agent delivered the formal sales presentation, a memorized monologue supported by charts and other illustrations in a presentation book. Fourth, the agent tried to close the sale. At this stage the agent usually had to deliver one or more rebuttals to objections raised by the customer and generally had to make several attempts to close. Next, if the prospect did agree to buy a policy, the agent filled out the application, carefully reviewed the policy's provisions with the prospect to "solidify the sale," "sowed the seeds" for future renewals and amendments of the policy, and took payment. Whether or not the agent succeeded in making a sale, the last stage of the routine was to ask the prospect for referrals to other potential customers and to leave on cordial terms.

12. In fact, agents were taught to be suspicious of people who showed no resistance to the sales routine, on the assumption that those most eager to buy life insurance might have serious health problems that made them poor risks. Insurance companies have long struggled with the problem of "adverse selection." (See Zelizer 1979: 121.)

13. Chapter 5 analyzes in detail how the agents' scripts increased their control over prospects.

14. The script called for agents to begin the sales call by saying, "I'd like to verify some information on my records, and I may have some good news for you." The fact-checking was actually entirely unnecessary and only served as a transition between the warm-up and the sales presentation.

The routine was necessarily quite flexible, but the company tried as far as possible to prescribe how agents would adjust the sales pitch and their self-presentations to adapt to various circumstances. In fact, the most striking thing about Combined Insurance's training for its life insurance agents was the amazing degree of standardization for which the company was striving. The agents were told, in almost hilarious detail, what to say and do. The standardization of the agents' job performance was carried out through three closely related practices: scripting; instruction about proper movement, body language, and intonation; and attitudinal training.

Scripting

Large parts of the agents' routines were supposed to be memorized and recited precisely as written. In training class, the new agents memorized a complete presentation for each of the two policies then available, rebuttals of the most common objections to each of the sales talks, and shorter scripts for renewing and amending policies. The trainees were expected to learn these speeches word for word. The trainer, Mark, conceded that in the field the agents could make small adjustments to the scripts based on what they found to work best, but he encouraged them to try to be word-perfect while in school.[15]

The stress on exact memorization underscored how far management went in trying to make skill and decision making unnecessary. The trainees were assured that the routines had been proven effective over many years and that anyone with the right personal characteristics who used the routines could succeed in selling insurance. The message, as one executive told me, was "If you follow this [sales presentation] precisely as it is, you'll win. If you start deviating, you'll get into trouble." Mark illustrated the power of the scripts (and of good mental attitudes) with stories of successful foreign-born agents:

---

15. Mark turned out to be relatively lenient. In his class, trainees were literally applauded if they were able to make it through a recitation of a section of the script, even if they made some errors. The trainer who took Mark's place one day when he was absent was much stricter, withholding praise and insisting on correction if a single word was changed. According to both trainers, Combined's accident and health insurance divisions stressed precision and standardization even more strongly than the life division did. All accident and health agents were expected to deliver their presentations in exactly the same way.

Mark tells us about a Czech guy who didn't know any English except for the sales talk. He learned the script phonetically and didn't even know what the words meant. . . . He sold twenty applications on his first day and is now a top executive. Combined also has an Iranian agent who is doing well. Mark says that when prospects say no, she claims not to be able to understand them.

The company gave several reasons for this strict scripting. The most important one was that the routines worked. If the agents used the presentations exactly as written, they were told, they would have fewer interruptions, they would be sure to cover all the necessary information, and they would sell policies. Having the presentations perfectly memorized would also give the agents the self-confidence necessary for success, since they would not have to fear being at a loss for words, offending anyone, or getting their facts wrong. Yet another benefit was that if the agents were so familiar with the scripts that they could rattle them off without having to think about them, their minds would be free to consider what strategies would help to make a particular sale (training manual).

The fear that agents might get the facts wrong was an important incentive for the company to script the sales presentations. The insurance business is subject to government regulation, and misrepresentation is a serious concern throughout the industry. The use of standard sales presentations made it less likely that agents would inadvertently misrepresent the policies.[16]

For the most part, the trainees accepted these justifications of the scripting and did not resist the standardization. Some of them did have reservations about it, though. For example, one trainee's reaction to the first day of training was, "It's OK if I can get past the phoniness"; he explained that he thought it would be hard to seem natural and casual if he was reciting a script. Mark undercut such feelings of discomfort by occasionally acknowledging that there was a comic element to the scripting. For instance, the script called

16. It was extremely easy to give a false impression of a policy feature through a careless choice of words. For example, I heard one agent explain a policy's Automatic Loan Provision to a prospect this way: "Say you buy the policy today, and in six months you're on vacation when we come to collect. We wouldn't cancel the policy." This statement was untrue, though the agent had not meant to mislead the prospect. Under the Automatic Loan Provision, the company could subtract the cost of a premium from the cash value that had accumulated in the policy. However, since cash value did not start building in this policy until two years after purchase, the agent misrepresented the policy feature when he ad-libbed the phrase "in six months."

for agents to ask, "Isn't that true?" and nod, as they made statements that anyone would have to agree with. This technique was supposed to put prospects in a "yes frame of mind." Mark sometimes used the technique jocularly in class, as in, "I bet you're ready for a break now, isn't that true?", thus giving trainees a chance to laugh at the scripting without calling its usefulness into question.

Some members of the class did resist specific elements of the script that they thought could not be delivered in a way that sounded natural. For instance, several people asserted during a class break that they would never use the introductory phrase they had just been taught for use in amending policies ("Pardon me a moment, if you will"), because they thought it sounded ridiculously stilted. There was more general resistance to the Standard Joke that was supposed to be included in every life insurance presentation:

> This policy is so good that the president of our company says . . . "Once you have it, you will live forever!!!" How's that? [original punctuation, including ellipses][17]

Upon hearing a salesman in a videotaped demonstration give a particularly wooden delivery of the joke, one trainee said firmly, "I'm not using that in the field. Forget it!" Mark willingly conceded that the joke was not funny, but he insisted that it worked well as a means of dispelling tension, especially when the agent laughed at it heartily himself. Mark recognized that this was hard to do:

> We don't care why you laugh, as long as you laugh. You can laugh at yourself for telling it. You can laugh at the customer for laughing at it.

This acknowledgment that some resistance to the standardization was understandable helped assuage the trainees' discontent.

Agents were supposed to use the scripts for sales presentations, rebuttals, renewals, and amendments according to fixed decision rules: if the prospect is more than sixty-five years old, give the presentation for the senior citizens' policy; if the prospect says she already has insurance, deliver Rebuttal Number One. In addition to these standard scripts, the agents learned a variety of less rigid subroutines they could choose from, using their own judgment about

17. The other sales divisions had their own Standard Jokes, of course. Health insurance agents said, "We pay if you're sick. We even pay if you're sick and tired! How's that?" and accident insurance agents said, "We pay if you're hurt. We even pay if your feelings are hurt! How's that?"

the specific context. For example, quite a bit of time was spent, in class and on homework assignments, on creating and learning "interruption-stoppers," quick phrases that allowed the agent to return to the sales presentation after a prospect interrupted him. Although one trainer told the class to practice them until "you become a computer and spit these things out," this part of the routine allowed agents some discretion. It was clear that any of a variety of responses might be used to deal with the same interruption successfully, and the agents were encouraged to experiment to find the ones that worked best for them. Similarly, Mark gave us a long list of suggestions on "How to Get the Money" when prospects who wanted to buy said that they did not have the cash. These scripts were presented as helpful suggestions, not as inflexible routines. They expanded the agents' ability to accomplish their work while allowing them some discretion.

Another way the trainers standardized agents' speech was by teaching them general rules about what sorts of things should and should not be said during sales calls, so that the agents could improvise on the job without alienating prospects. Among the rules the agents were taught were: never ask prospects why they have said no to a policy, since that would force them to solidify their reasons for saying no and make it harder for them to change their mind; literally "never say 'die'" when speaking to a prospect (given the nature of the product, this rule required a creative use of euphemism); respond to all questions from prospects by saying, "I'm glad you asked"; preface questions prospects might be reluctant to answer with a casual "By the way," or conclude them airily with "Do you remember offhand?"

These sorts of tips made the trainees feel better able to conduct their sales calls successfully without making them feel constrained by inflexible rules.

Standardizing Movement, Body Language, and Intonation

In *The Chronicles of Doodah*, a novel lampooning corporate efforts to demolish executives' individuality, George Walker gives this account (1985: 152–53) of the training that goes on in the company's Posturium:

The most difficult thing for me is Executive Stride. Conrad and I had talked jokingly about developing the perfect Executive Shuffle, to be used when approaching Marlott's desk or leaving his office. I was surprised, then, to discover that our fantasy was not so far from reality. Because, as I found out two days into this class, Executive Stride has certain variations, and one of them is, indeed, the proper way to enter and leave a superior's office.

Once more I am taught that subtlety is everything. . . . The Executive Shuffle cannot be obvious! The proper exit consists of an exactly timed period of standing before the Turn and Walkout are executed. It is during this Respectstand that one listens to additional details of the superior's instructions and gives assurances that everything will be done exactly as ordered. Then, and only then, does the careful about-face occur. The exit should not be that of a servant overcome by awe and humility, but that of the loyal functionary hurrying to carry out his mission.

Walker's fantasy was not so far from reality either. In addition to scripting the life insurance agents' words, Combined Insurance tried to standardize how the agents held themselves, how they delivered their lines, how they gestured, and how they used the physical setting. Consider, for example, my field notes from a class lecture on getting through the door:

After ringing the doorbell and opening the screen door, wait for them to answer with your side to the front of the door. Do a half-turn when they open it. It's almost as though they catch you by surprise—non-confrontational. Be casual.

Lean back a little when they open the door. Give them space.

Attitude: "Be as loose as a goose," Mark says. Be able to respond to what they say.

To get inside, use The Combined Shuffle. It has three steps:

1. Say, "Hi, I'm John Doe with Combined Insurance Company. May I come in?" Handshake is optional. Break eye contact when you say, "May I come in?"

2. Wipe your feet. This makes you seem considerate and also gives the impression that you don't doubt that you'll be coming in.

3. START WALKING. Don't wait for them to say yes. Walk right in. BUT—be very sensitive to someone who doesn't seem to want you to come in. In general, act like a friend; assume you'll come in. Mark demonstrates one effective technique: he keeps shaking hands while he's walking forward, which makes it hard to stop him.

The agents were also given instructions on how to seat themselves in relation to the prospect, how to position the sales materials, and precisely when to open the presentation book. Special attention was paid to the agent's speaking style. One of W. Clement Stone's "Seven Essentials" for successful selling is to "TALK IN A POSITIVE, ENTHUSIASTIC TONE OF VOICE," which, he said, means talking loudly, talking rapidly, keeping a smile in one's voice, emphasizing important words and phrases, hesitating deliberately for effect, and modulating one's voice (training manual). These techniques were intended both to make the agents more persuasive and to help them overcome their own timidity and fear.

The scripts of the sales presentations provided even more detailed instructions on exactly how to deliver the lines. Various kinds of typography (underlining, capitalization, boldface) were used to indicate which words should be memorized and which read from the presentation book, which should be emphasized, which should be pointed to in the presentation book, and which should be spoken while making eye contact with the prospect. The manual contained a full page of instructions on exactly how to deliver the Standard Joke. For example, the agents were supposed to "telegraph the joke" by starting to chuckle a moment before they began speaking, so that the prospects would know a joke was coming. The manual continued:

> A slight chuckle should be started and built up to a crescendo as you deliver the punch line, "How's that?"—continuously laughing with several "Ha-Ha's."

In addition to this training in the proper delivery of lines, a considerable amount of class time was devoted to practicing proper pointing and eye contact. For most of the presentation the agent was supposed to look intently at the presentation book, pointing to important words with a pen. This technique made it likely that the prospect would also focus attention on the book, while eye contact would make it easier for the prospect to interrupt. Nonetheless, at specified points the agent was supposed to make eye contact with the prospect. Mark said the way to do it was to raise your pen from the page of the presentation book and bring it up near your eyes, looking up from the book to the prospect's eyes. The prospect, he said, would automatically follow your pen and make eye contact. Then you could deliver such scripted lines as "Just think of it!" I found, during role plays, that this technique for forcing eye contact worked quite well.

Many details of the agents' physical comportment and way of

speaking were thus subject to routinization. The standardized techniques were usually designed to help the agents seem natural and spontaneous. Hiding the routinization of the work was an important part of the agents' job, which was not true for McDonald's workers. To conceal the routinization, the agents needed to do particular kinds of emotion work and to cultivate particular kinds of attitudes.

Standardizing Attitudes and Ways of Thinking

Combined's overall approach to standardizing its workers' characters and personalities was through Positive Mental Attitude training. That training was intended to ensure that the agents had the enthusiasm, optimism, and determination necessary for success in sales.

In addition to the general PMA orientation, Combined's training for its insurance agents included specific attitudinal guidelines and psychic strategies for dealing with the work. Some of these guidelines were intended, like PMA, to prevent the agents from becoming discouraged. For example, Mark advised the trainees never to tell themselves that they had been assigned a "bum town." Should they be assigned to work in a town with very high unemployment, they should not think, "Forget it, no one has any money, I'll never sell anything." Instead, they should keep in mind that many people will have lost the insurance benefits they had at work and that Combined's small policies would be attractive to them. Mark also taught the agents to protect their positive attitudes by quickly ending interactions with very negative prospects: "Spend the time with people who show interest, and get away from those who are giving you a hard time." He told the agents, "Reject them before they reject you. You can't sell everybody, and it's much better to leave graciously."

Similarly, Combined Insurance tried to control interactions among its employees in the field, so that they would not reinforce or transmit disappointment, cynicism, or other negative attitudes. At a morning sales meeting I attended, for example, the sales manager interrupted an agent who had started to criticize his own previous week's performance, reminding him that they were supposed to be sharing good news. The sales team I observed spent plenty of time grousing, but company policy encouraged agents to share goals and successes, not gripes.[18]

18. It is not unusual for companies to concern themselves with employee morale or with the potential damage malcontents can do, but this concern is likely

Much of the standardization of workers' attitudes and ways of thinking that Combined Insurance undertook was intended to persuade agents that their own interests coincided both with those of the prospects and with those of the company. If the company and the individual agents were to succeed, for example, the agents would have to be willing to put considerable pressure on prospects to buy. Combined Insurance trained its agents to think that they were acting in the prospects' interests even when the prospects clearly asserted that they did not wish to participate in the interaction. On the first day of class Mark emphasized that "people buy what they want; they have to be *sold* what they need." The agents were taught that everyone needs life insurance[19] and that Combined's policies were extremely good ones. If people showed reluctance to discuss buying life insurance—an understandable reaction, since such a discussion would make them think about their own death—it was the agents' duty to make them see the importance of protecting their loved ones from financial disaster. If people tried to brush off the agents by saying that they already had life insurance, it was important to find out whether their present policies were now inadequate because of inflation or changed financial responsibilities. Throughout the training the agents were frequently reminded that their services were needed and that a certain amount of persistence was not only morally justifiable but morally required.

The company tried to overcome the reluctance new agents might feel to put pressure on prospects, but it was equally concerned about the possibility that, in order to maximize their own profits, agents

---

to be especially salient when emotion work is crucial to workers' success in dealing with customers. Butterfield (1985), a former Amway distributor, provides an especially chilling account of the damage to personal integrity and the stifling of authentic connection with others that can result from organizational pressures to censor and standardize interactions with co-workers. Those pressures are especially strong when, as in Butterfield's case, one's income depends on the positive attitudes of others, but they are present in other settings as well. For example, a former telephone-company worker I interviewed told me she didn't know whether the women in her work group had shared her sense of anger and humiliation at their close scripting and intrusive supervision: "It was set up so you couldn't really be honest."

The preferred content of interactions among co-workers of course varies with organizational goals. A former canvasser for a feminist organization told me that, in addition to keeping the people in their work groups focused and enthusiastic, senior fund-raisers were expected to "keep the conversation political" during shared meals.

19. Kessler (1985) presents a comprehensive critique of life insurance.

would put too much pressure on prospects or would even try to cheat them.[20] Mark argued that it was in the agents' own interests to behave ethically and to refrain from high-pressure sales techniques. Although the agents were taught to create a sense of urgency about buying insurance, they were also taught that being too pushy would only increase prospects' resistance. A low-key approach was more likely to increase prospects' trust, Mark told us. He mentioned one successful agent who went so far as to yawn while waiting for the prospect to make a decision, to show that he was not overly concerned with making money on the sale. Ideally, the agents would not push prospects into buying but would lead them along so that they came to see why they should buy. That way, Mark said,

> the customer will feel good about the sale, and it will stick [he or she won't cancel the policy or fail to renew it]. If you put service and the customers' needs number one, your needs will be taken care of.

The agents were taught that the proper attitude was one of sincere interest in meeting prospects' needs. An overly insistent or demanding approach would make prospects wary and resentful, and prospects might cancel policies they had been bullied into buying.[21]

Combined's training emphasized business ethics. The agents were urged to "do the right thing because it is right" ("Statement on Representatives' Conduct") and also because it was in their own interest to behave ethically. Mark argued:

> If you're doing anything remotely unethical, it affects your sincerity, your confidence, and your commitment, and the customer can pick up on this.

Among the sales practices that were expressly forbidden were "abusive or overly aggressive sales tactics"; misrepresenting policy coverage, benefits, or premiums; encouraging prospects to cancel an existing policy in favor of a new one; and selling policies to people who were obviously too poor to afford them ("Statement on Representatives' Conduct").

Combined Insurance tried to make the agents identify their

---

20. Oakes (1990) provides an extended discussion of the contradictory ideals of commercialism and service that guide insurance agents.

21. Combined's new sales approach was designed to enhance the focus on the prospects' needs, guiding the prospects to provide their own rationale for buying life insurance.

interests with those of the company as well as with those of their prospects. For example, because Combined's life-insurance policies did not require medical examinations but became effective immediately upon issue, the company had to rely on its agents to follow its underwriting guidelines strictly, declining to sell policies to people whose health, as described by themselves, was not good enough to qualify them for coverage. "Always visualize that the claim is being paid out of your checking account," Mark urged the agents. He pointed out that Combined Insurance could preissue policies and keep its prices low (both important selling points) only if the agents followed the underwriting rules precisely. Therefore, he argued, it was not in the agents' long-term interests to maximize their commissions by increasing the company's risk.

Birth of a Salesman

The Combined Insurance trainees did not show much resistance to the intense routinization of their words, movements, and attitudes. Most were quite anxious about facing customers and were grateful to be told exactly what to say and do. As at McDonald's, the main justification employees were given for following the instructions exactly was that the routines worked. As Mark told our class on the first day of training, "It's not easy to sell life insurance, but we got a system, it's OK." To the trainees, the routine apparently seemed a lifeline rather than a constraint.

The two experienced Combined Insurance agents in the training class helped to dispel skepticism among the trainees. They strongly believed that the sales techniques worked, that Combined Insurance was a good company to work for, and that it was entirely possible to earn a lot of money as an agent. George, a highly successful accident insurance agent, softened other trainees' resistance to the corny Standard Joke. When several people groaned at the joke and declared that they would not use it, George said, "I love that joke. It works." He proved his point by telling the joke with extraordinary enthusiasm, laughing uproariously at it himself, so that no one could help laughing along with him, just as prospects are supposed to do. George was also a true believer in PMA:

> After lunch, George leads us in singing and cheers. We start with a PMA song that is sung with accompanying body motions—George

shouts out the body part to use before each verse, as in the Hokey Pokey: "Right elbow!" "Left arm!" The song goes:

"My philosophy is PMA
And we live it every day,
And if you look around [turning in a circle]
You'll see it's true,
With PMA you can't be blue!"

We sing many verses, and then George leads us in singing "If You're Happy and You Know It" and finishes up with some cheers, including, "Give me a P-M-A!" By the time he sits down, George looks ready to drop from exhaustion.[22]

To reinforce trainees' commitment to working hard on learning Combined's system and giving it their best efforts once training was over, Mark used many techniques of commitment well known to social psychologists.[23] Several of these techniques, including putting commitments in writing, saying them aloud to a group, and formulating compliance as a matter of free choice, were combined on the last day of class, when Mark had the trainees write down and read aloud a pledge of commitment:

Mark says, "Look how far you've come in the last two weeks. You've made quite an investment this week—one you expect to get a lot of returns on." He goes on to say that that goes for the company, too. They've also made an investment in us, and they expect to get returns. "Is it good for an agent to try it for a week or two, and then decide that it's not for them and turn tail and run?" Everyone says no, that would not be giving it a real chance. Mark asks, "How long would it take to be able to say you've really learned the system and given it a try?" People give various answers, ranging from three months to a year; Combined's answer is three months. "Do you think it's a good idea to make that commitment?" Everyone says yes. "Would you put it on paper?" "Yes." "Take out a clean sheet, and head it 'My Commitment for Success.'" Mark dictates the following statement, which we then read aloud:

22. This performance was all the more remarkable because it came immediately after a lunchtime conversation in which George had brought all talk to a halt by introducing the subject of his son's sudden death at the age of twenty-one. He described his reconciliation to this loss through a vision he had of Christ on the cross, which reminded him that he was not alone in losing an only son. The simple cheeriness of the PMA philosophy seemed pretty thin in the face of this revelation.

23. Social psychologists first gave serious attention to the matter when trying to explain how the Chinese were able to brainwash American prisoners of war captured during the Korean War (Cialdini 1984; Schein 1956).

"I, [*fill in name*], am making a commitment to succeeding with Combined Insurance Company by applying myself to the system, as learned in Chicago, in its entirety for eight hours a day, minimum, quality time, for five days a week, minimum, for three months. I will insure this commitment by:

"becoming a student of the business" by continuing to read and study the manual. (Mark gets people to say "yes" aloud to each item.)

"daily, reading some self-help material.

"playing self-improvement tapes and memorized [sales] material tapes."

Note that Mark enhanced the power of this pledge by framing it as a commitment to personal success, not to Combined Insurance, and by emphasizing that it would be up to each agent to choose how hard to work. Biggart (1989: 164–65) explains the principle:

> Self-control does not *feel* controlling. If an individual accepts the standards that attach to the social idea—and this is a critical hurdle—then there is a perception of self-determination. There is an experience of autonomous competence. In teaching [direct-sales] distributors strategies for self-control . . . the organization is perceived as helping individuals achieve their own goals, not as manipulating workers to an alien end established by management. The organization is a benevolent "helper," not a profit-seeking "controller."

Manipulation was part of the commitment process, whether or not the trainees experienced it that way. The training course facilitated trainees' embrace of their new identity as insurance agents by giving a somewhat rosy picture of what their work lives would be like. Mark never tried to make the work sound easy and never hid the reality that the agents would be turned down a lot more often than they would sell. But he tended to concentrate on the possibilities of the job, not on what it was like for most agents. He urged us, "Don't come home without $100 a day," even though "It's hard." He said that the company expected its agents to earn over $20,000 in their first year of work and that "the minimum" was $14,000, adding that he had seen first-year agents earn as much as $60,000. A company executive told me, however, that the average income for Life agents at that time was only $200 per week, or less than $10,000 per year. The agents on the sales team I studied were relatively successful; several of them brought in about $500 a week fairly consistently. The sales manager estimated that $50,000 per year was about the maximum someone could make as an agent, but the rapid promotion policies at Combined Insurance meant that many employees still in their first year would have an opportunity to increase their earnings by becoming managers and getting additional income from higher commissions and from their team members' sales. One team member estimated that the sales manager received $1,200 to $1,300 each month in overrides on the team's sales. The manager told me that his goal was to earn $35,000 to $40,000 that year. He said that to accomplish this goal he would have to bring in $25,000 himself. (Keep in mind that Combined Insurance encourages its employees to set their goals high. During the week I spent with the team, the sales manager, unlike the other agents, sold virtually nothing.)

The executive quoted above also told me that Mark underestimated the amount of time agents worked in the evenings. Mark made it sound as though work time was mostly a matter of personal preference and will—just tell yourself that you're going to make all the money you need before six o'clock, and make it happen—but I was told that it was common for salespeople to spend 75 percent of their time making home calls during evening hours. Furthermore, Mark assured the class that because there were so many more Combined Insurance accident agents than life agents, the life agents usually had more leads than they had time to contact, but the agents I worked with said that they commonly ran out of leads before the end of their week in an area.

More complete or more accurate information about their career prospects would not necessarily have dissuaded the trainees from committing themselves to selling for Combined Insurance. They had been trained to regard themselves as winners. They had heard a great many success stories, and they had been told that the key factors that brought success were under their control: their own attitudes, willingness to work, and belief in the system and in themselves. Just as test pilots can persuade themselves that colleagues killed in plane crashes must not have had "the right stuff" (Wolfe 1979), agents could take the view that those who had failed must not have had a sufficiently Positive Mental Attitude or a serious enough commitment to achieving success. The trainees were given a great deal of evidence that it was possible to succeed with Combined Insurance, and they were challenged to change themselves into the kinds of people who could realize that possibility.

The trainees wanted badly to succeed. On the last day of class, when, in a little graduation ceremony, Mark presented each new agent with a certificate, the trainees had the opportunity to say a few words to the class. These little speeches were unexpectedly moving. The trainees were very hopeful, full of resolutions of tenacity and full of gratitude for the opportunity they had been given. If Mark had asked me to speak, I would have said that I admired my classmates, that their willingness to leave behind jobs that had been unsatisfying to them and throw themselves into another kind of life seemed brave to me. One agent's speech captured especially well the sense of personal transformation and new beginning that the training had tried to engender. This trainee had formerly worked in a laboratory doing biological research. In the course of the sales training he had occasionally been teased by his classmates for asking so many questions and for speaking in a way that apparently struck them as overly intellectual and long-winded. In his graduation speech he thanked the class for putting up with his verbosity, which he now viewed as a thing of the past, explaining, "That's because I was a scientist. Now I can call myself a salesperson."

This agent's embrace of his new identity marked a success for Combined's training program, aimed as it was at fostering just such a personal transformation. The point of the training was to teach recruits to sell insurance by using routines that the company believed were effective. But for this kind of interactive service work, learning the routine meant much more than learning a script and some physical motions. Selling insurance demands particular kinds of emotional resources, habits of thinking, and ways of relating to other people (see Oakes 1990). Routinization at Combined Insurance, then, involved turning recruits into certain kinds of people.

OVERVIEW

Combined Insurance had much in common with McDonald's. Each company carried the routinization of the work of employees who deal with the public very far indeed, and in each company the routines were based on a system and rules developed by a charismatic founder who was held up as a model for employees and managers. In the company's view, its routines codified the best methods of accomplishing the interactive tasks necessary to establish good relations with customers and sell products. To the extent that workers could be made to use them, then, the routines gave the companies greater control over an important aspect of their business—relations with the public—than they would have had if employees were left to use their own judgments, personal styles, and inclinations.

Combined Insurance and McDonald's differ in organizational structure. While most McDonald's employees work for franchise owners who exercise some control over personnel policies, work rules, and other matters, Combined Insurance directly controls the hiring and training of its employees. Nevertheless, in neither company are work routines designed locally. Considering the tremendous geographic spread of the companies, especially McDonald's, it is striking that they have not found it necessary to pay more attention to variation in local tastes and interactive norms. (See Chandler 1962 for discussion of other responses to similar issues.)

Combined's life insurance agents and McDonald's window workers were predominantly young people with relatively little work experience. Both jobs were largely gender-segregated, but Combined's life insurance agents were almost all men and most of McDonald's window workers were women. Neither job is held in high esteem by the public, although working at McDonald's confers lower status on jobholders than selling insurance does, in large part because McDonald's jobs are known to be low-paying and low-skilled. The low status of these jobs can influence both how workers feel about their work and how they are treated by customers on the job (see Chapters 5 and 6). At both companies, very high employee turnover was the rule. At Combined Insurance and at those McDonald's stores where turnover is far above average, this pattern was considered a serious problem.

Despite these many similarities, the routinization of interactive service work took quite a different form at Combined Insurance than it did at McDonald's. While the training for McDonald's crew workers is in many ways similar to training for, say, assembly-line work, Combined's training calls to mind such transformative experiences as Marine boot camp or political reeducation. The insurance agents' routinization was aimed at the whole person, and it was expected to change the initiate's outlook in a global and permanent way. McDonald's made no such attempt to transform its window workers. Its managerial training program, however, had some elements of character standardization, and for the same reason that Combined's agent training did. The companies had to rely on these groups of workers to make decisions in the companies' interests.

Many of the major differences in how the two jobs were routinized stemmed from differences in how the two companies tried to ensure the stability of raw materials and product specifications, because that mechanism dictated the type of relations that were established between service workers and service-recipients. The standardization of service-recipients' behavior that is required for routinization was not, for the most part, the responsibility of McDonald's window workers. The customers who came to McDonald's did not need to be persuaded to take part in the service interactions, and they usually did not need much guidance from workers in order to play their part in the routine adequately. Advertising, restaurant design, past experience, and observation of other customers all teach McDonald's customers how to behave, and the customers are generally willing to cooperate. Because there was relatively little variation in customers' behavior and because the interactions were relatively simple, McDonald's was able to create a routine that gave workers little discretion and little control. The central task for McDonald's window workers was to serve the customers, not to control them. The customers could be regarded as superiors who specified the terms of the service interactions; the workers had to focus on controlling themselves. The workers' close supervision by managers and customers further minimized their autonomy.

In contrast, Combined's agents had to persuade prospects to participate in the service interactions and to cooperate with the routines. The agents had to be able to respond to a broad range of circumstances and of customer behavior, since the customers were neither trained nor motivated to fit into the agents' routines. These routines therefore had to be flexible, and the agents had to approach their customers in a different spirit than did McDonald's workers. Although the agents were trained to think of their work as that of serving customers, their central task was to sell. In these service interactions, the service-recipients were treated as raw materials to be manipulated, not as superiors to be obeyed. The agents had to exercise considerable self-control, but their focus was on controlling the customers. Although the agents' work was highly routinized, that routinization did not rob them of either discretion or a sense of autonomy.

Not surprisingly, the incentive systems for the two kinds of workers reflected the differences in their autonomy. The closely supervised McDonald's workers, whose routines allowed minimal discretion, had no real stake in the success of a given interaction, though managers did provide some modest incentives for good work. By contrast, because the insurance agents worked on their own, obliging the company to rely on their motivation and judgment, it was important to Combined Insurance that the agents cared deeply about how well they handled each interaction. Like most insurance companies, Combined Insurance therefore paid its agents on commission, making workers' income dependent on their discipline, energy, and skill. The company also provided numerous status ceremonies, contests, and prizes as incentives.

Because Combined's success rested largely on its agents' self-motivation, confidence, and persistence, the company's managers did not believe that either monetary incentives or superficial training would suffice to keep agents at their work in the face of repeated rejection. They therefore undertook, in addition to an extraordinarily detailed standardization of their agents' words and actions, an extensive effort to remake their trainees into the types of people who would be most likely to succeed. PMA training was intended to reshape new agents, changing not only the ways they interacted with people on the job but also the ways they approached life, viewed themselves, and thought about their experiences.

These cases are representative of two directions in which the routinization of work can be intensified. Combined Insurance went much further than McDonald's in trying to influence how their workers thought and felt, both on the job and off. To the extent that Combined's approach to creating the kinds of workers it wants was more far-reaching, the agents' job can be considered more highly routinized than that of McDonald's workers'. But since almost all decision making had been removed from the McDonald's window workers' job, their work seems in that sense to be more highly routinized than the work of Combined's agents, who did have significant discretion.

Combined Insurance went to some trouble to persuade trainees that their interests, those of the company, and those of prospective customers coincided and that the routines the company had developed served those interests reliably. If that were always in fact the case, routinized interactive work would provoke little resentment among either workers or customers, and service interactions would proceed smoothly. In reality, however, the three parties to the interactions have some interests in common and some that are opposed, and although management's strategies for controlling the behavior of workers and customers are many and powerful, workers and customers also try to exercise control over service interactions. Chapter 5 examines how the approaches to routinization at Combined and at McDonald's worked out in practice, focusing on the responses of workers and customers to the routines and on the degree to which the companies succeed in dominating the three-sided relations of service work.

5

Controlling Interests

The managements of McDonald's and Combined Insurance tried to implement work routines that were extraordinarily detailed and standardized. Describing the design of work routines is only the first step in analyzing the effects of routinization on interactive service work, however. Braverman (1974) has been rightly criticized for assuming that managers are so effective in implementing their programs that outcomes can be deduced from their intentions (see Littler 1990). Important as managerial designs are in determining the experiences of participants in interactive service work routines, a variety of other factors shape workplace outcomes as well. Only by looking at how routines actually function in given settings can the variable consequences of routinization be understood. How inflexible are the service routines? What are the sources of variation in service interactions? Do the routines serve only managerial interests, or can they benefit workers and service-recipients as well?

Braverman (1974), assuming that Frederick Taylor's views accurately represent employers' interests, argued that the intent of routinization is to banish decision-making from workers' jobs and to ensure strict standardization of procedures and output. Were he correct, managers would try to quash all variation in prescribed procedures. Other analysts, however, have shown that employers benefit from allowing workers some discretion to control their work. Burawoy (1979) sees limited worker decision-making as important for the construction of workers' consent to the premises of capitalist labor relations, since power to control even minor matters can engage workers' interest and mitigate discontent with hierarchical relations. Moreover, the tradition of "work to rule" labor actions provides clear evidence that employers depend on workers' exercise of discretion and good sense to compensate for divergences between rules and contextual contingencies (see Friedman 1977 for related arguments). That dependence is especially marked for employers of interactive service workers. Fuller and Smith (1991: 3) argue that these employers pursue policies that tend to "extinguish . . . sparks of worker self-direction and spontaneity" at their own risk:

> Quality service requires that workers rely on inner arsenals of affective and interpersonal skills, capabilities which cannot be successfully codified, standardized, or dissected into discrete components and set forth in a company handbook.

It is important, then, not to overstate employers' interest in standardizing work. To the extent that routines prevent or dissuade workers from using their own "ethnomethodological competence"[1] on the job (Stinchcombe 1990a), they do not serve the interests of either employers or service-recipients. Garson (1988: 65) makes this point in insisting that the strict routines of airline telephone-reservation workers are counterproductive. She told a manager:

> You hire human reservation agents because they are the only beings, organic or mechanical, that can respond with sufficient flexibility to an open-ended inquiry. Then you try in every possible way to restrict that flexibility.

But the manager she spoke with was sure that the benefits of uniformity outweighed the dangers of rigidity. Their disagreement points to a problem inherent in standardizing interactive service work. Well-designed routines ensure a minimal level of acceptable work performance. The same routines that keep less competent or dependable workers from undermining organizational standards, however, can prevent better workers from using their talents and common sense to meet the demands of particular situations. Employers pursuing the benefits of routinization, including protection from the incompetence of unskilled, unintelligent, or unmotivated workers, may sacrifice the responsiveness necessary for smooth organizational functioning and optimal service.

Service organizations are differentially sensitive to the dangers of limiting workers' initiative. Whether employers choose to err on the side of uniformity or on that of responsiveness in designing service

---

1. See p. 7 for a discussion of this concept.

routines and supervisory systems depends on such factors as the complexity and difficulty of interactive service workers' tasks, the qualifications of the labor force, the preferences of service-recipients, and the vulnerability of the organization to service-recipients' dissatisfaction. The two companies I studied illustrate contrasting approaches. Combined's routines were designed to allow for considerable customization to meet the demands of different situations, while McDonald's intended only minor variation in the execution of its routines.

Although departures from scripted routines do not necessarily undermine managerial interests, much variation in the execution of interactive service routines occurs despite managerial intentions, not because of them. The abilities and interests of workers and service-recipients determine in part whether or not routines are carried out according to management's specifications. Workers are not always able to execute the routines as planned, either because their own capacities are limited or because contingencies arise that the routine cannot accommodate. Moreover, when workers and customers believe that their own interests are not well served by the routines, they sometimes intentionally subvert them.

Analysis of routinization is too often cut short by the assumption that management has the capacity to impose routines unilaterally, an assumption that historical research on routinization has proven untenable.[2] Labor historians and sociologists of work who reject the portrayal of workers as hapless victims of managerial power have focused a good deal of attention on workers' capacity for resistance (Benson 1986; Edwards 1979; Halle 1984; Montgomery 1979). This research has been a useful corrective to earlier models that downplayed workers' agency, showing that workplace outcomes are shaped by a struggle for control of the work process. Nonetheless, the model of contestation it presents is fairly simple. It allows for variation in the resources workers and management bring to their struggles, but it takes for granted that the interests of the two groups are always opposed (though workers may be fooled into believing otherwise).

This conception of the struggle for control in the workplace is

---

2. Managers performing different functions often have competing interests as well, so official organizational policies are not always uniformly supported even within management.

inadequate for analyzing interactive service work. Because service-recipients have their own interests in how the work is carried out, the contest for control has three antagonists, whose alliances are variable (see Wouters 1989). Both workers and service-recipients sometimes try to subvert managerial goals, as in the "resistance" model, but they also sometimes try to subvert each other's goals. Under some circumstances workers see the struggle for control between themselves and service-recipients as primary. If managerially imposed routines protect workers from service-recipients or give them more power over service interactions, there is no reason to assume that workers will resist those routines. Even so, service-recipients' resistance may cause considerable variation in how the routines are carried out.

To understand the outcomes of routinization in interactive service work it is essential to pay attention to how the interests of workers, service-recipients, and managers align in particular settings, as well as to the constraints and resources of the actors. Although the alignment of interests of individuals in each of the three parties to service interactions is somewhat fluid, any organization is likely to have a dominant pattern of alliance that shapes the process of routinization. At McDonald's, the interests of managers and customers converged, diminishing workers' control and allowing customers to augment management's control strategies. At Combined Insurance, workers' and management's interests were most often aligned in the effort to persuade service-recipients to buy policies. The routines at each company reflected these alliances: McDonald's routines were concerned primarily with controlling workers, while Combined's focused on controlling prospects. The degree and kind of resistance to service routines varied accordingly.

How closely management's designs for service interactions, systems of controls, and incentives for workers approximate the actual workings of any given organization and the motivations of its workers are empirical questions. An accurate and nuanced understanding of how control over work is contested and conceded in interactive service jobs can emerge only through careful analysis of the resources, rewards, and strategies available to the parties involved in particular organizational settings. In analyzing service interactions at McDonald's and Combined Insurance, this chapter shows why workers at both companies were less resistant to routinization than labor-process theorists might have predicted.

McDONALD'S

Subservience and Skill

Because almost all McDonald's customers knew how to fit into the service routine and were willing to do so, the company did not depend on the window crew to regulate customer behavior. It therefore did not provide workers with routines that gave them leverage over customers. Instead, customers were granted the superordinate position in the service interactions, and workers were taught that they were to try to meet customers' expectations, not force customers to meet theirs. At the window training class, trainees were given Ten Commandments to guide them in dealing with customers. Such tenets as "The customer does us an honor when he calls; we are not doing him a favor by serving him," and "The customer is not someone to argue with or match wits with" were intended to shape workers' attitudes by emphasizing the primacy of customers' needs. The standardization of workers' attitudes thus served to curtail the workers' range of response, discouraging them from expressing disrespect, resentment, or annoyance.

McDonald's use of the term "guests" for customers reinforced the lesson that all customers were entitled to respectful and courteous treatment and that the workers were there to serve them. The terminology made it easier for workers to accept this role by equating it with a familiar situation in which deference does not imply inferiority. Hosts defer to guests because they are guests, regardless of their social status. Any inequality will be reversed when the host pays a visit. Of particular importance for McDonald's is the social obligation to be polite to guests whether or not they are favorites of the host. This formulation was a face-saving way for workers to think about their dealings with those customers who did not treat them respectfully.

The window workers' routine was intended, not to help them control customers, but to maximize workers' speed and efficiency in filling customers' orders and to discourage them from treating customers rudely. Since crew people had little stake in the outcomes of their interactions with customers, other than the desire to avoid unpleasantness, trying to influence customer behavior was a minor part of their work. The workers did direct the service interactions to some extent. They sometimes called customers over to their registers to keep the lines moving evenly, and if customers' orders were not specific enough they asked questions such as "For here or to go?" or "Will that be a large Coke?" Window crew could also exert some control over the interactions by trying to set their tone (see Whyte 1946). For instance, they might use a preemptive display of determined friendliness or helpfulness to discourage apparently irritable customers from becoming difficult. A few workers mentioned that they knew how to cheer guests up or head off trouble:

> Traci reports: "Some people you can tell—when they walk through the door, you know how to act with them. Like some people look in a bad mood, you know, just go easy with them. Don't aggravate them that much. And if anything is late, you know, try to talk with them. 'Cause you know they've had a hard day, too."

> Steve explains his approach: "Mainly people come in, they be mad, I just joke with them. And if they come in with an attitude, I tell them to smile. If they come in cursing and all—well, usually, when a customer come in, I'll look, and if they seem to be in a bad mood, I'll just work faster, so I can get 'em out, 'cause I know they're in a rush. And the people that come in with a smile, I just do my normal speed."

Workers who paid attention to customers' interactive cues and were willing to adjust their own behavior increased customer satisfaction and spared themselves angry outbursts. Although the work was defined as unskilled, crew members' skills in reading customers' moods and responding to them could be important to the smooth running of the store (see Kusterer 1978).

For the most part, though, as Traci put it, "We're sort of at their mercy." Well aware that their routine was not designed to give them leverage over customers, most of the workers felt they had little power to affect the behavior of customers who were rude or angry for no apparent reason. As Desmond told me:

> Some be polite, and they talk to you. . . . Some be very rude: they snatch their money from you, you know, they say things under their breath. But you ignore them and stuff, that's all.

Several workers used some variant of the phrase "he just went off" when speaking of customers who had suddenly become unreasonably irate. The expression nicely captures the workers' sense that they were handling explosive materials. They knew, too, that they had little means of shielding themselves from the fallout associated with customer outbursts.

Most customers did not cause any such problems, but the minority of difficult customers had a disproportionate effect on the window workers' experiences. Customers' familiarity with McDonald's routines meant that they had quite well-defined expectations. They were therefore easily frustrated, especially if service took longer than they thought was reasonable.

Since window workers were normally the only employees with whom customers interacted, they bore the brunt of customers' impatience and anger, whether or not they were to blame for a delay or mix-up (see Glenn and Feldberg 1979b). When customers were angered by delays caused by inefficient grill workers or managers who had underestimated the demand for a product, window workers were ready targets. Even when it was clear that the worker had no discretion in a matter, such as how late in the day a breakfast item could be ordered, the worker might be subjected to the display of temper or discourtesy that the inflexible routine provoked. Even workers who acknowledged that customers sometimes had reason to become impatient found their expressions of it hard to take:

RL: When do customers get annoyed?

CAROL: When their food is not ready. They get annoyed when they're waiting on food. If we go down product [don't have an item ready] it isn't our fault. And you might tell them [how long the wait will be], and when the time of it is up, they start to get hyper. Like, "Where's my food? You told me such-and-such a time, and it's not here yet. What happened?" And they're like, "Well, I can go to Burger King," or somewhere else, and they want their money back or something.

RL: Do you take it personally if they seem impatient or irritated?

CAROL: Yup. 'Cause they're looking at you. I mean everyone's just looking at you, 'cause you're taking their order and then they think it's your fault. And you have nothing to do with it. All you do is take their orders.

RL: When people get impatient or irritated, do you ever take it personally? Feel like they're getting mad at you?

EDWARD: They *are*. [We laugh.] . . . You know, it's like, "I'm not paranoid, I am being persecuted." I'm not paranoid, there are people hollering. No, but—they are mad. And whether they're mad at you or mad at some other thing, they're gonna direct it on you, it's gonna be focused on you—"Why haven't, why is this going wrong, why haven't *you* done this?" Because they aren't gonna turn and look at a wall and say, "I hate this whole place, why

> isn't the service good?" They're gonna take it out on you.
> So it is personal. And you know, you try to tell yourself
> it's not personal, but after, you know, a period of time,
> three or four times a day, you begin to take it *very* person-
> ally. [We laugh.] You feel like shouting back at these peo-
> ple, "This is not my fault."

The window workers were exposed to abuse, not just because
McDonald's service could be exasperating, but also because McDonald's customers were so often ready to express their exasperation
openly. The association of work at McDonald's with unskilled
young people meant that window crew completely lacked what
Hochschild (1983: 163) calls a "status shield." Some customers who
might have managed to be polite to higher-status workers had no
compunction about taking their anger out on McDonald's employees.[3] The extreme routinization of the work, as well as its low pay,
apparently led some customers to believe that anyone working at
McDonald's must be an idiot undeserving of consideration. Workers were therefore forced to endure rude, sarcastic, and insulting
remarks and behavior from a minority of customers. The crew people
were not permitted to yell back at customers, to insist that they
were in the right, or to make smart-alecky remarks. Moreover, they
usually could not withdraw physically from unpleasant interactions,
since they were trapped behind the counter.

A few workers mentioned that they did sometimes let customers
see their resentment. Claire not only refused to smile when customers kept changing their minds about their orders but also could be
mildly intimidating:

> Sometimes, I just look at them for a long time, you know, like—
> "Yeah." You know. And they say, "OK, I'm sorry," and all this.

If Marisa had an overly demanding customer, she felt entitled to try
to "show them who's boss." For example, she got out the scale and
weighed a bag of french fries when a customer challenged her judgment of what was a fair serving. But workers could not often show
their irritation with impunity.

> RL: Is there anything you enjoy least about working with the
>   public?

---

3. The tendency might have been exacerbated at the franchise where I
worked, since most window workers were young black women, vulnerable to
status slights based on age, race, and gender.

LORI: You have to take their crap. [Laughs.] I'm not the type of person to say, "OK, have it your way." I mean, I have to admit,
I'm tempted to backtalk a lot. So. That gets me in a lot of
trouble. So I mean, when a customer's rude to me I just have
to walk away and say, "Could you take this order please,
before I say something I'm not supposed to say?" I mean, I
think I'm a very nice person, but I find it hard to be nice to
other people when they aren't nice to me.

RL: So you have had some [laughing] "incidents" where you've
talked back to people?

LORI: Yeah, I've had a couple of incidents where I'm just like,
"Well, fine then! Get an application and get it yourself!"
[Laughs.] But I mean, it does get you in trouble, and it's not
always the best thing to do.

In the three-way relationship among workers, customers, and managers, window workers clearly had relatively little power. They were
subject to all three of the types of managerial control enumerated by
Edwards (1979: 18). Direct control was exercised by the managers
and trainers, who were constantly present; technological control
was built into the computerized cash registers that both dictated
how workers did their jobs and monitored their performance; and
bureaucratic control was embodied in the detailed sets of regulations
that described McDonald's standards for each task and criteria for
evaluating workers. Informal supervision by customers constituted
yet another form of control over the window workers, for customers
had the power to direct, evaluate, and reward or punish workers. In
fact, customers often punished window workers, by abusive or disrespectful behavior, for the mistakes of others or for policies over
which the crew had no control. Because McDonald's routines were
designed to give customers what they wanted (as long as their wants
were limited to fast and courteous service of standard items), the
interests of managers and customers in how window workers performed coincided to a great extent. Customer supervision therefore
tended to reinforce managerial control.

Benson (1986) has demonstrated that where management is
dependent on service workers' expertise and good will in managing
customers, the workers' culture can be a powerful force for resisting managerial demands. At McDonald's, however, workers did not
exercise much group control. Extensive routinization minimized
the store's dependence on the skills of individual workers, and
close supervision made it difficult for workers behind the counter to
to sustain the bravado some of them showed in the crew room.

Moreover, management's attempts to persuade workers to take the company's interests as their own were successful with some who took pleasure and pride in providing good service or who were interested in prizes or promotions. The peer culture was therefore not a unified one that could enforce alternative definitions of adequate work.

McDonaldland Morale

The assumptions common in the labor-process literature would lead us to expect McDonald's workers to be highly dissatisfied with their jobs. They lacked control over their work, had little freedom to make decisions, and had few opportunities for human contact that went beyond the most instrumental and superficial level. Moreover, they were closely supervised and subject to blame for things beyond their control. Garson (1988) argues that McDonald's exaggerated devotion to the values of uniformity and speed results, predictably, in alienation. The four present and former McDonald's employees she quotes all felt demeaned and discouraged by a system they saw as discounting their ability to think. Garson suggests that customers also suffer from the preposterous extreme to which McDonald's takes Taylorism. She notes how heartless and absurd routinized service can become when workers do not have the freedom to use common sense on the job: "I was almost fired for my attitude. Which was helping customers who had arthritis to open the little packets" (1988: 28). Customers and humane workers are on the same side, this anecdote implies, but the interests of both groups are thwarted by management's insistence on consistency and speed.

Although the technology, procedures, and rules Garson describes are essentially similar to those that were in use at the franchise I studied, my findings are markedly different. The workers' reactions to their jobs were quite varied, but few seemed to experience the workplace as generally oppressive. Resentment about unreasonable customers did not outweigh positive aspects of the job, and the workers expressed relatively little dissatisfaction with the extreme routinization. One reason was that, despite the constraints of the routine, some workers felt that their interactions with customers were more than mechanical and that they were able to express their personalities on the job. Other workers, in contrast, appreciated the routine precisely because it did not require that they treat exchanges with customers as full-fledged personal interactions.

Individual workers could act on their self-defined interests and exercise some control over their work in three ways. First, time permitting, they could go a bit beyond the routine in providing extra services, pleasantries, or conversation. Workers might choose to do these things if they wanted to minimize the likelihood of angering customers, if they found it satisfying to please customers, or if they wanted more scope for self-expression than the Six Steps of Window Service allow. Those who chose this approach served the interests of management and most customers as well as their own. Second, workers who resented the subordinate position in which the routine placed them or who simply had put up with all they could bear on a particular shift could do their best to resist the routine while avoiding punishment from managers or customers. They might withhold smiles, risk a show of impatience or irritation with a customer, or refuse to suggest additional purchases or to encourage return business. In most of these cases, workers clearly defined their interests in opposition to those of both managers and customers. Finally, crew members who were interested in demonstrating to themselves or others that they were good workers but who had no taste for displaying deference could concentrate on speedy service. Their desire for some sense of mastery of their work led them to serve management's and customers' interests to some extent, but they took advantage of McDonald's high valuation of speed to avoid working toward other values—service, friendliness, courtesy—whose enactment they found demeaning.

The use of a short, repetitive, tightly structured routine did create problems for workers, customers, and managers aiming for a high standard of quality in the service interactions, but for the most part these interactions were either pleasant or neutral for both workers and customers. Although McDonald's routines were quite limiting, they were not entirely mechanical; they allowed some room for workers to customize interactions, express their personalities, and make use of skills. Moreover, although it might seem that the interests of workers, customers, and managers would coincide in the creation of pleasant, friendly interactions, in fact both workers and customers often preferred to limit their involvement in the service routines. Neither all workers nor all customers wanted the service interactions to be spontaneous or idiosyncratic.

For those who preferred to expend as little emotional energy as possible, the formulaic routines had real benefits.

The Hamburger University instructors I observed stressed that managers should make their stores "fun places to work," and the people who ran the franchise I studied were fairly successful on that measure. Over half of the workers I interviewed (twelve out of twenty-three) volunteered the information that work at McDonald's was fun for them. For some, the fun derived from interacting with customers. Despite the specificity of the script and the brevity of most encounters with customers, the service interactions were not all alike and were not necessarily devoid of personal involvement. For example, Steve answered the question, "What do you enjoy about working with the public?" with great enthusiasm:

> It's just fun, the people are fun! . . . They make my day, they really do. I mean, sometimes, I can come to work—like yesterday, I wasn't really happy. I was somewhat in the middle. This guy came in, he was talking real low, and his friend said, "Why don't you talk up?" . . . I told him to turn his volume up [I laugh], and he said something . . . and I just started smiling. Ever since then, I've been happy. . . . The guests out here, . . . they're friendly and fun. I just love to meet them, you know? I mean, it's nice working for them, it's nice serving them. Some, you know—well, I'd say one out of ten guests will probably try to give you a bad time. But the rest of them, they'll just make my day.

A less effusive male window worker, Theo, shared Steve's view:

> Well, I enjoy working with the public, 'cause they're fun to be with. Some of them are a trip. So I enjoy it, find it very amusing.

Even some window workers who did not particularly like working with the public still enjoyed coming to work. For many of the crew people, work was a chance to see their friends from school and to meet other young people, and the worker culture that developed, full of good-natured teasing, was an important attraction. When I expressed surprise that one worker had come to the store two hours before the start of her shift, she told me, "I'd rather hang out here than at home." Several workers also mentioned that they were glad to have gotten to know crew people of different races or from different countries.

On the job, I found that for the most part the workers treated each other with consideration, though there were the usual jealousies and conflicts one would expect to find in a work group. I noted on my first day's work behind the counter that "the other crew people are quite nice and helpful," and this pattern proved to be typical. This support was no small thing at a time when I was constantly hitting the wrong button on the cash register or wondering where to find the supplies I needed. Alphonse, a new employee, told me that what he liked most was that

> everyone is kind to you. You know, if they see that you're having a hard time, you know, with the cash register, they'll come over and ask, "What's the matter?" and they'll give you a hand, and they'll explain it as they go along.

Workers certainly became annoyed with more experienced coworkers who avoided their share of the work, waiting for someone else to make a pot of coffee or restock the napkin dispensers, for instance. In general, though, the crew seemed to me to work together remarkably well.[4]

Workers' satisfaction at McDonald's should not be overestimated, however. The company's extremely high rate of employee turnover suggests that my interview sample probably excluded the most dissatisfied workers. Even among the people I interviewed, many resisted or expressed dissatisfaction with at least some aspects of the routine. Still, it is important not to discount the positive responses to working at McDonald's. Labor-process theorists who treat workers' preference for jobs that are varied, challenging, and personally involving as a constant have not provided a satisfactory account of those workers whose responses to routinization are not wholly negative. It is possible that satisfaction among my respondents at McDonald's reflected only the poverty of choices available to them or the effectiveness of their indoctrination. It is possible, too, that positive attitudes existed despite routinization, not because of it, deriving from residual opportunities for exercising discretion or

---

4. In part, the courtesy and cooperation that were the norm among crew people in this McDonald's were built into the routines they were taught. In the window training class, new workers were told that the proper phrasing for giving an order to a grill person was, for example, "Two Big Breakfasts, please," to which the grill person would respond "Thank you" to indicate that he had heard the message. This courteous protocol was used consistently. Also, window workers were taught that they should use any spare time to back up other workers, by, for instance, assembling an order for a second worker while she set up the tray and handled the monetary transaction.

from the social and monetary rewards of the job rather than from the work itself. The possibility that even highly constraining routines can provide some benefits to workers should, however, also be considered seriously.

Because of the positive skew in my data, I will focus more on the range of responses to McDonald's work I found than on the prevalence of various attitudes and types of behavior, but it is clear that more than a small minority of the workers I interviewed seemed to like their jobs. Moreover, despite the common view of social critics that McDonald's routines make workers behave like robots, few window workers complained about the degree of routinization of their work. Virtually all of the workers I interviewed said in response to a direct question that the Six Steps of Window Service, their basic routine, were effective and that they felt comfortable using them. For example, Luella replied:

> Yes, they work well. You ask them may you help them, and then they ask you [for what they want. You say] "Just a moment, please." They do help. They wouldn't want you to say [harshly], "Just come over here. Whatchu want?" That's not very polite. This works well.

Several workers mentioned that they were able to personalize the routine, thus exercising some discretion, albeit minor. Madeleine said:

> I think [the routine for dealing with guests] is perfect. . . . It's really nice. Because then you can use the Six Steps in your own way. Just do the Six Steps, but do it in your own way. It's not like you have to say, "Hi, welcome to McDonald's." You can say, "Hi, how you doing?" or "Good morning," "Good afternoon," "Good evening," things like that. But it's real nice.

In contrast, Edward especially appreciated not having to make decisions:

> What I like most about working here is when everything is going right. It's like . . . in any other activity, if you can hit a groove . . . it's a kind of high. Because you have hit that groove, and you're not really having to think about it any more, things are just happening and it's all going very smoothly. I think that's what I like the most.

Although most workers claimed to appreciate the routine, not all of them behaved accordingly. Whenever possible, crew members eliminated parts of the routine that they disliked, and some followed the letter of the law with no expression of the spirit of friendly service. One section of the routine was widely disliked by workers, in part because it was widely disliked by customers. Suggestive selling—recommending that the customer take an extra product or a larger size of one already ordered—was supposed to be a part of every interaction except those with small children.[5] Sometimes even the wording was inflexible. During a special promotion the window workers were required to ask every customer, "Would you like to try our Bacon Double Cheeseburger?" Ten of the twenty-three workers I interviewed criticized the suggestive-selling requirement, and five more said that they frequently "forgot" that part of the routine.

It was easy to understand why many customers responded to suggestive selling with irritation. It was the one element of the window workers' routine that departed significantly from the pattern of cheerful responsiveness to customers' wishes. People sometimes responded snappishly when workers asked, "Would you like a hot apple pie with that?" or "Will that be a *large* fries?" Customers seemed irritated in part because the workers were stepping out of the role of passive servant by questioning the customers' decisions and delaying the delivery of the food. Suggestive selling was also annoying because it was obviously intended not to please customers but to increase sales. An exception to the usual congruity of customer and management interests, it was the one point in the interaction at which the organization's interest in controlling customers came to the surface. Although managers tried to finesse this incongruity of interests by presenting suggestive selling as a service that reminded customers of available products or introduced them to new ones, many customers perceived the practice as an attempt to manipulate them, and they resented it. Finally, suggestive selling irritated some people precisely because it was so clearly part of a

---

5. The instructors at Hamburger University taught that suggestive selling should be used only "when appropriate," but it was a required part of every interaction with an adult at the franchise I studied. According to the manager, the raters from regional headquarters, who visited periodically, took off points if workers did not try to increase the size of every sale. Corporate directives also presented suggestive selling as mandatory: a crew-room poster describing special Halloween promotions depicted a bat saying, "Don't be scared—suggestive sell to EVERY adult."

scripted routine. Customers who felt that they had been engaged in a genuine conversation with a worker might be deflated when a line such as "Would you like to try our Bacon Double Cheeseburger?" called that premise into question.

Some workers hated suggestive selling under any circumstances, dreading the possibility that a customer would snap, "If I wanted it, I'd have ordered it." Other workers didn't mind suggestive selling when there was an obvious gap in the order—no fries, for instance—but thought it was ridiculous to suggest something extra when the order was for a complete meal or when the customer had already said, "That's it." In cases like these, management's stress on suggestive selling tended to heighten the sense of distance between scripted interactions and ordinary conversations. Under other circumstances it would be considered odd or rude to disregard an explicit statement such as "That's it." The store's manager conceded that "it really would be better if counter people just used their common sense about this," but he justified the inflexibility of the suggestive-selling rule by saying, "Unfortunately, if you just leave it to them, they stop doing it altogether."

This observation was perfectly true. Workers disobeyed the rule about suggestive selling whenever they could get away with it. Since in this case following management's rules tended to annoy customers, window workers were put in the difficult position of having to please one party at the expense of the other. They were likely to resolve this dilemma in the customers' favor, because management had not created any incentives that brought the workers' interests into line with their own.

The window workers voiced few complaints about the constraints of their service routine other than the rule about suggestive selling. Although, by and large, service interactions at McDonald's were highly repetitive and minimally involving, workers and customers who chose to could turn them into something more. First, regular customers could establish ongoing relationships with workers, as do customers of conventional restaurants. Superficial though the relationships might be, they allowed for interactions that were not entirely anonymous and perfunctory. For example, Rosalie almost always worked the breakfast shift, and some people who stopped by on their way to work every morning always got in her line and addressed her by name. A few workers mentioned that they enjoyed this continuity and the chance to deliver personal service, whether or not the customers showed a preference for a particular worker. Matthew told me:

> What I like [is that] when you work window you get to know every customer that come in here every day. You get to remember their faces, you get to know what they want . . . , and all they have to [do is] just show their faces, and you just grab the tray and set up everything they need, 'cause they get everything the same every day.

Furthermore, some workers enjoyed chatting or joking with customers, finding satisfaction in providing a pleasant moment in a customer's day or simply trying to make their own day go faster. In response to my question about how their "ideal customer" behaved, the majority of respondents expressed some preference for customers who were friendly or at least responsive, and about a third said that their ideal customer chatted with them.

Notwithstanding the tendency of routinization to establish a ceiling on the quality of customer service, some workers were willing to go out of their way to please customers who were looking for individualized service. It sometimes happened, though, that the strict routines and computerized systems made it impossible for workers to provide extra courtesies without involving a manager, as was required in these incidents during my work shifts:

> A little girl tells me that she wants "a hamburger in a box." I say that they usually come wrapped up, and I explain to her mother which products come in boxes. The mother just wants to order hamburgers but says, "She's just fascinated by those boxes." I ask Jim (the manager) if I can get a hamburger in a box, and he obliges by putting a burger in a Big Mac box for the child.

> One child specifically requests a plastic shovel instead of a rake with her Happy Meal beach pail. Charlene (a manager who overhears the request) tells her she's too late, we don't have shovels any more. However, Charlene makes a special effort to go find one, and she returns with a shovel, telling the girl it's the last one.

I could not meet these requests myself because, in the first case, I did not have the authority to confuse the inventory by using a Big Mac box without serving a Big Mac, and, in the second case, I neither knew where to look for a shovel nor felt I could leave my post at the counter.

Window workers could provide some nonroutine services on their own. I learned of them only from coworkers, however, not from managers. One worker, hearing me tell a customer that her meal would be ready in a few minutes, told me that when one item in an order was delayed, I could give the customer the rest of the meal and offer to deliver the delayed item when it was ready. I was surprised to hear of this option, since I had had no idea that it was ever permissible to leave the counter, but I found that it could both ease tensions with customers and make the job more enjoyable. Customers who declined the offer were unlikely to complain about having to wait for their food, and customers who accepted it obviously felt that I was doing them a favor and responded with appreciation.

I found out for myself that the store had items that could be given away to children:

> I notice another counter person going by with a plastic Ronald McDonald hand puppet, which I didn't know we had. I see that there are Ronald McDonald Fun Times booklets under the counter at some of the registers, so I take some for my station. I have fun giving them out to little kids, presenting them with a flourish as a special surprise. I'm rewarded with some very big smiles and thank yous, sometimes even before the parents say, "Say thank you."

I enjoyed providing these extra services for several reasons: they provided a little break from the routine; customers responded with more personal thanks than usual; and, because they were extras, I could decide when to volunteer them. Since the managers at this store were eager to please customers, it was striking that they did not make more of a point of letting workers know of these options.

I appreciated breaks from routine and took satisfaction in pleasing customers, but not all of my coworkers felt the same way. Most of the window workers preferred friendly customers, but some cared only that customers not be bothersome. Almost a third of my respondents' descriptions of their "ideal customers" suggested that the best they hoped for was customers who were not actively annoying. They merely wanted customers who were polite, prepared to order, and patient during delays. Most window workers valued predictability in customers' behavior, so even those who enjoyed personalizing their interactions greatly preferred dealing with well-trained customers. Eighteen of the workers I interviewed mentioned that they did not like customers who were slow, imprecise, or indecisive. For example, Luella described her ideal customers:

They're ready to give their order [snaps fingers]. Most people, when they walk in here, they should know this is McDonald's and what McDonald's should have. Don't ask me how much things are, because it says so right up there, and they're watching me punch it in [so they can see the prices on the cash register]. I say, "Thank you, have a nice day," and they tell me [that] back, and then they're gone, or they go sit down. But most people come up, and they're playing with their hands, they're playing with their money, they're counting their toes [pantomimes customers taking their time]. And there's a line behind them.

The window crew liked people who knew what they wanted when they came up to the counter, who ordered things in the expected sequence, who gave specific orders that kept the workers from having to ask a series of clarifying questions, and who did not change their minds after the order had been assembled. In fact, some workers told me that they became quite irritated with people who were not ready to play their parts properly. They were contemptuous of customers who "took forever," and they spoke as though indecisiveness or confusion were a mark of stupidity.

Workers' hostility to customers who slowed them down had several sources. First, during busy periods, other customers exerted silent pressure to hurry. Workers were quite reasonably concerned that time-consuming interactions would make those waiting in line impatient, increasing the likelihood that service encounters would be tense. However, workers often seemed impatient with slow-thinking customers even when the store was uncrowded. That might be explained by managers' focus on speed. Although they wanted the workers to maintain cheerful demeanors and "good attitudes," managers' primary concern was to make sure that long lines did not develop, or, during rush periods, that the lines moved quickly. The pressure on workers to hurry, exerted by managers as well as customers, was therefore more implacable than the pressure to be friendly and personable. In fact, several fast workers who seemed quite rude to customers were promoted.

Finally, some workers resented customers who slowed them down because they prided themselves on their speedy service. In this highly routinized job, the most significant way that workers could challenge themselves or display excellence was to strive for greater efficiency, so they sometimes spurred themselves to hurry.

Like the factory workers described by Burawoy (1979) who willingly worked harder than they had to because they wanted to "make out,"[6] these McDonald's workers pushed themselves to ever higher levels of productivity in order to derive some satisfaction from their work.

In the McDonald's case, however, this speed-up was not an unalloyed benefit to managers and customers, since workers who focused exclusively on speed sometimes overlooked or overruled customers' convenience or preferences. Instructed by managers to perform at top speed and never to keep customers waiting, window workers often went overboard and annoyed customers by pressuring them to hurry. When customers were met by a chorus of workers demanding, "May I take your order?" the moment they entered the store, the crew's eagerness to serve could take on the character of harassment rather than solicitude. Sometimes it was merely funny:

> At one point, two teenage girls pause near my register, looking up at the menu. I ask if I can take their order. They say they don't know what they want, and I say, "Whenever you're ready." In quick succession, though, Emma, Mark, and Diana all ask for their order, and they keep repeating that they're not ready. I joke with them about the "great service."

On one occasion, customers who were trying to give me their orders were subjected to questioning in stereo because of my trainer's insistence on speed:

> Diana is standing next to me listening to the orders so that she can race off to get the items while I ring them up. She is impatient to get all the information she needs and apparently doesn't believe she can count on me to ask the right questions. We therefore frequently speak in unison: "Large?" "Cream and sugar?" "For here or to go?" The customers look astonished.

In these cases the window workers expected the customers to be aware of their concern for speed and to be ready to fit into the routines. Although their behavior was demanding, the workers apparently did not see themselves as imposing their priorities on

6. When piece-rate workers speak of "making out," they refer to reaching the production targets they set for themselves and hence meeting their incentive-pay goals. Although the workers think of such success as beating the piece-rate system, Burawoy (1979: 91–92) argues that the workers' absorption in the game of making out benefits management by obscuring the conflicting interests inherent in capitalist workplace relations and by generating consent to the social relations of production.

customers. They believed, probably correctly, that most customers came to McDonald's because they wanted to be served quickly. However, sometimes the goals of speed and responsiveness to customer wishes subverted rather than supported one another. Workers who came to define their task as delivering speedy service rather than as pleasing customers sometimes treated slow customers as obstacles, not as types of customers requiring a somewhat modified approach. When that happened, the demands of the routine superseded rather than facilitated "quality service."

At McDonald's, the involvement of service-recipients in the work process changed the usual dynamic of workers resisting management's efforts to impose routines and raise productivity. Instead of resenting the extent to which good work was judged by speed rather than by pleasing customers, many window workers focused their irritation on customers who slowed them down. Overall, the object of disgruntled workers' resentment was much more likely to be customers' behavior than the constraints of the routine imposed by management. Luella, for example, had little sympathy for customers, finding interactions with them more irritating than enjoyable:

> The customers are terrible. (Another worker present laughs.) I'm serious. I can't stand them. The old people, I have to give them a little credit. But the other people, I don't give them no credit at all.[7]

Her generalized hostility was unusual, but most workers, taking the basic structure of their job as given, regarded customers as the main source of unreasonable demands. When customers were impatient because the line was long or angry because no Big Macs were ready, workers resented them, not corporate advertising that promised fast service or store managers who scheduled as few grill workers as possible to keep labor costs low. During "window contests," when workers competed to see who could take in the most money during a given period of time, they became irritated with people who took a long time to order or who changed their minds, not with managers who created incentives for speed instead of customer satisfaction.

The pressures put on workers by the design of the service routine

7. Unlike Luella, many workers singled out older people for disparagement, because they "take forever," have trouble hearing, are too picky, are officious about their special rights (including, at this franchise, free coffee), and initiate long, dull conversations because "they have nothing better to do."

and the system of supervision help explain why many workers disliked or were ambivalent toward the kind of individualized, open-ended conversations that critics of routinization assume workers prefer. Although many workers said that they liked getting into conversations with customers, just as many said that there were times when they preferred to stick with the routine. Several mentioned that they did not like it when customers tried to strike up a conversation when the store was busy. Not only did the conversation slow them down, but some feared that supervisors would interpret their chatting as wasting time rather than as responsiveness to customers.

The unequal power of workers and customers also made some workers prefer routine interactions to more extended ones. If crew people found particular conversations boring (an elderly person going on and on), uncomfortable (comments to a young woman worker about her appearance), or inconvenient (when it was time for the worker's break), they might feel trapped, unable to escape the unwelcome situation, criticize the customer, or cut the interaction short. Workers who preferred to avoid such interactions therefore looked on the scripted routine, with its much-criticized limitation of personal contact, with favor. They saw the routine as a protection against intrusive conversations.

Many customers also seemed to prefer highly routinized interactions with window workers. Some, clearly determined to avoid personal contact, approached the service interactions with the complete lack of affect ordinarily used for dealing with inanimate objects. Not only did they make no attempt to treat the stylized dialogue as though it were a genuine conversation, they made no acknowledgment that the workers were human. They avoided eye contact with the workers who were speaking to them, ignored greetings and questions, and offered no thanks. Some workers resented such treatment, but others did not mind these stripped-down interactions, since they were efficient and required no emotional energy.

The reactions of McDonald's window workers to their routinized work were more varied than company critics might have predicted. Although the routine reflected the shared interest of management and customers in regulating workers' behavior, by and large the workers did not see their own interests as compromised by routinization, and they were not generally hostile to it. Some found satisfaction in the modest adjustments they could make to customize service, and others appreciated the routine's limited demand for personal involvement.[8] Workers did generally resist suggestive selling, however, the part of the routine they saw as incurring the greatest risks and offering the least possibility of reward. In this regard, customers' and managers' interests were at odds, subjecting workers to cross-pressures. Although the routine officially barred workers from deciding for themselves when to use suggestive selling, most workers, dreading retorts from customers more than reprimands from managers, followed their own predilections.

COMBINED INSURANCE

The alignment of interests among the three parties to the service interactions at Combined Insurance was very different from that at McDonald's, and the routines reflected the difference. At Combined Insurance, management and agents shared an interest in controlling the behavior of prospective customers in order to sell as much insurance as possible. At times this basic alignment of interests shifted: for instance, when a technically ineligible prospect wanted to buy a policy, the agent's desire for the commission conflicted with management's responsibility for limiting the company's risk. Agents' primary focus, however, was on overcoming prospects' resistance. This focus typically led them to embrace rather than resist their routines, because those routines were designed to enhance agents' control over the service interactions, not to limit it.

Moreover, since Combined's prospects' behavior varied much more than the behavior of McDonald's customers did, the insurance agents' routines were designed to be considerably more flexible than the window crew's. Despite the agents' freedom from direct supervision, much of the variation in their execution of their standard routines was unproblematic for management. To regulate workers' behavior, the management of Combined Insurance concentrated on persuading agents that their routines served their own interests.

---

8. Individual workers' preferences also fluctuated. The same workers who sometimes enlivened the routine with individualized embellishments might retreat behind the routine and decline personal involvement at other times. Their behavior depended on such factors as their mood, how much time was left on their work shift, their assessment of whether they were being treated fairly by managers, and their preferences for various types of customers.

Autonomy, Control, and the
Response to Routinization

The routinization of the life insurance agents' job was both extensive and intensive. It delved deeply into the selves of the workers, standardizing their words, gestures, personal styles, and attitudes, and it affected minute details of conduct as well as general character traits. Throughout the training period and during my work with the sales team, I was struck by how little the trainees and agents seemed to resent or resist this strict routinization. Their acceptance of the work routines bore no resemblance to the hostility with which industrial workers have historically reacted to managerially imposed work routines. The agents also seemed considerably more eager to shape themselves to the requirements of their routines than did McDonald's window workers. There were three reasons for the trainees' and agents' lack of resistance to the routinization: they retained significant decision-making power, they believed that they needed the routines in order to succeed at their work, and they understood that the routines increased their control over prospects.

Despite the extensive scope and intensive detail of the routinization, the agents' jobs allowed them considerable discretion. First, as the trainees were aware, agents almost always worked on their own, without supervision. No one watched to make sure they followed all instructions to the letter. Furthermore, although Mark, the trainer, wanted the trainees to learn the scripts as precisely as possible, he wrote on the board the main question to ask about an agent's presentation: "WILL IT $ELL?" He told the class, "No one will hit you if you slip on a word or two. Salespersonship is what counts." Under some circumstances, he said, it might not even be necessary to use the complete sales presentation: "You must respond to the situation. Go with your instincts." This message was comforting for trainees, making them feel that they were both being credited with some intelligence and also being given the tools they needed to do the job.

It was clear to trainees that although Combined Insurance specified as much of the interactions as possible, agents still had to make many decisions on the job. They were responsible for deciding whom to call on when (although they were given a system for planning their calls), and they certainly needed to keep thinking as they interacted with customers. The agents had scripts to follow, but they either had to choose particular lines from those scripts to fit the situation or had to construct suitable dialogue on the spot. Agents had to decide, in response to what they learned about customers' circumstances and personalities, which policy features to stress, which arguments to make, whether or not to try to sell policies for other family members, and what sort of persona to project. The necessity for decision making meant that the job was never entirely mechanical, even though the decision making was kept within well-defined limits. As Mark put it, "We could train a parrot to recite, but I doubt we could train a parrot to sell." Combined's reliance on the motivation and discretion of its unsupervised workers explains the company's efforts to transform the workers through Positive Mental Attitude training.

In the field, the agents I observed did feel free to alter their routines, yet they continued to have faith in the basic routine. "If you're making money, you don't make any changes," Chuck told me, but he felt that he had the leeway to made adjustments based on the lessons of experience. Kevin said, "Every house is different. Every person is different. Every selling situation is different. It's never gonna be the same." Nevertheless, he was a firm believer in the routine, explaining that the responsiveness he spoke of was a matter of adapting the routine to each situation, not of abandoning it. He argued that the agents who stick the closest to the presentations, the rebuttals, and the systems "do the best." His feeling that some of the rebuttals, for instance, sounded artificial or were too wordy did not contradict his strong faith in the basic framework of the selling system or in the utility of scripts. The discretion that agents felt to adapt the routines undercut any resentment they might have felt about being programmed and any doubts they had about whether all contingencies could be handled with a prepared script. The very freedom to change the script seemed to strengthen their belief in it, bolstering their sense that they freely chose the routinization.

A second reason that the trainees and agents did not resent Combined's routinization was their belief that they needed the routines to succeed at their work. The trainees were eager for information, the more concrete the better, on what to do to overcome resistance from prospects. Far from regarding the routinization as an affront to their dignity or intelligence, the novice agents welcomed instructions and hints of all kinds. They did not feel that they were being treated as idiots. When it came to selling insurance, the new agents felt that they *were* idiots, and they wanted the security of what the manual called "a track to run on."

The trainees were acutely aware that their income would depend entirely on how successfully they conducted these interactions. They therefore wanted to be told exactly how to warm up prospects, what phrases to use to counter particular arguments, and how to turn uncomfortable situations to their own advantage.[9] Combined's trainers and printed training materials stressed that the company's methods, originally called "Mr. Stone's Scientific Sales Approach," had been proven effective over years of use, and the trainees were persuaded that embracing the routine was the surest way to guarantee a steady income from sales commissions. Several of the agents in the field told me that the key to success was to "put pressure on the system, not on yourself," meaning that as long as agents depended on the system, faithfully doing ten full presentations a day, they would be ensured enough sales to be "a winner" regardless of their level of talent.

Furthermore, the trainees understood that the service interactions would be difficult. Unlike McDonald's customers, most of their prospects would be neither trained nor inclined to make the job easier. Since the agents did not work in an environment controlled by the company, even sales calls with cooperative prospects could present many difficulties, as I learned on the very first call I made:

> I get a good demonstration of stressful, distracting conditions at this house. It's the home of a Spanish-speaking family, and lots of relatives are present. The person whose name is on the lead card does not live here any more, but Kevin goes ahead and tries to sell to this family. When we arrive, three women and six small children are in the living room, and the TV is on at high volume. During our call, two men come in at separate times. The women ask the kids to turn the TV down (at Kevin's request, which is part of the routine). The children do, but they soon turn it back up again, and they make a lot of noise.

Several difficulties combined to make this call unusually challenging, including the noise and activity, the frequent interruptions, the

---

9. The trainees' perception that using the right words could enhance their control over interactions was quite accurate. In Milgram's experiments on compliance with authority (1965), he found that subjects' ability to resist the authority figure's demands depended in part on whether or not they could find a verbal formula to counter his orders.

lack of clarity about the relations among those present (information which, ideally, could be used in determining to whom the presentation should be addressed and which policies to offer), and the intermittent presence of people who might comment on the policies or challenge the decision makers' judgment. Most calls were far less confusing than this one, but agents could never predict what they would find when a prospect opened a door, and having a routine and a set of decision rules helped them proceed with equanimity.[10]

Whether or not particular gestures and lines of script actually increased the likelihood that a prospect would buy a policy, the trainees' belief in the efficacy of the sales routine was important in itself. Having a clear set of instructions and assurances that they would be successful in the long run could help to give agents the confidence and security they needed to keep at their work. As Malinowski (1954 [1948]: 31) found in his study of the Trobriand Islanders, ritual can be an important comfort when the success of a crucial activity is uncertain:

> In the lagoon fishing, where man can rely completely upon his knowledge and skill, magic does not exist, while in the open-sea fishing, full of danger and uncertainty, there is extensive magical ritual to secure safety and good results.

Given the uncertainty of the agents' work, the trainees' eager acceptance of the routine may have reflected a desire for ritual assurance as well as for technical knowledge.

The third reason that Combined's trainees were generally not resistant to routinization was that their routines were intended to increase the agents' control over prospects. Work routinization is generally associated with a loss of workers' autonomy and control, but in this case the routines were designed to give workers more control over prospects and hence over their conditions of work.[11] That control over prospects seemed to compensate for the self-control that the routines demanded of the agents, for their loss of

10. In fact, Kevin handled even this call with aplomb. He gamely gave the presentation to two of the women, focusing on the one who showed the most interest, and he maintained a cheerful and positive attitude throughout. By the end of the call, the woman wanted to buy a policy, but she could not work out payment.

11. The value interactive service workers place on opportunities to control interactions is suggested by Van Maanen and Kunda's report (1989: 61) that the more prestigious jobs at Disneyland are those that allow workers to shape customer behavior instead of just responding to it.

autonomy vis-à-vis management, and for any loss of dignity entailed by standardization.

The training classes continually stressed the importance of establishing control over interactions with prospects. On the first day, we were taught that W. Clement Stone became a successful insurance salesman only when he learned not to give prospects a chance to say no. The lesson came from a prospect Stone had approached by asking, "May I take a moment of your time?" He told Stone, "Young man, as long as you live, never ask for a man's time—TAKE IT!" Taking charge of interactions was essential for Combined's agents because it was up to them not only to enlist but also to organize the prospect's cooperation. The routines were therefore designed to make it as difficult as possible for prospects to refuse to listen to the agent, to cut the presentation short, or to decline to buy. At the same time, though, the routines were designed to avoid making prospects feel that they were being controlled. Mark told the training class that "the rebuttals that work best are the ones that pressurize the customer the least, and give the customer the least control."

The principle of never giving prospects a chance to say no, but avoiding obvious pressure, is well illustrated by the Assumptive Close, which Mark considered the best approach to closing a sale. After completing the sales presentation, the agent was supposed to break eye contact with the prospect and begin writing out the policy application. The agent then asked "noncommittal questions," such as height and state of birth, and entered the responses on the application—he did not look up at the prospect, but acted as though he took it for granted that the prospect would answer the questions. Eventually, if the prospect did answer the questions without protest, the agent asked "committal questions," including name of beneficiary and doctor's name. The idea was for agents to proceed to the application without ever asking prospects whether they wanted to buy a policy, and to get the prospects to answer questions as if they were going along with the sale. This technique challenged the prospects to protest if they objected to the sale, and protest was made more difficult by the agents' avoidance of eye contact.

The trainees were taught that most prospects would try to prevent the agent from proceeding with the routine long before he reached the stage of closing the sale. The agents were trained to use carefully rehearsed "interruption-stoppers" in such cases, to keep the prospect from taking control of the interaction. These interruption-stoppers were designed to allow the agent to pursue the agenda, overriding the prospect's stated wishes. For example, if a prospect said, "I'm really not interested," the agent could respond, "I'm not surprised to hear that. I wouldn't expect you to be interested until you know more about it. As I was saying . . ." An interruption-stopper was supposed to "knock the prospect off his feet": the agent's acceptance of the prospect's objection would be so unexpected that momentary disorientation would stanch resistance long enough for the agent to rush ahead with the routine. This sort of quick rejoinder put the burden on the prospect to continue to voice objections, an effort that required more forcefulness than some prospects could, or wanted to, muster.

As this last point illustrates, customer resistance to compliance with the routines was entirely expected, and strategies for counter-ing resistance were themselves routinized. The short interruption-stoppers were used before and during the presentations to allow the agents to get through their sales talk. For objections made after the presentation was complete, the agents used Rebuttals Number One through Number Five, which were longer speeches. For those customer objections that did not fit any of the five categories for which the rebuttals were created, the agents were taught to use a formula to construct a rebuttal on the spot. As at McDonald's, then, common problems were handled through standardized subroutines, but the agents' subroutines allowed them considerably more range for decision making than the window crew's did.

Combined's routines were carefully designed to augment agents' control over the service interactions. Cialdini (1984) has investigated how people can be made to comply with others' wishes regardless of their own and has enumerated the principles by which would-be persuaders can construct "compliance techniques." In *Influence: How and Why People Agree to Things*, he argues that the main categories of compliance techniques are those based on liking, social proof, authority, consistency, scarcity, and reciprocation. Although Com-bined's routines were not designed by social psychologists, they made use of each of these principles of compliance to help the agents control the interactions and to make prospects' behavior more predictable.

Liking

Combined's training course emphasized that people buy from those they like, and the "warming up the prospect" stage of the routine was created to encourage such liking. The Standard Joke was included in the routine to create a comfortable, friendly atmosphere because, as the trainees were taught, people like those they laugh with. The agents were trained to be outgoing and affable and were never supposed to be antagonistic or insistent. The idea was to make sales by making friends. Some of the agents I worked with had learned to use a show of good humor to establish rapport quickly and even to disarm prospects who were distrustful. For example, when a man challengingly asked, "How much?" as soon as Tom identified himself as an insurance agent, Tom answered jovially, "A million dollars." The prospect laughed and allowed him to give the presentation.

Social Proof

Cialdini demonstrates that people look to others to determine the proper way to behave in a given situation: the mere fact that others have chosen a particular course of action is taken as evidence of the rightness of that choice. Combined Insurance takes advantage of this principle by having agents show prospects lists of names of Combined Insurance policyholders, as part of the sales presentation. This technique was said to be most effective when the lists included the names of neighbors, relatives, and other townspeople the prospect knew personally. The lists of names were supposed to make the prospects less hesitant about buying, since they would assume that the other people must have had good reason for thinking that the policies were worthwhile. Kevin took advantage of a particularly useful model. On every sales call, he made a point of mentioning that one of the people he would be calling on that week had already purchased fifteen policies for family members, including all of his grandchildren.

The agents' routines also called on them to make casual assertions about what "most people" do:

> Tom very smoothly tells the policyholder, a young working-class man with a boastful manner, that he is now eligible to get his first increase in coverage. Tom says something like, "You'll probably want to raise it to $20,000 [from $10,000], that's what most people do." He gives the price of the new premium, and the guy simply nods as if there is no question that he's the sort of person who would want as much life insurance as possible.

Here the principle of social proof was exploited without any proof actually being offered.

Authority

People are more likely to comply with a course of action when it is advocated by someone in a position of authority. Combined's agents were trained to present an authoritative persona themselves, to convey that they were knowledgeable and trustworthy professionals. The agents' routines also borrowed others' authority. On the lists of Combined Insurance policyholders shown to prospects, the names mentioned first were supposed to be "Power Names," people who were especially influential in the community, such as the mayor, the president of the bank, and other prominent citizens (training manual).[12] It was hoped that prospects would be swayed by the knowledge that respected members of the community, who could be expected to be wise decision makers, had chosen to buy Combined's policies.

Consistency

Cialdini provides evidence that, in order to avoid seeming inconsistent, people often comply with requests they would prefer to decline. Combined's routines made extensive use of this tendency, leading up to a sale by getting prospects to agree with a series of general statements. The sales talks were peppered with statements and questions that called for agreement:

> Many people lose their lives in accidents every day, isn't that true?
>
> That's certainly the kind of feature you'd want in your financial plan, isn't it?
>
> Sounds pretty good, doesn't it?
>
> Isn't that the sort of protection you want for your family?[13]

The idea, as Mark explained it, was to get the prospect in a "yes

12. Insurance agents were considered especially useful "power names," since prospects would assume that insurance professionals would not have bought policies that were not worthwhile.

13. Combined Insurance refers to this questioning technique as the Socratic method.

frame of mind," to make buying the policy seem like the logical step to take, and to make the prospect feel that it would be inconsistent to answer no to the final committal question.

Scarcity

Since people are more likely to want things that are scarce, stressing that certain items are available "for a limited time only" or "in limited quantities" is a common compliance technique. The technique was especially well suited to life insurance sales and was incorporated into the sales routines in several ways. The agents were supposed to emphasize the unpredictability of the future health of prospects and their families, pointing out that if they did not buy policies today, they might not be eligible for coverage at standard rates in the future. Similarly, because of the age-based pricing system for life insurance, agents could truthfully argue that delaying the purchase of a policy would mean paying higher rates.

In another appeal to scarcity, Mark taught the class to "milk a medical condition" in order to give senior citizens the impression that the policies were hard to get. The agents were instructed to express serious concern about any health problem mentioned, even when they were well aware that the health problem would not disqualify the prospect. The idea, Mark said, was to make the policy sound terrific and then "make them think, 'Oh no, I might not get it.'" He gave a hilarious demonstration of how to milk a medical condition:

> Mark asks one of the trainees, playing the role of the prospect, if he'd been treated for any problem within the last five years. The trainee answers facetiously, "A skinned knee." Mark simultaneously acts out and explains his technique. He says quietly, "'I see.' Pause. Look serious. Think it over. Sigh. Then ask, 'Does it look like it's gonna come out OK?' Bite the lip. Tap the policy with your pen. Set the pen down. Ask, 'That's all you've had in the last five years, just that skinned knee?' [The class is cracking up at this performance.] Look at the prospect. Look at the lead card. Look at the prospect. Finally give in and say, 'OK, I'll do it for you.'"

Reciprocation

Combined Insurance made relatively little use of the tactic of making prospects feel obliged to comply with a request by first doing them a favor, although in the example given above Mark made the offer of the policy itself seem like a personal favor. The company's new Financial Needs Analysis sales routine (see Appendix 2) does make use of the principle of reciprocity. Early in the interaction, the agents are supposed to tell prospects how much money the Social Security Administration credits incorrectly each year, and then give them a postcard, addressed to the Social Security Administration, requesting information on their account. This free service was intended to create a sense of obligation in prospects, so that they would at least listen to the rest of the presentation.

Combined's agents' routines, unlike McDonald's window workers', were full of compliance techniques, because inducing the prospects to cooperate was part of the work process. The main imperative the agents faced on the job was to control interactions with prospects without making them feel bullied. The tactics described above, and numerous other techniques either built into the sales presentations or taught as subroutines to be used when necessary, helped the agents to assert and maintain control of the interactions and therefore gave the agents more control over their work. In the course of their training, though, Combined's agents were manipulated just as they were trained to manipulate others. As Chapter 4 makes evident, the company used every one of the compliance techniques enumerated by Cialdini in an effort to ensure that their investment in each agent's training would not be wasted and that the agents would follow their routines even without direct supervision.

PATTERNS OF INTEREST AND RESOURCES FOR CONTROL

The compliance techniques built into the sales routines were effective to the extent that prospects felt bound by the social norms the routines were designed to manipulate. When prospects said, "I'm not interested," what they meant was, "I don't want to be rude, but I don't want to hear your sales talk," yet the agents were trained to turn these polite demurrals into a rationale for going on with the presentation. While overriding the prospects' clear wishes, the agents counted on prospects' unwillingness to be similarly impolite themselves. In fact many prospects did seem to find it hard to interrupt an agent, to refuse to listen to him, or simply to close the door in the agent's face. The routine forced prospects to insist on ending the interaction if they hoped to override the agent's determination to continue, thus inhibiting those who were tongue-tied, timid, or disinclined to be rude.

Although the numerous compliance techniques increased agents' control over their interactions with prospects, they certainly did not prevent determined prospects from thwarting the agents' intentions. Some prospects, who had apparently learned from experience that only active and determined resistance would spare them an unwanted sales pitch, forcefully denied the agent any opportunity to lure them into compliance:

> A middle-aged woman in a waitress's uniform answers the door. As soon as Tom identifies himself, she says, loudly and firmly, "No. I have two minutes to get to work. I already sent in my money [for the Combined accident policy she owned]. I don't want to talk." She is obviously quite adamant, so we just leave. Tom and I laugh ruefully at our warm reception, and Tom jokes that he should go around to the back door and tell the woman when she answers that door, "Wow, you should have seen the bitch who lives up front."

Some prospects were not just adamant but hostile:

> After a long pause, a woman in her fifties or sixties, walking with crutches, answers the door. When Chuck introduces himself and asks to come in, she says coldly, "What for, may I ask?" He says that he just wants to verify some information.[14] She says that he can do that in the doorway, "because I'm *not* gonna buy anything." She is quite angry and says that the last guy who came from Combined "stayed for two hours, and the son of a bitch still didn't know enough to leave. What kind of information? I'll answer right here." Chuck says curtly, "Never mind," wheels around, and walks away. She yells after us, "They should have that information at the office." Chuck turns and calls back, "Thank you," and we hurry away. Chuck comments, "I can't believe I said thank you. I saw she was handicapped and felt sorry for her, so I didn't abuse her." He went on, though, "I can see why she was mad. Someone probably went in and pounded on her for two hours." Chuck surmised that the agent had really thought she should buy because her health problems would make it hard for her to get coverage elsewhere.[15]

14. Chuck's answer was at odds with company policy. Although the introductory part of the sales script does say, "I'd like to verify some information, and I may have some good news for you," trainees were specifically taught not to mislead prospects who asked the reason for the visit by implying that it was not a sales call.

15. Here Chuck did not follow the rule, taught in training, to "leave graciously" no matter what the circumstances. Agents' strategies for maintaining face

Some prospects who were willing to listen to the sales presentation found ways to resist the compliance techniques embedded in them by refusing to play along with the scripts. For example, when Tom tried to show one man the list of names of Combined Insurance policyholders, the prospect interrupted with, "Skip all that and just tell me what it is. I don't care who has it." This man also refused to be drawn into verbal agreement with the list of statements that were supposed to put him in a "yes frame of mind." When Tom said, "Many people lose their lives in accidents every day, isn't that true?" he answered noncommittally, "You'd know better than I." The prospect clearly conveyed that although he was willing to hear about the policy, he would not tolerate being manipulated or having his time wasted. Others were less confrontational. When Kevin urged a young woman to insure the life of her baby daughter, stressing the policy's low cost, she disarmed his persuasive technique by calling attention to it:

> Kevin whips out a calculator and figures out the cost of the policy per day, then says, "Let me ask you something—I know you're going to say yes. Is Jennifer worth 18 cents?" Instead of answering, the woman turns to me and says, "Oh, he's good." I can't help laughing and agreeing.[16]

The company was well aware that resistance and disrespectful treatment from prospects could undermine agents' Positive Mental Attitude and their belief in the efficacy of the sales routines. To help agents maintain company-approved attitudes and work habits when out in the field alone, Combined Insurance recommended a variety of techniques designed to reinforce standards and provide inspiration. During training, Mark urged agents to buy motivational audiotapes and to make tapes of their sales routines to play while driving on their rounds. Listening to these tapes, he said, would not only reinforce the agents' knowledge of their routines and confidence in themselves, it would replace radio programming that might threaten

---

and smoothing over discord in difficult interactions are discussed further in Chapter 6.

16. As is mentioned in Appendix 1, Kevin had told me he was concerned that prospects might "look to you for an out." This call was the only occasion on which that happened. Kevin did not imply that he held me responsible for his inability to close the sale, though. Instead, he mused about how he could have done a better job of minimizing the prospect's resistance.

their Positive Mental Attitude. Mark specifically warned the agents to avoid listening to "negative newscasts" (a weather report in particular could provide an easy excuse for stopping work early) or country and western music (its focus on heartbreak replaces productive thoughts with depressing ones).

Combined Insurance also tried to reinforce agents' enthusiasm and dedication by means of regular group meetings.[17] Sales teams were supposed to hold weekly meetings, ideally on Mondays, for programmed training exercises. They also held morning meetings several times a week at which agents could revive their sense of collective purpose, report results, receive praise for their efforts, and publicly announce their goals. In addition to team meetings, the agents regularly attended sessions that brought agents from a wider area together for one or more days of instruction, cheerleading, and competitive selling.

Several of the agents on the team I studied mentioned that some of these recommended practices had proved useful to them. Tom said he found regional meetings "very inspiring," and he and Kevin both regularly reviewed motivational books by Stone and other star salespeople. Moreover, all the agents made some conscious use of the principles of PMA to keep their spirits up in the field. When tempted to slack off, Josh, Kevin, and Tom drew resolve from the chant "Do it now, do it now." Josh and Chuck literally "kept their goals in front of them." Josh taped pictures of his children to the dashboard to remind himself of the importance of earning money for their support, and Chuck stuck up a note reading "$250 to finish Thursday," a reminder that if he worked hard enough early in the week he could afford to take a day off. Kevin's self-conditioning was spoken aloud:

> I'd like to have about three senior sales and wrap up my Winner's Score [$1,000 worth of new sales for the week]. I have $400 to go. I once did that in forty-five minutes. . . . Lately I've had a lot of $150, $200, $250 days, so the odds are, I'm due for a big day.

He also took to heart the PMA principle of turning a negative into a positive:

> Kevin says he has found that he actually sells more when he was

17. Most of these techniques are widely used by direct-sales organizations (Biggart 1989).

originally hesitant about making a particular call, those times when he sees the place and thinks, "You gotta be kidding." Kevin thinks it's fun when the customer says, "I'm letting you in, but I'm not buying." He takes this as a challenge and, he says, "I make the sale."

Even agents who believed in PMA did not always use it consistently in ways that the company would have approved, however. For example, Josh found a number of excuses for not working very hard the day I accompanied him. He had made a big sale early in the morning, which he treated as a justification for easing up rather than as an incentive to exceed past records, and he blamed his lackadaisical attitude on the rainy weather.

Despite the company's efforts to manage the agents' attitudes, not all the agents shared Kevin's faith that they could turn difficulties to advantage. Several of the agents mentioned categories of calls they had come to hate—rural calls, calls on businesses, calls where the Combined Insurance policyholder was not in—and they clearly approached these calls with a Negative Mental Attitude.[18] The sales team I studied had apparently developed some shared evaluations of types of prospects, beliefs which survived despite evidence to the contrary:

> The next lead card is for an auto body shop. Chuck says that he hates auto body shops. I say that Tom and Ralph told me the same thing and ask what's so awful about body shops. Chuck says that he doesn't know why they're so bad; in fact, he once made a sale at one. He then realizes that the lead card shows that the man at this body shop is fifty-nine years old (the highest age at which regular, rather than senior, policies were available). He could be a really good sale, since he would pay the highest premiums available for the larger policies.

Tom approached an auto body shop with a negative attitude and then surprised me by citing the prospect's behavior, which I thought was firm but not insulting, as evidence that people in these shops always treat insurance agents badly. Nonetheless, he credited Positive Mental Attitude precepts with allowing him to maintain his equanimity:

> Tom tells me, "On that last call, I kept my attitude up by saying, 'I'm better than this guy. He's being a jerk, and I'm gonna be a jerk back to

18. See Davis on the tendency of service workers to develop typologies of service-recipients in an effort to "order experience, reduce uncertainty, and further calculability" (1959–60: 163).

to him.' . . . At the beginning [of his career] I would have gotten pissed off. You have to have that Positive Mental Attitude."

Rather than using PMA as the company intended, to approach each sales call in a spirit of confident optimism, Tom seemed to define PMA as any psychological process that allowed him to maintain his sense of dignity, even if it excused a hostile and defeatist approach. From the company's point of view, though, that approach served no one.

Combined Insurance tried to persuade agents that their interests and those of prospects and the company were congruent, arguing that all would benefit if agents adopted an ethic of service and put the prospects' needs first. In fact, though, agents' interests sometimes coincided with those of prospects, sometimes with those of the company, and sometimes were in opposition to both. Protecting the interests of the company, its policyholders, and its prospective customers was an important problem for Combined's managers, since the agents' relative freedom from supervision gave them scope to pursue their own interests.

One area in which the interests of the agents differed from those of the company was in determining which sales calls to make. Combined's trainers encouraged agents to treat every meeting with a policyholder as a chance to sell more insurance, either by increasing the size of the current policy or by selling policies for other family members, but the agents I observed generally regarded calls to current life policyholders as less central to their jobs than calls to potential policyholders. The simple reason was that the commission on premiums collected for new policies was much higher than on premiums for existing policies: 50–65 percent versus 7 percent.[19] Similarly, although Josh assured me that he usually used every lead card he had, on the day I was with him he explained that he was "headhunting," calling only on older people because sales to them were more lucrative. He felt that he had earned this indulgence by selling an expensive policy first thing in the morning.

Conflicting interests among the three parties to the interactions could lead to more serious breaches of ethics. The commission system of compensation gave the agents a significant stake in the

19. Under the new sales system described in Appendix 2, the commission structure has been revised to give agents a stake in the persistency of the policies they sell, thus increasing their incentive to provide ongoing service to policyholders.

outcome of interactions with prospects, and, because these interactions took place beyond the scope of direct supervision, some agents were tempted to cheat customers or the company. Combined's requirement that agents sign a "Statement on Representative's Conduct" that clearly described impermissible activities acknowledged this temptation. Predictably, I did not observe any agents engaged in unlawful or clearly unethical conduct, and I had no reason to suspect that they did so when unobserved.[20] However, I heard about and saw evidence of past dishonesty in the field by former or current Combined Insurance agents. Agents told me that, despite the company's clear rules, in the recent past a local sales manager had encouraged the agents on his team to cheat customers. Ralph reported that five people had been fired because of such "bad work habits," some had quit before they were fired, and others had been given a second chance, and that, since this incident had occurred, ethics were being stressed strongly in their district. In a meeting I attended, the district manager called ethics their "number one priority."[21]

One way agents had swindled customers was by misleading them into thinking they were buying health or accident insurance rather than life. According to the sales manager, though, the biggest problem was with "replacing" existing life policies. Chuck and I called on one family that had been the victim of that practice. The lead card showed that they had bought their policies only six months earlier, but the woman to whom we spoke said they had had them for years. It turned out that instead of increasing the family's coverage by selling them amendments to the existing policies at the rates applicable at the time of the original sale, the agent had tricked the woman into canceling those policies and replacing them with new ones. These were more costly to the family, since the policyholders'

20. The only incident that even came close to such conduct was one in which Tom felt that he had "blown ethics." During a call on a married couple, some ambiguity emerged concerning the man's medical eligibility. The underwriting rules prohibited sales to people who had received advice or treatment for heart trouble within five years. Gerald and Helen had trouble remembering how long it had been since Gerald had consulted a doctor about his heart; at first they seemed to believe it had been three years, but eventually they said it had been five. Tom went ahead and wrote the policy. Since the company could rescind the policy if they discovered upon checking Gerald's medical history that there had been misrepresentation, I thought Tom was being rather hard on himself in doubting the ethics of accepting their statements as truthful.

21. Two agents independently mentioned that members of a local team supervised by a different district manager still routinely engaged in unethical practices.

increased ages raised their rates, but much more profitable for the agent, who got the high commission paid for new policies. Furthermore, he had told the woman that the cash value she would receive for the paid-up portion of the old whole-life policies was higher than the actual payment.

> The woman eventually finds her copy of one of the policies. Chuck looks over the application and finds that the agent's signature is totally illegible—just a scribble. He points out to us that the agent didn't even fill in his four-digit agent number, so he obviously didn't want to be tracked down. Chuck notices that although the rest of the writing on the application is in carbon, the agent's signature is in ink: he must have signed the copy of the application that went to the company separately, and presumably legibly, so that he would be credited for the sale. (To my surprise, Chuck is able to get the woman to renew these policies.)

This practice would no longer be tolerated, Chuck told me. "Now, if you get caught replacing policies like that, you'd get fired right away." Team, district, and regional managers could be held accountable for agents' breaches of ethics, and they were responsible for screening agents' applications for irregularities. The company provided incentives for ethical behavior, rewarding agents who had low cancellation rates and high policy-renewal rates.

The company, as well as its customers, could be the victim of unethical agents, through damage to its reputation and also more directly. The commission system tended to synchronize the interests of agents with those of the company, but the company's interest in minimizing risk competed with the agents' desire to sell as many policies as possible. Since the policies were "preapproved" (effective as soon as the contract was signed, revokable only if material misrepresentation by the prospect was discovered), agents' honesty and good judgment were crucial to the company, and no more than three "underwriting mistakes" per agent were tolerated. Josh and I discovered one such "mistake," obviously intentional, when we visited a family that included a man in a wheelchair:

> When inquiring about the family members' health, Josh asks the man, "Were you in an accident or something?" The man replies that he was in a work-related accident a long time ago—he'd been in the wheelchair for twenty-two years. Since the policy is not nearly that old, it is clear that it should never have been written to begin with, because the underwriting rules prohibit sales of these policies to

wheelchair-bound people. . . . Furthermore, the previous agent had apparently lied to the policyholders as well as to the company. The woman has two life policies, but she should not have been sold the second one before she had taken all of the amendments available on the first one at its lower rates. She had also been misinformed about how soon the second whole life policy would be paid up.

The team I observed was, as Josh put it, "cleaning up the mess" left by dishonest agents, and they had to face the distrust of policy-holders who had been misled in the past. The agents did not have a script for dealing with this extremely awkward situation, a problem they discussed at the team training session I attended. Nevertheless, several of the agents reported that they had good records of "turning around" such policyholders, persuading them not to cancel their policies and sometimes even increasing their coverage.[22]

Agents could also take advantage of the elaborate system of incentives Combined Insurance offered its sales force. Like most commission-sales businesses (see Biggart 1989; Oakes 1990), the company offered both material and status rewards to individual agents and teams. For example, frequent sales promotions provided special awards for achieving a high level of sales within a limited period of time. The rewards given in the various incentive programs sponsored by the company or by individual managers ranged from pens featuring the president's picture and lapel pins symbolizing status rank to expensive prizes such as vacation trips and stereo systems. These lures could prompt some agents to cheat the company, though without cheating particular policyholders:

> Looking at a lead card, Chuck says that he thinks it is for a fake policy: the address of the policyholder is apparently nonexistent. He explains that the agent could have handed in a counter check on a non-existent account, which would bounce. I ask what good that would do the agent, since the commission would be taken away from him when the check bounced. Chuck explains that by the time that happened, the agent would have gotten his award.

These instances of dishonesty, although not typical of the behavior of Combined's agents, are nevertheless illuminating. They point to the

---

22. The new sales system, which encourages agents to build their own clientele and rewards them for keeping policies in force, was designed to minimize the temptation to make quick but short-lived sales. (See Appendix 2.)

complexities introduced by the three-way contest of control among workers, management, and service-recipients. The commission system created an overall commonality of interest among management and workers that partially compensated for the company's inability to supervise agents' activities directly. Even so, some interests did diverge and alliances could shift in particular situations, leaving both the organization and its service-recipients vulnerable to workers' violations of the routine.

Variations on a Theme

Agents' departures from the routine did not necessarily constitute violations. It was an article of faith at Combined Insurance that methodical use of the scripted routine would produce a profitable level of sales, but the scripts were intended to be flexible. Combined gave its agents considerably more leeway to alter their routines than McDonald's gave its workers, and with good reason. Combined's agents were encouraged to establish rapport by engaging the prospects in personal conversation at the beginning of the sales call, and they were supposed to choose from among subroutines, adapting them when necessary to suit particular circumstances. Therefore, despite extensive routinization, Combined Insurance still had to rely on its agents' finesse, sensitivity to context, and personal ethics.

It was no surprise, then, that the scripts taught in class were altered in the field. Some of the changes were made at the direction of managers, who had developed their own ideas about what worked in making sales. The district manager who supervised the sales team I studied had instructed the agents to eliminate several pages of the presentation that he believed wasted time or provoked resistance. Agents made many changes on their own initiative as well. All of them had firm opinions about what worked for them and what did not, and they were quick to drop parts of the routine that they believed held things up or caused them to lose control of interactions. For example, some of the agents used the Standard Joke, but when I asked Kevin about it he grimaced and said that he preferred to use his own jokes to warm up prospects. He still believed in the principle, however: "If I can't make them laugh before we're sitting down, forget it." Chuck stopped using the introductory phrase, "and I may have some good news for you," when he found that some prospects asked at the end of the presentation, "What's the good news?"

Agents also dropped potentially useful parts of the routine that made them feel uncomfortable. For instance, all but one of the team members disregarded the prescribed request for referrals at the end of each sales call.

The agents developed flexible routines of their own, eagerly gathering information from their coworkers and managers about techniques or phrases that worked in particular situations and evolving their own responses. For example, although the script called for agents to find out about prospects' eligibility for the standard policy only at the end of the presentation, Kevin preferred to "qualify the prospect up front." That way, he could incorporate facts he had picked up, such as a fixed income or particular health problems, into his presentation. One of the experienced agents in my training class advised the other trainees to use a standard line when their regular script eluded them: "If you forget what you're saying, it works to just say, 'I forgot what I was supposed to say. Oh, yes—,' as long as you laugh when you say it."

Not all of the agents were equally adept at improvising lines or choosing appropriate ones from their memorized repertoires. Kevin, a methodical worker, carefully devised what he called "the respect rebuttal" to use with women prospects, a script he taught other agents at a district meeting. I heard him use it on two calls:

> Kevin says to the woman, "I have a lot of respect for you. You remind me of my grandmother [alternatively, "sister"]. She's an intelligent businesswoman, like you, and she likes to review all the facts before making a decision. So, knowing your situation won't be any different tomorrow than it is today, look it over now. Take all the time you need."

Kevin told me that after delivering this speech the agent should "shut up and wait in the corner." The main idea, he said, was to "show that you respect their decision and let them take their time."

Other agents believed they were at their best when improvising. Some of their impromptu dialogue, however, made me appreciate the value of memorized scripts:

> Chuck and I chat with a woman about a Mexican blanket hanging on her wall, and she tells us how she bargained to get a good price. Later, when "verifying information" on the lead card, Chuck says, "And your name is Susan T. Jones. . . . " She says, "No, it's Susan J. Jones." He makes the correction on the card, saying, "Oh yeah, I should have known: J for Jew." I am dumbfounded and assume I've

heard wrong, but Chuck goes on, "Like the way you jewed down the price of that blanket." I am in shock, but Susan just laughs.

Like McDonald's workers, then, the agents changed their routines to suit themselves, but they had much greater scope for editing and improvising than McDonald's workers did. Since they were greatly concerned about the outcome of their interactions, the agents were more likely than the window crew to make changes based on perceived efficacy as well as on comfort, though their alterations were not necessarily improvements.

Because there was a great deal of variation both in prospects' behavior and in the ways the agents used the routines, it is difficult to judge how useful the basic routines were in helping agents overcome resistance and close sales. My impression, based on both positive and negative evidence, was that at least some aspects of the routines worked effectively, if not altogether reliably, to enhance the agents' control of the interactions. The positive examples were interactions in which agents, by acting in accordance with their training rather than adhering to ordinary rules of interaction, led unwilling prospects to conform to the agent's agenda instead of carrying out their intended lines of action. For example:

> The woman who answers the door tells Chuck firmly, "If you're selling something, I'll tell you right now, I'm not buying." Chuck goes on with his "verifying information" routine, then goes into the presentation. I expect her to get annoyed at this point, since she had said that she didn't want to buy anything, but instead she seems quite interested. She warms up a little and follows what he's saying closely. (Although Chuck succeeds in "getting off the presentation" despite her resistance, he doesn't change the prospect's opinion that she has enough insurance.)

During a long and difficult sales call, when a man was interested in buying policies but his wife was firmly opposed, Tom's routine helped him block the prospects' move to bring the interaction to an inconclusive end:

> After much discussion, Gerald says that he'd want to talk it over with Helen before making a decision. Tom closes the presentation book, calmly tells them to take all the time they need to talk it over, and stays put. (Gerald decides to buy two policies.)

Negative evidence of the usefulness of some aspects of the sales routines came from instances in which agents' abandonment of the procedures they had been taught clearly undermined their efforts. Failure to use techniques designed to minimize the prospect's opportunities to say no, such as avoiding eye contact when attempting to get into the house, predictably allowed prospects to assert their preferences more easily. For example, Ralph, the sales manager, gave a prospect many opportunities to end the interaction, and that is what eventually happened:

> A man who says he was just on his way out agrees to spend five minutes with Ralph, who tells him that he "just wants to verify some information." After doing so, Ralph admits that he has a life insurance policy to sell and asks, "Could I come back later in the week to show it to you?" (failing to follow through with the presentation while the man was listening but instead giving him the chance to veto a return visit). The man says that he has "plenty of life." Instead of using the scripted rebuttal, Ralph asks, "Your wife, too?" The man thinks carefully and then says yes. Ralph says, "OK, thanks. I didn't want to take up your time."

In cases like this one, the agents deferred to prospects instead of attempting to control them. Their behavior met ordinary norms of politeness and did not displease the prospects, but it gave the agents no chance to change the minds of prospects who were not already interested in buying insurance.

As these examples suggest, despite their use of detailed scripts each agent handled sales calls differently. Their sales styles, ability, and judgment all varied, and it seemed to me that even extensive routinization had not rendered this variation irrelevant.

Tom and Ralph seemed ill at ease with small talk, and they followed the scripts closely, going through them methodically and seriously. Tom even recited the Standard Joke without a smile, though he did insert some humorous lines into his presentation; Ralph rarely displayed any affect at all. In contrast, Chuck and Josh enjoyed talking to people and approached their work more playfully, and both could veer quite far from the routine. They ad-libbed with a confident bluster in difficult situations, and each sometimes put his foot in his mouth:

> A prospect has a question about the Combined accident policy he owns. He's had the policy for fourteen years and has always paid the premium when a salesman called. However, he recently got a bill in the mail, which he paid. He is confused about what the bill was for and why it came in the mail. Chuck asks how much it was for and says

that it was probably a particular kind of supplement to the accident policy. If so, Chuck says, the prospect didn't have to pay it. The man is quite indignant and says that sending the bill was a sneaky way of doing business. Chuck doesn't seem sure about the bill, and I am surprised that he would offer annoying information when he's not convinced he's right. . . . When we get outside, I ask Chuck if he really knew anything about the mailed bill. He says, "Fuck, no!" and laughs.

A fifty-four-year-old woman says that she now has $3,000 worth of life insurance. Josh tells her that if she adds to her current policies the amendment he's trying to sell, she'll have "enough for a really nice funeral, I mean, nothing cut-rate." I am *amazed*. (Agents were trained never to make explicit references to a prospect's death.)

Kevin struck me as the ideal Combined Insurance agent. He used the routine conscientiously, spoke fluently, was good at making prospects like him right away, and came across as sincere, smooth, and interested in the prospects' welfare. When he did depart from the routine, he consciously chose adjustments to meet various circumstances, based on what he had learned from previous sales calls.

As would be expected, the agents on the team were not equally successful. What accounted for the variation in their success is not self-evident, however: faithfulness to the routines? attitude? skill? If in fact the routines made workers' skill irrelevant, willingness to implement the routines conscientiously would be an important determinant of success at Combined Insurance. The company itself argued that the main determinant of agents' success was attitude, a term meant to encompass agents' belief in the routines, their persistence and dedication, and their infusion of conviction and simulated spontaneity into the scripts. Combined Insurance argued that anyone with PMA and a willingness to follow the company's instructions day in and day out could succeed as an agent.

Considering the room for variation allowed in the agents' scripts, though, skill would also seem to be an important determinant of agents' success. The meaning of "skill" is elusive in interactive service jobs, however. Researchers generally distinguish skill from attitude (see, for example, Finlay and Martin 1991), but these dimensions are inseparable when the job requires workers to manipulate their own mood, demeanor, or style. Stinchcombe (1990b: 33) suggests that skill consists of knowledge of how a task can be carried out in a wide range of circumstances, the capacity to execute the work under a variety of conditions, and the ability to choose among the range of techniques based on a correct reading of the requirements of the situation. According to these criteria, it would seem that, beyond knowledge of their routines, skill for insurance agents corresponds to sensitivity to the demands of varied social situations, responsiveness to cues, the capacity to monitor and adjust behavior to produce desired responses in others, quick-wittedness, verbal dexterity, and likability—the range of capacities usually described as "social skills," plus some intelligence. Since Combined Insurance had not eliminated discretion from the agents' jobs, we would expect skill of this sort to be an important determinant of success.

My observations of five agents would obviously be an inadequate basis for untangling the relative importance of attitude, skill, and the routines themselves in shaping outcomes, even if I had a reliable measure of skill unrelated to success at sales. Nonetheless, a comparison of the two most successful agents on the sales team is suggestive, though it necessarily relies on my own impressions of their skill in handling interactions.

My admiration of Kevin's good sense and interpersonal skill, as well as his discipline, made it easy for me to understand why he had one of the highest sales records in the region, and I was not surprised to learn two years later that he had gone on to win a national award. Josh was also one of the top salespeople in the region, however, and the reasons for his success were less apparent to me. My first reaction to hearing him give a presentation was, "There's no way I would buy anything from him." He did not use the scripts precisely, but the changes he made, unlike Kevin's, seemed to be the first words that came into his head rather than conscious choices. His descriptions of policy features trailed off to "and stuff like that," and his efforts to ad-lib struck me as utterly inarticulate. In short, although he spoke with great confidence, I thought he sounded as though he did not know what he was talking about.

I was not the only one to notice the sharp contrast between Kevin's and Josh's handling of their job or to feel that Josh's success required some explanation. Several of the agents spoke of Josh having incredible luck, but luck would probably not explain long-term success, and two years after my fieldwork ended Josh was still doing well. The regional manager then supervising Kevin and Josh believed that different attributes accounted for the success of each:

> One is finesse and tact and professionalism, the other one is brawn, bowl 'em over, "let's do it."

Even so, given strong supervision, Josh was able to adapt to the less aggressive style called for by the new sales system:

> He's so aggressive and competitive that when he saw Kevin pulling [ahead], he said, "I will forgo my personal beliefs to win." He's a big winner and a big competitor.

It seemed that the flexibility of Combined's routine allowed the company to benefit from Kevin's skill, while the routine's structure allowed Josh to compensate for relatively poor skills with such PMA-related attributes as enthusiasm, drive, and confidence. These agents, among the most successful in the company, were clearly extraordinary. In their cases at least, Combined Insurance managed to gain the benefits of routinization while avoiding its worst pitfall. The scripting and standardization of attitude decreased the company's dependence on agents' skills without wasting competent workers' capacity to improve upon the routine.

By and large, though, the company had not resolved the dilemma inherent in balancing standardization with flexibility. In allowing workers to make adaptations to the routine, Combined Insurance gave agents the freedom to improve on their scripts, but the company thereby forfeited the protection the routine might have provided against the effects of unskilled agents' poor decision making or execution.[23] Combined Insurance had not devised a system that could differentially enforce adherence to the scripts so as to allow the company to take advantage of the skills of its best employees while holding those lacking in judgment or finesse to the proven routines.

OVERVIEW

The relative interests and power of the three parties to interactive service work routines are widely discussed, but broad generalizations hamper analysis and little agreement has been reached on basic questions. Managers directly responsible for supervising interactive service workers often claim that the interests of managers, workers, and customers are ultimately consistent, particularly in consumer

---

23. The commission system of compensation did insulate the company from some of the damaging effects of its workers' poor judgment, since it did not pay for the time of workers who did not make sales. It did pay for these workers' training, fringe benefits, and supervision and did forfeit possible sales, however, and misbehaving agents could damage customer goodwill and the company's reputation.

service organizations whose survival depends on pleasing customers. Contradictory arguments about the alignment of interests in
interactive service work abound, however. Whyte (1946) and Glenn
and Feldberg (1979b), for example, note that service workers who
deal with the public are likely to find themselves caught between
the competing interests of service-recipients and managers or other
workers. Consumers often feel that their own interest in receiving
good service is outweighed by management's determination to lower
costs, workers' desire to minimize their own exertion, or implacable
bureaucratic perversity (Koepp 1987b). Similarly, a variety of commentators (e.g., Albrecht 1988; Garson 1988) describe service-
recipients as sometimes victimized by managerial commitment to
routinization, since they are forced to make do with standardized
responses that may not address their situation. In stark contrast,
Roman (1979: 26), writing about telephone marketing, describes
workers' deviations from the script as an unethical waste of a prospect's time. Labor-process writers generally do not consider the
interests of service-recipients at all, but take for granted that the interests of workers and management are diametrically opposed. Literature in this tradition typically treats routinization as oppressive to
workers, robbing them of both power and creativity (see Thompson
1989 for an overview).

The picture is equally contradictory with regard to the resources
of the three groups. Some stress the power of consumers to force
organizations in competitive markets to adapt to their wishes, while
others portray consumers as being at the mercy of bureaucracies.
Some scholars of the sociology and history of work seem to assume
that managers are almost inevitably able to impose their routines on
workers, but others assume that a culture of resistance among workers often offsets the power of management.

The limits of generalizations about interests and power in service
work become apparent when we examine routines in action. The two
case studies show that the alignment of interests among workers,
service-recipients, and managers varies in different kinds of service
work, as does the balance of power. Moreover, the participants in
the interactions are likely to have an assortment of interests, some
of which align them with one party, some with the other, some with
neither. Individuals in each group also differ in their evaluations of
the benefits and costs of compliance or resistance. Labor-process
theory's standard model of power dynamics in the workplace—that

of management and labor contesting control over the work process and its rewards, their interests fundamentally at odds—clearly needs to be modified to make sense of interactive service work. The struggle for control between managers and workers does not disappear in this kind of workplace, nor do the parties' conflicting interests in matters of wages and work effort. Both groups, however, also have to reckon with the aims, expectations, and demands of service-recipients.

The case studies show that when the interests of management and workers differ, workers try to pursue their own interests, sometimes succeeding in undermining managerial plans, as the resistance model would predict. To minimize such noncooperation, managers often create incentives that give workers a stake in the company's success, or otherwise try to persuade workers that their interests coincide with the company's. In interactive service work, the resistance model must be extended to encompass service-recipients as well. Customers may share interests with managers, workers, or both, but it is not uncommon for the aims of the three parties to diverge. Under some circumstances, then, service-recipients resist workers' attempts to implement organizational routines, but in others they insist that routines be followed properly. If service routines are more varied in execution than they are in design, it is in part because workers and service-recipients deliberately try to evade the constraints managerially designed routines impose on their actions. Which of the three parties to service interactions achieves their goals depends on the resources available to them in particular settings and on their willingness to use those resources.

Research on interactive service work also suggests that sociologists and historians of work have given insufficient attention to the concrete benefits workers may derive from routinization. Underlying much labor-process research is the assumption that workers comply with routinized work regimens only because they have no choice. In this view, it is taken for granted that workers prefer work that is challenging, varied, autonomous, and personally engaging. Since routinization destroys just these qualities of work, workers are assumed to try to resist all efforts to usurp their decision-making power and trivialize their skills through standardization.

The studies of McDonald's and Combined Insurance do not support the view that workers are uniformly hostile to routinization, or even that the conflicts of interest between workers and management are necessarily more salient than the interests they share. To assume that workers will resist the constraints of routinization unless they misunderstand their own interests is to give them too little credit. In interactive service work, both managers and workers generally wish to regulate the behavior of service-recipients. When routines are designed to give workers more power over service-recipients, as those at Combined Insurance were, the benefits routinization provides for workers are apparent. The workers may even see the routines as giving them skills. McDonald's routines did not generally empower workers, but they did allow workers to limit their involvement in unequal relations, providing a shield behind which workers could withdraw. Whether or not the workers would have preferred more varied and challenging jobs, my fieldwork provides ample evidence that even strict routinization can serve some interests of interactive service workers.

Under some circumstances, then, interactive service routines can enhance workers' control over the labor process. Under others, routines protect rather than undermine workers' personal dignity. Furthermore, the studies of McDonald's and Combined Insurance suggest that to the extent that routinized interactive service work is frustrating or demeaning, workers are likely to direct their resentment toward service-recipients who make it difficult to carry out the routine rather than toward management for imposing it.

One reason workers' dissatisfaction with routinized work is relatively muted is that even the most routinized work is likely to keep remnants of decision-making and skill requirements. My research supports the argument that employers' interests are not always best served by eliminating workers' opportunities for exercising discretion (cf. Burawoy 1979; Friedman 1977; Fuller and Smith 1991). Limited discretion can mitigate workers' discontent by increasing their sense of control. It also makes it possible for routinized work to proceed in the face of contingencies, including the sometimes unpredictable demands of service-recipients. The salience of these benefits varies in different kinds of interactive service work. Because of differences in the workers' tasks and in the service-recipients' commitment to the service interactions, flexibility and responsiveness were more important to Combined Insurance than to McDonald's.

Combined Insurance found ways to make routinization workable even under relatively varied and unpredictable conditions. Organizations that want to allow for customization can encourage flexible use of routines, as Combined Insurance did, in several ways. They can carefully delineate areas of worker discretion within the routine; they can issue rules to guide adaptation and improvisation; or they can provide menus of subroutines with decision rules for choosing among them. Even organizations that do not explicitly build flexibility into their routines can provide tacit support for adaptation to circumstances, by choosing methods of supervision and work evaluation that do not penalize workers for departures from their scripts. McDonald's supervision was unusually tight, however. Since only minor variations in workers' manner and wording were sanctioned, the company relied on the intercession of managers for much of the flexibility in its service system.

Routinization limits flexibility and responsiveness, but it need not eliminate them. Skill requirements, Kusterer (1978) argues, cannot be eradicated even in highly routinized jobs, and my fieldwork supports this contention. However, analysis of interactive service work requires a reexamination of the meaning of the term "skill." Many of the capacities required to accomplish such work appear to be features of personality or attitude, dimensions usually considered to be distinct from work skills.[24] How able workers are to control their emotions, to read and respond to various situations, and to manipulate their presentations of self partially determines their success in carrying out service interactions. These capacities are not easily distinguishable from disposition, attitude toward work, and acceptance of organizational definitions and goals, so workers who exercise them may not be acknowledged as skilled.[25] Indeed, workers themselves may not recognize these capacities as skills. Combined's agents generally saw their ability to read situational cues and manipulate responses as valuable and understood that this skill could be honed and developed. McDonald's workers, by contrast, more often spoke of their handling of interactions as a function of the "kind of person" they were than of their skill.

Although routinized interactive service work need not be as objectionable to workers as labor-process theorists assume, such

24. DeVault (1991) discusses a similar problem in analyzing the care women provide for their families. Although family care is work that requires effort and skill, a requirement of the work is that its activities be constructed as an expression of women's personal characteristics and their devotion to their families.

25. These qualities are more likely to be recognized and rewarded as skills in, for example, managerial or therapeutic work than in low-level interactive service work.

work does remain problematic precisely because it raises questions about the kind of person each worker is. Whether particular workers experience their routines as helpful or as humiliating, the routines force them to take on a persona distinct from their usual identity. The varied adaptations workers make to jobs that require them to cede control of their self-representation are examined in Chapter 6.

6

Meanings of Routinized Work
Authenticity, Identity, and Gender

Interactive service work is work on people, since service-recipients are the raw materials of the labor process. When such work is routinized, quality control inevitably involves standardizing some aspects of the workers themselves, including personal attributes that would not otherwise be subject to employer control. Because the selves of the workers are closely bound up with the quality of the work they do, employers work on the people they hire, and the employees generally need to work on themselves to do their jobs well.

C. Wright Mills noted in *White Collar* (1951: 185) that "the real opportunities for rationalization and expropriation are in the field of the human personality," and, increasingly, employers are taking advantage of those opportunities. The routinization of human interactions by corporations and other large bureaucracies can be seen as a disturbing trend, one that epitomizes the kind of depersonalization, dehumanization, manipulativeness, and superficiality that critics of late-twentieth-century United States culture deplore. Ironically, much of the standardization of workers' behavior and identity that service businesses undertake is intended as an antidote, or at least a sugar-coating, to the perceived impersonality of mass-produced services. Organizations that routinize service interactions are acting on contradictory impulses. They want to treat customers as interchangeable units, but they also want to make the customers feel that they are receiving personal service. The tension inherent in this project was apparent when I asked one of the trainers at Hamburger University about McDonald's goals for customer service. He told me quite sincerely, "We want to treat each customer as an individual, in sixty seconds or less"—thirty seconds, for drive-thru. He was confident that this goal could be achieved through the proper enactment of McDonald's Six Steps of Window Service. It is clear that even if organizations recognize that customers' individuality must be acknowledged in order to create high-quality service interactions, the meaning of "individuality" is greatly attenuated when interactive service work is routinized.

For workers, the routinization of interactive service work makes individuality, authenticity, and identity everyday concerns. For example, I noticed that one of Combined's agents, Kevin, had a little note stuck to the dashboard of his car that said, "BE KEVIN." As he explained it, this was not a statement of a metaphysical imperative, but a practical reminder. When how one presents oneself is minutely prescribed, being oneself is problematic, so Kevin had to work at it. Furthermore, he did not want to be himself so that he would *feel* better, but so that he would *do* better. He had found he was more likely to sell policies when more of himself came through, so he consciously worked on being genuine.

In all areas of social life, people have to struggle with the relation between what they do and say and what sorts of people they want to be. Erving Goffman, who regarded organizations as "place[s] for generating assumptions about identity" (1961c: 186), analyzed the problems faced by people who do not want to accept the assumptions that are generated by their participation in an organization. The mental patients he observed found ways to discount the implications participation had for their self-definitions. Similarly, for both the worker and the person being served, highly routinized service interactions can create tensions between the ways they want to think about themselves and what the situation implies about them.

Consumers of services, by and large, have already accepted the overriding assumption built into service routines, that people are generally interchangeable, at least for the limited purposes of the organization. Consumers do not approach encounters with representatives of large bureaucratic organizations with the expectation that they will be treated as whole individuals or that they will be allowed to define what matters will be considered relevant. A counterexample may clarify this point. The following letter was sent to *The Times* of London in 1915, when passports were first being introduced in England and the rest of Europe (cited in Fussell 1980: 29):

> Sir,
>   A little light might be shed, with advantage, upon the high-handed methods of the Passports Department at the Foreign Office. On the form provided for the purpose I described my face as "intelligent." Instead of finding this characterization entered, I have received

a passport on which some official utterly unknown to me has taken it upon himself to call my face "oval."

Yours very truly,
Bassett Digby

The letter is amusing now because that sort of outrage at the very premises of bureaucratization would be rare today. As a rule, people understand that bureaucracies do not regard them as whole and unique individuals. They do not waste their energy struggling against *Gesellschaft*. Instead, they accept the anonymous status large bureaucracies accord them, and they try to adapt themselves to the requirements of the organization. Thus, even where interactive service workers have to guide people to behave in ways that are convenient for the organizations, a large part of that work has already been done for them.

Service organizations that have to compete for customers realize that although most customers accept anonymity, the implications of interchangeability are not flattering or pleasing to them. Such organizations try to construct routines in which workers uniformly inject into the interactions some of the attributes of authentic humanity, such as friendliness, consideration, and personal attention (see Hochschild 1983). The idea is to make standardization more palatable by reliably producing good feelings without greatly interfering with efficiency, which remains the dominant goal.

The implications of participation in routinized interactions are different for workers. Although the effects vary according to the nature of the job, all sorts of interactive service workers face tensions resulting from the discrepancy between how they normally deal with people and how they are required by the routines to deal with them. Inevitably, then, employers who routinize interactions create problems of identity and authenticity for their workers. One such problem is the necessity of disguising some feelings and simulating others.

Whether workers experience the discrepancy between their authentic feelings and the feelings they need to express as part of the job as a problem is, to some extent, culturally variable. According to Trilling (1972), personal authenticity is a relatively new cultural ideal. Hochschild (1983) argues that contemporary Americans are unusually concerned with authenticity, and she analyzes the socioeconomic determinants of this preoccupation. Since "phoniness" is considered a serious failing in the United States, jobs that require the manipulation of one's own and others' feelings may raise painful questions of identity for workers in this culture.[1] In contrast, Dalby (1983: 157–58) reports that Japanese geishas were genuinely puzzled by the hostility of American women who seemed to find the geishas' work reprehensible because it involved "insincere flattery." Dalby describes the difference between the Japanese and the American understanding of "the wide gap between true intentions and social facades":

- The Japanese express this human dilemma by the concept of *honne* versus *tatemae*, the truly felt as against the socially required, and they see the dichotomy as a necessity of civilized life. . . . Japanese know that certain kinds of social situations demand tatemae. There is nothing insincere about facades. They are a ready-made way of helping people through social occasions. One simply cannot get by wearing one's honne on one's sleeve.

  The American version of this human predicament casts suspicion on the social facade and tends to view it as deception, in opposition to true intentions. We feel that bad faith has intervened if the gap between honne and tatemae becomes too wide.

The emotion work required of the geishas was therefore not a challenge to their sense of authenticity. In the United States, the cultural emphasis on individuality and sincerity (Lamont 1992), which encourages employers to try to ensure that customers receive "personal service," also makes the standardization of such interactions especially troubling for workers.

As the example of the geishas illustrates, constructions of gender are also at issue in the design and implementation of interactive service routines. In many cases, these routines draw on widely accepted understandings of how men and women think and behave. Workers' and service-recipients' enactment of the routines can bolster the taken-for-granted status of these beliefs. The case studies of McDonald's and Combined Insurance suggest, however, that cultural definitions of masculine and feminine work are quite elastic, allowing workers to interpret their jobs as expressive of their gendered nature regardless of content. Nevertheless, even when women's and men's jobs draw on skills or traits usually associated with the other gender, the gender segregation of jobs helps sustain the notion that women and men have essentially different characters.

1. Wouters (1989) argues that Hochschild overstates workers' discomfort with emotional labor.

PROBLEMS OF IDENTITY

McDonald's window workers and Combined's agents had to find ways to reconcile their sense of themselves with the identity their job conferred upon them. Some of their difficulties arose because neither job was held in high esteem by the public. This low public regard affected both customers' treatment of workers and the workers' responses to their roles:

> Traci tells me, "Some people seem to look down on [McDonald's] employees. Like I was working one night, and . . . we were really busy. My friend had taken this one girl's order, and she [the worker] picked up a straw and she laid it on the counter. And the girl [customer] got mad and said that she threw the straw at her. And she started calling her ignorant for working at McDonald's. Some people look down on us, [and] some people think, 'It's just a job, I have a job too.'"

> Dennis, a host, speaks very disparagingly about working at McDonald's. He says, "This isn't really a job." I ask what he means, and he says, "It's about as low as you can get. Everyone knows it."

Although the Combined Insurance salesmen did not regard their work as low-status, they were well aware that insurance agents are widely regarded as bores or pests, to be avoided if possible.[2] Moreover, they frequently had to deal with rude and dismissive behavior from prospects. Some of the hostility insurance agents face is based on mistrust of their motives (Oakes 1990; Zelizer 1979). The intelligence of McDonald's workers was doubted, but it was the integrity of Combined's agents that was suspect.

Further challenges to identity were raised by the companies' extensive attempts to control their workers' self-presentation, including the workers' looks, demeanor, and personal style. For example, many McDonald's workers regarded the polyester tunic outfits they had to wear as ugly and degrading, and they were greatly cheered when those uniforms were replaced by ones that more closely resembled ordinary street clothes. The lack of control the window workers had over self-presentation was brought home most clearly

---

2. See, for example, Keegan (1976: 23): "We are most of us capable of compartmentalizing our minds, would find the living of our lives impossible if we could not, and flee the company of those who can't or won't: zealots, monomaniacs, hypochondriacs, insurance salesmen, the love-sick, the compulsively argumentative." Woody Allen expressed a similar view even more bluntly in his movie *Love and Death*: "There are worse things in life than death. If you've ever spent an evening with an insurance salesman, you know what I mean."

during a special promotion of "Shanghai McNuggets," when they were forced to wear big Chinese peasant hats made of styrofoam. Most of the workers felt that the hats made them ridiculous:

> Katie says that McDonald's ought to pay another ten cents an hour for making them wear the hats: "No one should have to wear those. It's TORTURE."

The selfhood of the workers was challenged most severely by routines that imposed particular types of interaction with other people. The problems of identity set up by McDonald's differed from those created by Combined Insurance.

The central duty of McDonald's window workers was to serve, and their major psychic task was to control or suppress the self. Their job required them to be nice to one person after another in a way that was necessarily quite unindividualized, and to keep their temper no matter how they were treated. What McDonald's demanded of its workers was a very stripped-down kind of interactive style, with some pseudo-*Gemeinschaft* thrown in. The workers were supposed to be efficient, courteous, and friendly in short bursts and within a very narrow range. They were told to be themselves, but their routines gave them little scope to express their personality.

Combined Insurance placed very different sorts of demands on its workers. While McDonald's merely instructed workers to smile and behave pleasantly to customers, Combined Insurance tried to affect its employees' psyches quite fundamentally through Positive Mental Attitude training. The company strove to inculcate optimism, determination, enthusiasm, and confidence and to destroy habits of negative thinking. The message for agents was somewhat paradoxical: you should do everything exactly the way we tell you to, but success depends on your own strength of character.

The main task for Combined's agents was not to serve but to sell, to take prospects and turn them into customers. Since the salesmen normally faced substantial resistance, their routines were designed to make it easier for them to impose their wills on prospects. Furthermore, the agents worked on their own rather than in a central workplace, and their interactions with customers could be much longer and cover a broader range than the McDonald's workers' did, so the agents were called on to use much more of their selves than were the window workers. They had to motivate themselves and keep up their enthusiasm, and they had to adjust their behavior to respond to the problems presented by each prospect. Although their basic routine was unvaried, they needed to be chameleonlike to a certain extent and adapt to circumstances. As Tom put it, "You have to learn to read people, to figure out what they want in a salesperson and BE that person." Like the workers at McDonald's, the agents were required to control themselves, but their focus was always on controlling the prospect and the interaction.

These two jobs, then, posed distinct problems of identity for the workers. At McDonald's, workers needed to suppress the self and to serve others. The implications for the self that the window workers might have wished to resist were self-abnegation and depersonalization. Workers in nonroutinized service jobs also face the problem of having to enact self-abnegation, but the sense of depersonalization is especially acute for workers who must speak sentences they have not constructed to people who take no notice of them as people. For Combined's agents, the job was not so much to suppress the self as to transform it, and not so much to serve others as to control them. In these circumstances the basic danger for workers was self-alienation: having to be, while at work, someone they did not want to be. To do their job well, the agents were required to be insincere and manipulative. That problem might well be shared by other salespeople, even those working on their own. Combined's agents, however, faced the additional problem of holding on to their sense of themselves as autonomous and authentic people while reciting a script. Kevin's efforts to be himself inside the bounds of his script reflected this difficulty. Scripting could also challenge the agents' sense of manliness.

These problems arose in concrete ways during the work process. The companies, aware of the problems, tried to provide workers with psychic strategies that minimized some of the difficulties, and workers looked for ways to reconcile their sense of themselves with the identity they enacted on the job.[3] Because the service interactions often bore little resemblance to genuine interpersonal exchanges, they raised questions about workers' real selves.

One question both workers and customers had to confront in every interaction was whether it was a real conversation. At McDonald's, the lines window workers used were extremely schematic: "Welcome to McDonald's"; "Will that be a *large* Coke?"; "For

3. Oakes (1990) discusses the dilemmas of identity and ethics faced by insurance agents, but he does not analyze how they deal with them.

here or to go?" These standard lines, repeated over and over again, were extremely familiar to workers and customers, and both parties, as a rule, maintained a lesser degree of engagement in the interactions than they would in ordinary conversations. The mechanical nature of the exchange was highlighted, to my embarrassment, in one exchange I had with a customer:

CUSTOMER: A hamburger and a large Coke.
RL: (while punching the order into the cash register): Something to drink?
CUSTOMER: I said, a Coke.
RL: Oh, I meant to say, "For here or to go?"

I had, in fact, heard and understood the order. Not giving my full attention to the conversation, I had absent-mindedly said the wrong line when it was my turn to speak, just as if I had pushed the wrong button on a tape recorder.

Not only did the form of the interactions tend to highlight the distance between these exchanges and ordinary conversations, but the content of the scripts also violated conversational norms, as when the workers were required to try suggestive selling to customers who had said, "That's it." This difficulty was especially acute during a promotion of Bacon Double Cheeseburgers, when the window workers were directed to suggest that product to every customer. Since it was summertime, when many customers stopped in just for a cold drink or an ice cream cone, the managers soon recognized that it was ridiculous for workers to respond to such orders by asking, "Would you like to try our Bacon Double Cheeseburger?" The solution they provided was for workers to ask this question *before* the customer gave the order. Customers, unfortunately, were likely to respond to a hurriedly delivered "Hi-welcome-to-McDonald's-would-you-like-to-try-our-Bacon-Double-Cheeseburger?" with a baffled "What?" Nevertheless, this practice was enforced, the goal of actual communication having been abandoned.

Under these circumstances, some customers did not even attempt to treat their interactions with workers as real conversations. They would fail to answer direct questions, for example, or even to look at the workers:

While observing service interactions from the customers' side of the counter, I see that some customers make no response at all to Edward's spirited, "Good afternoon, can I take your order here, please?" I occasionally catch his eye and laugh when this happens; he shrugs and tells me, "Sometimes they just ignore you."

Such customers apparently were not looking for personalized human contact. They wanted to expend a minimum of emotional effort in the service interactions, and they did not pretend that the encounters were anything but anonymous and routine. McDonald's attempts to standardize good cheer and enthusiasm were wasted on people who simply wanted to get their food as quickly as possible, with no emotional involvement whatever. Indeed, some of these customers seemed to regard the forms of routinized friendliness as intrusive, impertinent, or a waste of time.

Some workers also conducted the interactions by rote, withholding full involvement (see Goffman 1961b). I was surprised, for instance, at how a worker I knew treated me as a customer:

> I stand on line to buy a meal. Marisa recognizes me but waits on me without any variation in her routine or manner that would indicate that she's serving someone she knows—"Will that be all?" . . . "Have a nice day."

Even though some workers tried to divorce their selves from the service interactions, the divergence of the routine from the practices of ordinary conversation presented problems for workers' sense of self. Being treated as non-people by some customers could be hurtful in itself:

> Pat complains about suggestive selling: "I say, 'Would you like to try the raspberry shake?' They ignore you." She laughs. "They just go ahead on and give you their order. You'll be, like, 'Well—guess they didn't want it.' It makes you feel so embarrassed, 'cause . . . they just ignore you."

Furthermore, in enacting the routine workers were made to behave as though they did not know any better than to violate taken-for-granted interaction practices—to behave, in short, like badly socialized idiots. They felt some pressure to devise strategies to undercut this impression. For example, I found myself actively striving *not to* sound natural:

> As I'm taking an order, one of the crew trainers (I don't even have a moment to turn around to see who it is) says in my ear, "You have to push the Bacon Double Cheeseburgers." . . . I do start some of my orders by saying, "Would you like to try our Bacon Double

Cheeseburger today?" I sometimes camp it up a bit—sort of saying the line in quotes, with a big smile and a "have-I-got-an-offer-for-you" tone of voice. Some guests smile or laugh in response, especially if they just want an ice cream cone. Most say "No" or "No, thank you," and go on to give their orders. One guy says, "You read my mind!" I reply, "We do our best." I don't say the line to everyone, though, by a long shot. I'm especially reluctant to do so when there are lines of people who can hear what I've said to the previous customer.

The intention of my humorous delivery was to convey that, although it was part of my job to deliver the line, I realized it was slightly ridiculous.[4]

For the Combined Insurance agents, the question of whether they were involved in real conversations arose in drawing the boundary between genuine, relatively noninstrumental conversation and the sales pitch. During the "warming up the prospect" portion of the sales calls, the agents engaged in friendly, apparently idle chat that seemed to be at least as "real" as much social interaction. At a certain point, however, they needed to shift into the sales presentation. This transition was especially clear-cut in the presentation for the Senior Citizens' Policy. On these calls, the agents wanted to find out relatively early in the visit whether the prospect was healthy enough to qualify for the policy, so they would not waste a lot of time talking with someone who could not become a customer. They might ask casually, "How have you been feeling lately?" and listen sympathetically to the prospects' descriptions of their health. At some point, though, the agents would have to ask, "More specifically, during the last five years, have you had any advice or treatment for stroke? heart attack or heart condition? cancer or any malignant growth?" It would then be clear that the previous conversation had not been idle talk at all, but part of the sales process. The transition had to be handled somewhat delicately, lest the prospect be offended by the now-apparent insincerity of the agent.

Beyond this issue of how real their conversations were, the work roles of interactive service workers presented broader questions for the job-holders. What is their relation to other people? How do they treat them? At McDonald's, the workers' task was to serve others.

---

4. Cf. Goffman (1961b: 105): "By introducing an unserious style, the individual can project the claim that nothing happening at the moment to him or through him should be taken as a direct reflection of him, but rather of the person-in-situation that he is mimicking."

The design of the window workers' routines, including the requirement of constant cheerfulness, was intended to convey deference to customers. Since the workers were at the command of anyone who chose to come into the restaurant, they had to serve, politely, even those they considered to be their social inferiors, such as small children or homeless people, and even those who treated them disrespectfully. The servile behavior demanded of window workers could certainly be considered demeaning.

Combined's agents were expected to relate to other people by controlling them. The numerous compliance techniques built into their routines helped the agents to maintain control of interactions and prevent prospects from gaining the upper hand. A determined prospect could manage to get rid of an agent despite his use of clever interruption-stoppers, of course, but the agent's practiced tactics for turning prospects' responses to his own purposes and his refusal to accept the intended message of interruptions made it more difficult for prospects to control events. To carry out their routines the agents had to be pushy and manipulative, qualities some agents might not care to embrace.[5] The lack of autonomy inherent in following a detailed script could further challenge agents' images of themselves.

The routines of interactive service workers, in short, are structured to make them *be* certain kinds of people. Some of the qualities built into their routines are ones that workers might well judge positively—cheerfulness or aggressiveness, helpfulness or control. Similarly, routines may match workers' ideas of appropriate manliness or womanliness. Other aspects of the routines, such as those demanding subordination, passivity, or insincerity, may be harder for workers to incorporate into their self-images. Interactive service workers have to determine whether they want to be the kinds of people their routines demand, and whether it is possible for them, while at work, to be the kinds of people they do want to be. When their job makes them behave in ways that do not coincide with their preferred identity, they must determine whether it will still be possible for them to hold on to the belief that they really are the kinds

---

5. A district manager told me how hard it had been for him to learn to "keep his head down" during the Assumptive Close, so as not to give the prospect an opening to decline. "The first time I did it, I was shaking," he said. "I'm not a pushy person. I'm not overly aggressive." He explained that he had felt that the technique implied a lack of respect for the prospect.

of people they want to be, and not the kinds they are constrained to be at work.

Organizations want to make it easy for their workers to accept the identity embodied in their routines, or at least to minimize workers' resistance to doing their jobs. Employers therefore provide psychic strategies to help workers reconcile their work with their self-image. They supply ways of thinking about the work and of interpreting events that are palatable to workers. For instance, since both Combined Insurance and McDonald's workers sometimes had to deal with insulting or even abusive behavior, the companies provided practical ways for the workers to deal with the assault on the self such incidents represented without responding in kind. They defined acceptance of abuse, not as demeaning oneself, but as proving oneself to be better than the customer exhibiting a lack of self-control. Mark, the Combined Insurance trainer, told the agents they should be glad that some people gave them a hard time: "If people bought insurance without help, there would be no need for representatives to sell it." Similarly, the Combined Insurance agents were taught to think of their work, not as manipulating people, but as keeping control, achieving their goals, and being winners.

Despite employers' efforts to provide face-saving psychic strategies, workers may still not be entirely happy with the identity implied by their routines. In that case, how did workers think about themselves and what they were doing? How could they maintain their dignity while enacting a script? The high turnover rates at McDonald's and Combined Insurance suggest that the modal response to these particular jobs was to leave. Those who stayed used diverse strategies to cope with the strains of their work, but the structure of each job closed off some possibilities and made others more likely.

At McDonald's, workers took a variety of approaches to reconciling the way they had to act with the self they wanted to be. Some workers tried to be good actors, delivering the standard lines with enthusiasm and a degree of sincerity. The struggle for verisimilitude could be rather difficult to sustain, though, given how unlifelike some aspects of the routines were and how frenetic the pace could get. I sometimes had a hard time sounding natural on the job:

> It seems to me that my voice is getting higher all the time—"Can I help you, sir?" with the "sir" ascending to the upper octaves.

A related strategy for coping with the routine was to use the script as a starting point and inject one's own personality into the interactions. Thus, some window workers joked or chatted with customers and tried to make the exchanges enjoyable for both parties. This stance implied an assertion of equality with customers and a refusal to suppress the self completely. The problem, from the workers' point of view, was that the more workers were themselves on the job and the greater their efforts to make the interactions pleasant, the more painful or infuriating it was when customers were unresponsive or mean:

> I am pleased when people are responsive to my cheery greeting and feel annoyed if they don't smile or say thank you.

Both of these strategies involved a large degree of acceptance of the terms of the interactions set by management. The workers tried to match the cheery, efficient, eager-to-please image that McDonald's advertises. Other workers tried to establish greater distance from that role (see Goffman 1961b). One strategy, familiar to most fast-food customers, was to refuse to take on the upbeat, enthusiastic persona that management tried to impose. Thus, some workers delivered their lines and carried out their tasks as assigned, but they did so with a minimum of emotional commitment. Their unsmiling faces conveyed the message, "I have to do this, but I don't have to like it."

> Traci tells me, "If a customer's nice, OK, I smile. I don't smile unless something makes me laugh or somebody's just nice."

Even workers who were usually willing to be cheerful and smiling might make subtle adjustments in their manner to protect their sense of dignity. The window workers were in the position of servant to all customers, but when the customers were perceived to have a lower social standing than the workers or were unappreciative of the crew's efforts, workers could try to distance themselves from the extra indignity that role implied:

> The homeless woman I've served before comes into the store. She's barefoot, and despite the heat she's wearing a down jacket. She asks Edward for a key to the downstairs washroom. He answers her, but I notice that he's less nice to her than he is to "respectable" customers.

One especially self-aware worker described how she varied her manner to deal with different kinds of customers:

RL: Does how guests act affect you?

TINA: Yes, definitely. If they're rude or impatient, I will get upset. I
        will try and keep my cool and try to keep calm, but I will
        either snip at them, if they're going to snip at me, or when
        they leave I complain about them to the other people work-
        ing there.

RL: What might you say when you snip?

TINA: Well, just like, when you're answering them or something,
        or asking them for their order.

RL: Oh, just be brusque.

TINA: Yeah, be kind of short with them.

RL: I see. And how about in less extreme situations, do you
        adjust your behavior for different sorts of people?

TINA: Yes, I do. With college students [like herself], I tend to be
        more open, joking, and kind of freer with them, because I
        can identify with them. With older people, I try to be a little
        more deferring, a little more polite. With high school stu-
        dents [laughing], I tend to put on a small air of superiority.
        Not much, but I notice it.

As limiting as McDonald's routine was, within its constraints the
workers did find ways to express their sense of themselves and to
protect their dignity.

Another strategy by which workers avoided enacting deference
was to concentrate on an aspect of the routine that did allow them
to feel that they were in charge and that they were good at their work.
At McDonald's, this most often meant focusing on speed of service.
Some workers barked questions at customers in a no-nonsense
manner, making it clear to customers that by hesitating over their
order or neglecting to give sufficiently detailed information they
were holding things up. In this way the workers tried to impose their
priorities on the service interactions. Since speed of service was a
primary value at McDonald's, the managers at the franchise where
I worked held up some of these extremely efficient but minimally
civil workers as positive examples.

An especially interesting worker strategy was one that combined
complete detachment with perfect enactment of the role. For example, Edward told me that when he came to work he assumed a
McDonald's persona quite separate from his own. This practice enabled him to execute his duties with a show of good cheer and with
consistent courtesy, but without thinking much and without engaging his personality:

RL: You save yourself stress by doing that?

EDWARD: Yeah. [Laughs.] You put on the uniform, you have an identity, you have that whole persona, you know: you work for McDonald's. You don't have to worry about what happened before or after, you know—you're here, and you go.

When I asked Edward how he dealt with difficult customers, he answered, "I become a smiling little toady. . . . 'Whatever you say, sir. You're right and I'm an asshole.'" His detachment enabled him to enact subservience in these situations without feeling that his act was an acknowledgment of true inferiority. Edward did not perceive either the false cheeriness or the false self-abnegation as touching his real self.

This strategy of distancing, however good a shield against injuries to the self, also acted as a shield against some of the pleasures the job could provide. In contrast to the great majority of workers I interviewed, who said they frequently found it pleasant to deal with customers, Edward said, "It's almost too clinical for that. . . . Is it pleasant, is it unpleasant, I don't think about that."

How willing a worker was to accept the persona McDonald's prescribed was related not only to whether the worker was normally outgoing and personable but also to how much that worker was in fact defined by the job. Edward, who willingly became "a smiling little toady," was a part-time college student majoring in psychology. His acceptance of the McDonald's role was relatively untroubled because he did not see working at McDonald's as defining the limits of his talents and prospects. Furthermore, Edward was the only white male window worker in my sample. Shows of deference might well have a different meaning for him than they would for nonwhite and female workers, especially those for whom this job was the best available.

For the Combined Insurance agents it was a great deal more difficult to hold the self in reserve, because their job demanded that they throw themselves into their role to a much greater extent than the McDonald's workers did. If they were unwilling to be pushy or manipulative or if they recited their lines mechanically and without conviction, they could not sell insurance. Because their job required them to use a lot of themselves, they needed to find ways to reconcile their self-concept with the qualities their routines required them to embody. The agents I met therefore consciously worked on their selves in a way that was not necessary for most McDonald's workers. The agents saw it as a process of transformation to a better self, a more skillful and successful self. Most of them used the terminology of Combined's Positive Mental Attitude ideology in conversations and recognized that it was up to them to keep their spirits and their motivation high.

The transformation of their selves into the kinds of personalities that could succeed in Combined's system presented two related problems for the agents' self-identities. First, agents might wish to avoid thinking of themselves as manipulative and insincere. Second, they might find it hard to hold on to a sense of autonomy and of manliness while enacting their routines. Agents responded to the issue of manipulativeness in two ways. Some fully embraced this aspect of their roles. They took pleasure in outmaneuvering prospects and believed that Combined's routines enabled them to be smarter, smoother, more effective people than they were before. Other agents, who valued sincerity and ethical behavior more highly, discounted the manipulativeness of the role by interpreting their work as providing an important service. Despite the manipulativeness built into their sales routines, Tom and Kevin both believed that they could do their job without compromising their ethics. As Tom told me:

> I'm big on ethics. I don't push if people don't need it, if they have enough insurance. I'm not pushy at all—I won't waste my time or theirs.

Kevin expressed a similar attitude, adding that good intentions promote his own interests:

> It's not worth it to me to lie. I'm *big* on ethics. . . . When you push real hard, and there's greed in your eyes, and you're really struggling for the money, the sales won't be there. If you're more laid-back, it starts to happen. [Kevin criticizes himself for his attitude during a call that morning:] I had money on my mind.

Even these agents took pleasure in their ability to manipulate prospects, though. For example, Kevin, noticing that a prospect's car had a garter hanging from the rear-view mirror and a license-plate frame reading "No Fat Chicks," gleefully said, "OK, a stud. I'll melt him."

The second problem, that of reconciling autonomy and manliness with the agent role, had two elements. The recitation of a script and the enactment of carefully prescribed movements always imply a lack of self-determination that can be demeaning in itself. In addition, several requirements of the Combined Insurance routine could be seen as further undercutting the workers' sense of dignity and of manliness. An analysis of the agents' responses to this dilemma requires a broader discussion of the relevance of gender to both the construction of work roles and workers' reactions to those roles.

JOBS, GENDER, AND IDENTITY

One of the most important determinants of the meaning of a type of work, as well as of how that work is conducted and rewarded, is its association with a particular gender. The degree to which workers accept the identity implied by a job is therefore determined in part by the degree to which they can interpret the job as expressing their gender in a satisfying way.

Much contemporary sociological theory and research on gender shares an emphasis on the active and continual construction of gender through social interaction (Garfinkel 1967; Goffman 1977; Kessler and McKenna 1978; West and Zimmerman 1987). West and Zimmerman (1987: 127) argue:

> Participants in interaction organize their various and manifold activities to reflect or express gender, and they are disposed to perceive the behavior of others in a similar light.

One of the most striking aspects of the social construction of gender is that its accomplishment creates the impression that gender differences in personality, interests, character, appearance, manner, and competence are natural, and not social constructions at all. Gender segregation of work reinforces this appearance of naturalness. When jobholders are all of the same gender, it seems as though people of that gender must be especially well suited to the work, even if at other times and places the other gender does the same work. Thus, Milkman's analysis of industrial work during World War II demonstrates "how idioms of sex-typing can be flexibly applied to whatever jobs women and men happen to be doing" (1987: 50).

I will argue that jobholders and other audiences may make this interpretation of appropriateness even under the most unlikely conditions: when the work might easily be interpreted as more suitable for the other gender, and when many aspects of the workers' presentation of self are closely dictated by superiors and are clearly not spontaneous expressions of the workers' characters, interests, or personalities.

Gender is necessarily implicated in the design and enactment of service interactions. In order to construct routines, especially scripts, for interactions, organizations must make many assumptions about what customers like, what motivates them, and what they consider normal interactive behavior. Some of the assumptions employers make concern how men and women should behave. Once these assumptions about proper gender behavior have been built into workers' routines, service recipients may have to accept them if they are to fit smoothly into the service interaction. For example, employees of Gloria Marshall Figure Salons were expected to ask their customers, "Have you and your husband discussed your figure needs?" (Lally-Benedetto 1985). The question implies several layers of assumptions about the natures of women and men and the power relations between them.

As this example illustrates, scripts can embody assumptions about proper gendered behavior in fairly obvious ways. To perform such jobs as intended, workers must do gender in a particular way. (On "doing gender," see Berk 1985b; West and Zimmerman 1987.) Even in jobs where the gender component is less obvious, workers need to consider how their work relates to their own identity, including their gender identity. Whether workers take pride in the work itself or see it as stigmatizing, whether they work harder than is required or put in the least possible effort, whether they identify themselves with the job or seek self-definition elsewhere, are related not just to job tasks and working conditions but to the extent that the jobs can be interpreted as honorable, worthwhile, and suitable for persons of their gender (Ouellet 1986). Such factors are likely to be especially salient in interactive service work, where employers try to influence how workers present themselves and how they think about their jobs.

Gender is more salient in some service jobs than others. Telephone interviewing, for example, is apparently gender-neutral and is done by men and women. However, the gender of workers is not irrelevant in these jobs, since respondents may react differently to men than to women interviewers. Similarly, although airline flight attendant is a job currently held by men as well as women, Hochschild found that male flight attendants were more likely to have their authority respected and less likely to be subjected to emotional outbursts from passengers than were their female coworkers (Hochschild 1983). At the other extreme are jobs that are gender-segregated and that would be virtually incomprehensible without extensive assumptions about how both workers and customers enact gender. The Gloria Marshall Salon workers' job assumed that both workers and customers would be women. The script used by Playboy Bunnies, who were trained to respond to being molested by saying, "Please, sir, you are not allowed to touch the Bunnies" (Steinem 1983: 48), took for granted a male customer (see also Spradley and Mann 1975). Both scripts dictated "common understandings" about what men and women are like and how power is distributed between them.

The jobs of the McDonald's and Combined Insurance workers fell between these two extremes. They were neither gender-neutral nor entirely saturated with assumptions about gender. Furthermore, although neither job was entirely gender-segregated, each was held predominantly either by men or by women, which influenced how workers, employers, and customers thought about the jobs. The gender attributes of McDonald's window crew people and Combined's agents were not essential to their jobs, however. In fact, both jobs can be gender-typed in the opposite direction. In its early years, McDonald's hired only men (Love 1986: 142), and in Japan, door-to-door insurance sales is a woman's job (Life Assurance Association of Japan 1988).

Workers for both McDonald's and Combined Insurance try to make sense of de facto job segregation by gender, interpreting their jobs as congruent with proper gender enactment. Examination of these two jobs and of how workers thought about them highlights a central paradox in the construction of gender: the considerable flexibility of notions of proper gender enactment does not undermine the appearance of inevitability and naturalness that continues to support the division of labor by gender. Although the work of the insurance agents required many of the same kinds of interactive behavior as the McDonald's job, including behavior that would ordinarily be considered feminine, the agents were able to interpret the work as suitable only for men. They did so by emphasizing aspects of their job that required attributes they considered manly and by thinking about their interactive work in terms of control rather than deference. Their interpretation suggests not only the plasticity of gender idioms but the asymmetry of those idioms: defining work as masculine has a very different meaning for male workers than defining work as feminine has for female workers.

Because interactive service work by definition involves nonemployees in the work process, the implications of the gender constructions of the routines extend beyond the workers themselves. When service jobs are done predominantly by men or predominantly by women, the gender segregation provides confirming "evidence" to the public that men and women have different natures and capabilities. This appearance is especially ironic where employers, treating their workers' selves as fairly malleable, reshape the self-presentations and interactional styles of the service workers.

Doing Gender While Doing the Job

Although their jobs were largely segregated by gender, McDonald's and Combined Insurance workers interacted with both men and women as customers or prospects. Neither company suggested that significantly different approaches be used for men and women service-recipients.[6] Although the gender of the service-recipient might well have influenced how the workers experienced their interactions, I did not find consistent patterns of variation in workers' behavior along this dimension.

At McDonald's, most of the window crew took the division of labor by gender for granted and did not seem to feel any need to account for it. Since the pay and prestige of window work and grill work were the same, and since there were exceptions to the pattern of gender segregation, few workers considered the division of labor by gender unfair.[7] When I asked the workers what they thought was the reason there were more women than men working window, about two-thirds said they did not know, with about half of that group offering a guess based on stereotypes about proper gender roles. About one-quarter of the sample, though, stated explicitly that they disapproved of the division of labor by gender, and three

6. The Combined Insurance trainer did recommend slightly varied techniques for persuading men and women to buy policies without first consulting their spouse.

7. The job of "host," however, was viewed as less prestigious by some workers. When one woman took this job, I heard two women window workers express their disapproval; they felt that "girls" shouldn't have to do the dirty work of handling garbage.

women said they had asked a manager about it. The store's manager told me that women were typically assigned to start work on the window because "more females have an aversion to grill." Two of the window workers, however (both black men), thought that, on the contrary, men might have an aversion to window, because that job required swallowing one's pride and accepting abuse calmly. Theo explained:

[More women than men work window] because women are afraid of getting burned [on the grill], and men are afraid of getting aggravated and going over the counter and smacking someone.

Alphonse supported Theo's view:

I found the men who work here on window have a real quick temper. You know, all of them. And women can take a lot more. They deal with a lot of things, you know.

Although I never heard the masculinity of the few male window workers impugned, it was commonly assumed that men were naturally more explosive than women and would find it more difficult to accept abuse without answering back. The male window workers were usually able to reconcile themselves to swallowing insults, as the women were, either by dissociating themselves from their role or by telling themselves that by keeping their tempers they were proving themselves superior to the rude customers.[8] Thus, although the job did not allow workers to try to get the better of opponents, its demands were not seen as irreconcilable with enacting masculinity. However, no workers argued that men's capacity to tolerate abuse made them especially well-suited to the job, and the men quoted above made the opposite argument.

Other explanations given by workers for the predominance of women on window crew included assertions that women were more interested in dealing with people, that women "were more presentable" and looked better on window,[9] that their nimble fingers were

8. Refusing to become riled when provoked is consistent with "the cool pose," which Majors says black men use to "fight to preserve their dignity, pride, respect and masculinity" by enacting an imperviousness to hurt (1989: 86). However, the job requirements of smiling and otherwise demonstrating deference are not in keeping with the cool pose. Those committed to that stance might well find such behavior demeaning, especially in interactions with white customers or those of apparently higher status.

9. Three female window workers complained about being hassled by male customers who liked the way they looked. The workers were not given instructions on how to deal with these nonroutine interactions.

better suited than men's to work the registers, and that customers were more likely to find them trustworthy. Several of the workers who offered stereotyped responses like these indicated, however, that they did not believe that the stereotypes were sufficient justification for the predominance of women on the window crew.

It might easily have been argued that men were unsuited to work on the grill, since cooking, after all, is usually considered women's work. As the work was understood at McDonald's, however, cooking presented no challenge to masculinity. Serving customers, which involved adopting an ingratiating manner, taking orders from anyone who chose to give them, and holding one's tongue when insulted, was more difficult to conceive as congruent with the proper enactment of manliness. Thus, although the crew people did not argue that window work was especially expressive of femininity, most found it unremarkable that women predominated in that job.

The work of Combined's agents, in contrast, was defined as properly manly, even though the job presented interactive imperatives that are generally identified with femininity, along with stereotypically masculine elements. The Combined life insurance sales force was almost entirely made up of men, and the agents on the sales team I observed felt strongly that women would be unlikely to succeed in the job.[10] Moreover, Ralph, the twenty-two-year-old manager of this sales team, told me bluntly (without my having raised the question) that he "would never hire a woman."[11] Since some aspects of the agents' job require skills that are not generally considered manly, the agents' understanding of the job as demanding masculine attributes meant that these skills had to be reinterpreted or deemphasized.

Like many other kinds of interactive service jobs, including McDonald's window work, insurance sales requires that workers adopt an attitude of congeniality and eagerness to please. This

10. I learned, in fact, that the two other women in my training class had lasted, respectively, only one day and three weeks in the field.

Managers interviewed in 1989 reported that the number of female agents had increased since the new selling system had been introduced, although women were still a small minority on the sales force. Reduced travel demands were one reason given for the job's increasing attractiveness to women. See also note 11, below.

11. The higher-level managers I interviewed did not endorse these discriminatory views, and some commented on the many successful women in the insurance industry. See Thomas (1990) for a discussion of the growth of women's employment in insurance sales. She shows that, by 1980, 25 percent of U.S. insurance agents were women.

element of the job may strike some men as incompatible with the proper enactment of gender, since masculinity is often associated with toughness and detachment. In *America's Working Man*, David Halle records that a few of the chemical workers he studied did not support Jimmy Carter's presidential candidacy because they "suspected that a man who smiled all the time might be a homosexual" (Halle 1984: 246). To them, behavior that was transparently intended to please others, to encourage liking, was not considered masculine. Toughness, gruffness, and pride are taken-for-granted elements of masculinity to many blue-collar men, and Combined's agents come largely from blue-collar or agricultural backgrounds. For such men, deferential behavior and forced amiability are often associated with servility, and occasions that call for these attitudes—dealings with superiors, for instance—may feel humiliating. Such behavior is not easy to reconcile with the autonomy and assertiveness that are considered central to "acting like a man." The rebellious working-class "lads" Willis studied were concerned to find jobs with "an essentially masculine ethos," jobs "where you would not be expected to be subservient" (1977: 96). Sennett and Cobb, drawing on their interviews with blue-collar men, interpret the low prestige ratings of many service jobs relative to blue-collar jobs as a response to the perceived dependence of service workers on other people, whose shifting demands they must meet (1972: 236).

In the same way, the glad-handing insincerity required of many sorts of businessmen seems effete and demeaning to many working-class men. The job of salesman, which is on the low end of the white-collar hierarchy, would seem especially degrading from this point of view. Ingratiating oneself with customers is an essential part of the job, rather than just a demand of the social milieu. Salesmen must swallow insults, treat even perceived inferiors with deference, and keep smiling.

These aspects of the sales job were quite pronounced for Combined Life Insurance. The "warming up the prospect" phase of the routine called for agents to figure out what topics might interest the prospects and then to display a flattering enthusiasm for those topics and for the prospects' accomplishments. In order to ingratiate themselves, agents had to be willing to disguise their true feelings and to seem to accept the prospects' view of the world. It was crucial that they not lose their tempers with prospects, that they remain respectful at all times. Like most salespeople, they had to try to change prospective customers' minds while never seeming to argue with them and to stay pleasant even when rudely dismissed (see Prus 1989a).

The skills required for establishing and maintaining rapport—including drawing people out, bolstering their egos, displaying interest in their interests, and carefully monitoring one's own behavior so as not to offend—are usually considered womanly arts. Moreover, women may need well-developed verbal skills simply in order to be heard, not just to please. In analyses of a small sample of conversations, Fishman (1978) found that women had to do much more interactive work than men did to sustain dialogues; men largely took for granted that their conversational attempts would engage their partner's interest. Judging only by these interactive demands of insurance sales work, it would seem that women are especially well-suited to be agents. We might even expect that the association of ingratiating conversational tactics with women would lead men to view the extensive interactive work required of salespeople as degrading, since it requires that they assume the role of the interactive inferior who must constantly negotiate permission to proceed. Considering the additional attack on personal autonomy implicit in Combined's programming of employees to follow scripts, it would seem to be difficult for men to combine successful enactment of the role of Combined Insurance agent with successful enactment of gender. On the contrary, however, Combined's trainers and agents interpreted the agent's job as demanding manly attributes. They assigned a heroic character to the job, framing interactions with customers as contests of will. To succeed, they emphasized, required determination, aggressiveness, persistence, and stoicism. Qualities in which women excel, including sensitivity to nuance and verbal dexterity, were also important for success. The sales training did include tips on building such skills, but determination and aggressiveness were treated as the decisive factors for career success. It was largely this need for toughness that allowed the agents to interpret their work as manly.[12]

Of course it was quite true that considerable determination, self-motivation, and persistence were required to do this job. The agents had to make numerous sales calls every day, despite the knowledge

---

12. Some managers believed that the new needs selling-approach described in Appendix 2 is better suited to women agents, because it requires a less domineering stance and allows women to draw on their presumed understanding of families' needs.

that many people would be far from glad to see them. They had to keep making calls, even after meeting with repeated rejection and sometimes hostility. And in sales interactions they had to stick to their objectives even when prospects displayed reluctance to continue the conversation, as most did.

Some agents and managers believed that women were unlikely to meet these job demands because they are too sensitive, too unaggressive, and not able to withstand repeated rejection. Josh, one of the agents, claimed, "Most girls don't have what it takes. They don't have that killer instinct." Josh had, however, recruited a woman he knew to join Combined's sales force. "She does have [the killer instinct], if I can bring it out," he said. Ralph, the sales manager, also acknowledged that there might be some exceptional women who could do the job. He amended his statement that he would never hire a woman by saying, "Only if she had a kind of bitchy attitude." "A biker woman" is the kind he meant, he said, "someone hardcore." Obviously, he did not believe it was possible to combine femininity with the traits necessary for success as an agent.[13]

One manager attributed these assumed deficiencies not to women's nature but to economics, arguing that women whose husbands provided an income were unlikely to have the requisite "burning need" to succeed that a financial goad provides. An obvious factor that would prevent most mothers from taking the job— at least one week a month was spent away from home—was not mentioned by any agent in explaining the dearth of female agents, but two managers did mention it. Two agents told me that they "wouldn't want their wives doing this" work because of the unpleasant or potentially dangerous places agents must sometimes visit.[14]

13. Similarly, Williams (1989: 32) reports that during World War II military men claimed that female soldiers must be unfeminine, because the men did not want to accept the alternative explanation for the women's presence—that military service is not inherently masculine.

14. The work culture of the sales team was itself decidedly masculine and therefore unlikely to make a woman agent feel welcome. For example, at a team meeting Hal, the district manager, asked the agents what sort of reward they would like as an incentive for a new program. My notes report: "Kevin suggests some sort of group activity, like going to a baseball game. Hal suggests a survival game and talks a bit about his experience attending a survival game somewhere downstate. The guys are very interested and excited about this." Before another meeting officially began, "Chuck and Josh tell all about Wrestlemania, which they watched on screens at some arena on Sunday. They go on about this at great length. Chuck particularly enjoyed watching a midget wrestler 'get creamed.'" One agent also mentioned that when the team members were away for a weekend training program they went to a strip joint together.

This emphasis on aggression, domination, and danger is only one possible construction of sales work. Biggart (1989) and Connelly and Rhoton (1988) discuss in detail the very different ways direct-sales organizations that rely on a female labor force characterize sales work. These organizations, some of which are hugely successful, emphasize nurturance, helpfulness, and service both in relations with customers and among salespeople. Combined's training also encouraged agents to think of themselves as providing a service to prospective customers, largely in order to overcome trainees' reluctance to impose on others, and some of the agents I spoke with did use the service ideology to counter demeaning images of insurance sales as high-pressure hucksterism (see Oakes 1990). For the most part, however, the agents emphasized the more "manly" dimensions of the work, even though there is ample evidence that women can succeed in life insurance sales. For example, Thomas (1990) notes that after the Equitable Life Assurance Society made a commitment to recruiting and supporting women agents, the company's saleswomen outperformed salesmen in both sales and commissions.[15]

Most agents would not feel the need, on a daily basis, to construct an explanation for why so few women sold life insurance for their company. But if they were to maintain their positive attitude and do well at their job, which required much more self-motivation than did McDonald's jobs, they did need to construct an interpretation of their work as honorable and fitting for a man. The element of competition, the battle of wills implicit in their interactions with customers, seemed to be a major factor that allowed the agents to interpret their work as manly. Virtually every step of the interaction was understood as a challenge to be met: getting through the door, making the prospect relax and warm up, being allowed to start the presentation, getting through the presentation despite interruptions, overcoming prospects' objections and actually making the sale, and perhaps even increasing the size of the sale. Because many prospects did their best to prevent the agents from continuing, going through these steps did not simply represent following a prescribed routine; attaining each step was experienced by agents as proof of their skill and a victory of their will. Each sales call seemed an uphill battle, since the interactions took place on the prospects' turf and prospects

---

15. One of the Combined district managers I interviewed in 1989 reported that the top agent in his district was a woman.

always had the option of telling the agent to leave. If a customer seemed impatient or hostile and the agent got her to laugh, he won. If a customer tried to cut off a sales talk but the agent's clever response allowed him to continue the presentation, he won. If a customer claimed that he already had life insurance and the agent persuaded him to consider buying more, he won.

This spirit of jousting was especially clear in some of the techniques taught for closing sales, such as the Assumptive Close described in Chapter 5. As Mark explained it, the agents were supposed to "challenge customers"; it was up to the prospects to object if they did not want to go along with the sale. The routine allowed agents to limit the customers' options without seeming to do so, to let prospects believe that they were making decisions while the agent remained in control of the interaction. The pattern bears some resemblance to the seduction of an initially unwilling partner, and the satisfaction the agents took in winning such encounters is perhaps similar to the satisfaction some men take in thinking of sexual encounters as conquests. The agents seemed to approach sales interactions with men in much the same spirit as they did those with women, however, although they often adjusted their presentation of self to suit a particular prospect's gender, age, and manner: subtly flirtatious, respectfully deferential, or efficient and businesslike.

This sort of manipulation of interactions required a peculiar combination of sensitivity to other people and callousness. The agent had to figure out which approach would work best at any given moment and avoid seeming cold or aggressive, but he still had to disregard the customers' stated wishes. The required mix of deference and ruthlessness was well illustrated in an exchange that took place during a sales team training session. The agents were discussing how to deal with interruptions during a presentation. One of their superiors had advised ignoring them altogether, but the "training module" stated that it was insulting to fail to acknowledge a prospect's comment. When the sales manager instructed, "You have to let them know that you heard them," one of the agents finished the sentence for him: ". . . and that you don't give a shit."

All kinds of interactive service workers, including the McDonald's window crews, try to exercise control over their interactions with customers, although not all of them are given organizational resources to help them do so. (See, for example, Whyte 1946 on waitresses and Benson 1986 on department-store saleswomen.) Women who can dominate interactions at work may well take pleasure in doing so, as Combined's life insurance agents did. However, it is unlikely that these women's capacity to control other people would be taken as evidence that the work was womanly, unless it were reinterpreted in less aggressive terms as "skill in dealing with people."

If following a script could be given a manly cast when it involved asserting one's will through controlling an interaction, it was more difficult to do so when the interactions did not go agents' way. Refusals were such a routine part of the job, though, that agents could accept most of them as inevitable rather than as a result of lack of skill or determination. In sales school, the trainers emphasized that not everyone was going to buy. Some people really do not need or cannot afford the product; some are just closed-minded and would not listen to any salesperson. A greater challenge to the agent's definition of himself was presented by prospects who were actively hostile. Some people were angry at having been interrupted; some had a grievance against the company; some became furious when they felt that they were being manipulated. It was not unusual for agents to meet with loud insults, condescending sneers, and slammed doors. To accept this sort of treatment passively could certainly be seen as unmanly. However, the agents were expected to keep calm, refrain from rudeness, and leave graciously.

Some agents did tell me with glee of instances when, in response to particularly outrageous treatment from a customer, they shouted obscenities once they got outside the door. For the most part, though, passive acceptance of ill-treatment was reconciled with manly honor by defining it as maintaining control and a positive attitude, a strategy similar to that used by both male and female McDonald's workers. In this view, screaming back at a customer would be considered, not standing up for yourself, but letting the customer get the better of you, "letting them blow your attitude." Agents proved themselves to be above combative and insulting customers by maintaining their dignity and holding on to their self-concept as a winner, not by sinking to the customers' level.[16]

16. Although the agents spoke about the difficulty of controlling their anger in response to abusive customers, they did not necessarily experience prospects' denunciations as challenges to their self-image or even as threats to their self-confidence. For instance, when Chuck told me about a prospect whose behavior he apparently considered exceptionally abusive: "I ask, 'How do you keep your spirits up?' He seems puzzled by the question, and asks what I mean. I say that I think I would find tirades like that hard to take. Chuck looks genuinely surprised;

Other attributes of the job, not directly connected with job routinization, contributed to the salesmen's ability to define their jobs as compatible with proper enactment of gender. The most important of these were the sense of independence agents felt and their belief that they could earn as much as they were worth. Within the limits of their work assignments, agents could set their own schedules, behave as they chose, and work only as hard as they wished to work. Because of the importance of self-motivation to success, those who did well could feel justifiably proud, and those lacking in motivation could appreciate the freedom they had to relax if they did not want to push themselves. The agents thus felt that their job provided some of the benefits of self-employment. As long as there was the possibility of making it big, they could live with the knowledge that many people looked down on them, put up with insults, endure days of failure, and still maintain a sense that their work was compatible with manliness and social honor.

Interpreting Gender

Until the 1970s, most sociological work concerning the connection between workers' genders and their jobs mirrored the commonsense view that men and women hold different sorts of jobs because of differing physical capacities, psychological orientations, and family responsibilities. Rosabeth Moss Kanter (1977) reversed the traditional argument that women's traits determine the sorts of jobs they hold, claiming instead that the structural features of most women's jobs determine characteristic attitudinal and behavioral responses which are then interpreted as reflecting women's nature. She focused on power, opportunity, and numbers of like individuals in the workplace as the factors determining workers' response to jobs. According to her analysis, preexisting gender segregation leads workers, managers, and observers to believe, incorrectly, that gender explains how workers respond to their jobs. As Berk (1985b) has argued, Kanter understated the distinctive properties of gender and minimized the extent to which gender assumptions are built into jobs by work organizations (see also Acker 1990).

---

obviously he doesn't feel that way at all. He says, 'I think it's funnier than hell! Maybe there's something wrong with me.' He shrugs. 'You can't take it to heart. You just gotta realize the guy's an asshole, he's always been an asshole, he always will be an asshole.' "

More recently, analysts have called attention to the ways that jobs themselves are gendered, in the sense that they are designed and evolve in particular ways because of the gender of typical incumbents (Cockburn 1985; Reverby 1987). Moreover, theorists have argued that gender is not simply imported into the workplace. Rather, gender is constructed in part through work (Beechey 1988; Berk 1985b). This argument, which applies both to the gender identities of individual workers and to cultural understandings of women's and men's natures and capacities, is supported by the cases of McDonald's and Combined Insurance.

Just how jobs are gendered and how doing these jobs affects workers' gender identities remain to be clarified, however. Cockburn (1985: 169) describes the gendering of jobs and people as a two-way process: "People have a gender and their gender rubs off on the jobs they mainly do. The jobs in turn have a gender character which rubs off on the people who do them." Although she acknowledges that the gender designation of jobs, tools, fields of knowledge, and activities may shift over time, she treats these designations as cultural givens. For example, she writes (1985: 170):

> An eighteenth-century man no doubt felt effeminate using a spinning wheel, though he would have felt comfortable enough repairing one. Today it is difficult to get a teenage lad to use a floor mop or a typewriter because they contradict his own gender identity.

Cockburn correctly perceives the relevance of work tasks to the worker's gender identity, but she overstates the rigidity of the gender-typing of those tasks: at McDonald's, mopping has largely become low-status men's work. I argue that despite the existence of culturally shaped gender designations of work activities, employers and workers retain the flexibility to reinterpret them in ways that support workers' gender identities. However, the gender designation of work is likely to have different kinds of significance for women than for men.

Workers at both McDonald's and Combined Insurance were expected to adjust their mood and demeanor to the demands of their jobs, and to learn to deal with customers in ways that might be very different from their ordinary style of interaction. To some extent, workers in both jobs had to take on the role of interactive inferior, adjusting themselves to the styles and apparent preferences of their customers. They were supposed to paste on smiles when they did not feel like smiling and to behave cheerfully and deferentially to people of every status and with every attitude. The workers were not officially permitted to respond to rudeness in kind, but had to try to remain pleasant even in the face of insult.

This sort of behavior is usually associated with femininity, but in fact the two jobs were interpreted quite differently. At McDonald's, many workers and managers considered it natural, even self-evident, that women were best suited to deal with customers. At Combined Insurance, women were generally seen as ill-equipped to handle such work. The insurance agents were able to define their job as masculine by emphasizing those aspects of the work that require such "manly" traits as control and self-direction and by reinterpreting some of the more "feminine" job requirements in ways that did not feel degrading.

McDonald's workers' superiors emphasized that the crew's role was to serve, and attempts by window workers to assert their will in interactions with customers were strongly discouraged. Combined's agents, on the other hand, were taught that their job was to establish and maintain control in interactions with prospects. They were told that they control their own destiny, and they were urged to cultivate the qualities of aggressiveness, persistence, and belief in themselves. Success required that they behave deferentially, but this was seen as a matter of skill in manipulating situations, not as servility, and therefore it was not taken to be inconsistent with manliness. Similarly, accepting abuse calmly was interpreted as a refusal to let someone else dictate the terms of the interaction, not as a loss of control. This conceptualization of the work as an arena for enacting masculinity allowed the agents to accept working conditions that might otherwise have been seen as unacceptably frustrating and demeaning.

When Hughes (1984 [1951]: 342) called attention to the "social and social-psychological arrangements and devices by which men make their work tolerable, or even make it glorious to themselves and others," he apparently meant "men" to include men and women. In fact, the case of Combined's agents suggests that defining a job as "men's work" is precisely how some men make their work tolerable or even glorious. Willis (1977) and Ouellet (1986) have shown how ideas about masculinity can transform what otherwise might be considered negative job features, such as danger, hard physical labor, or dirt, into badges of honor. In other circumstances, work that seems "glorious" on its own merits, because it is understood to be

important, highly skilled, responsible, powerful, is defined as masculine (see, e.g., Cockburn 1985). Identifying work as manly, then,
can compensate male workers for hardships, but it also justifies
privilege.

Some working-class boys and men insist that only jobs that are
physically demanding, exhausting, or dangerous can be considered
manly (cf. Halle 1984; Willis 1977), but in fact the gender designation of particular job tasks is quite plastic, a matter of interpretation
in which workers, employers, and customers may participate. The
actual features of the work do not rigidly determine its gender designation. Nevertheless, the association of a job with manliness
serves to elevate the work itself and allows men to construe success
on the job as proof of masculinity. The importance of manly work
for constructing and maintaining masculine identity may explain
some of the resistance men working in gender-segregated occupations display toward female coworkers; they tend to define their
work not just as particularly appropriate for men, but as work that
women would not be able to do (Cockburn 1983, 1985; Halle 1984;
Swerdlow 1989; Willis 1977). The experiences of women entering
previously male-dominated occupations bear out this interpretation.
For example, Schroedel (1985: 20–21) quotes a female pipefitter:

> You see it is just very hard for them to work with me because they're
> really into proving their masculinity and being tough. And when a
> woman comes on a job that can work, get something done as fast and
> efficiently, as well, as they can, it really affects them. Somehow if a
> woman can do it, it ain't that masculine, not that tough.

The Combined Insurance agents were able to make this claim even
in a job that required skills and qualities typically associated with
women.

Interpreting work as womanly has a different meaning for women
than interpreting work as manly has for men. Certain jobs, including
nursing and elementary school teaching, are understood to require
some positively valued "female" trait such as nurturance or sensitivity, and the identification of the work with femininity significantly determines how the work is organized (Melosh 1982; Reverby
1987). Even when the work is seen as expressive of feminine
capacities, however, it is not seen as offering proof of female identity
in quite the same way that manly work supports male identity. That
is because adult female identity has not traditionally been regarded

as something that is achieved through paid work. In other words, although women in jobs traditionally defined as suitable for females may well take pleasure in doing work that supports their self-identification as feminine, they are unlikely to think of such work as a necessary part of their gender identity. Thus, men and women respond differently to challenges to gender segregation of work.[17]

The different cultural valuation of behavior labeled masculine from that labeled feminine also contributes to the different meanings men and women assign to enacting gender at work. The constant "doing" of gender is mandatory for everyone, but, as many theorists have noted, the effects of this demand are asymmetrical, since doing masculinity generally means asserting dominance, while doing femininity often means enacting submission (Acker 1990; Berk 1985a). Frye (1983: 33) claims that the female "cannot move or speak within the usual cultural norms without engaging in self-deprecation. The male cannot move or speak without engaging in self-aggrandizement." Thus, many men value the opportunity to do work that supports cultural understandings of masculinity and their own sense of manliness, but we cannot assume that job features that allow or require gender-appropriate behavior will necessarily be welcomed by women workers in the same way. On the one hand, some women may appreciate the opportunity to enact such "womanly" attributes as nurturance, helpfulness, or sexiness at work because that behavior affirms their gender identity. On the other hand, servility may be congruent with femininity, but we would hardly expect female McDonald's workers to take the same pleasure in enacting it at work that Combined's agents take in asserting control.

17. Williams (1989) found that although women nurses did not feel threatened when men joined their ranks, male Marines much preferred to keep women out of the Corps. Furthermore, male nurses were concerned to differentiate their activities from those of their women coworkers, but female Marines did not feel that doing quintessentially masculine work was a challenge to their femininity.

Williams draws on the work of Nancy Chodorow (1978) to provide a psychoanalytic explanation for male workers' concern with defining their work as masculine and with maintaining gender segregation at work. Williams argues that because men, whose original identification is with a female caretaker, must achieve masculinity by distancing themselves from femininity, they are psychologically threatened when one proof of their masculinity is challenged by evidence that women can do the work they have defined as manly. Women, who need not alter their original identification with a female caretaker, have no corresponding need to prove their femininity: "What one *does* has little or no bearing on how feminine one is" (Williams 1989: 140). Whether or not the psychoanalytic explanation is valid, Williams persuasively demonstrates that gendered jobs have different meanings for men than they have for women.

Job features that allow or require gender-appropriate behaviors are not necessarily welcomed, then, but work routines that prevent workers from enacting gender in ways that make them comfortable are resented and may contribute to workers' decisions to limit their investment of energy, effort, and self-definition in their jobs. Job features that allow gender enactment in ways workers find gratifying, by contrast, may make up for deficiencies in more objective job benefits. In any case, the variation in the interpretations of similar job demands at McDonald's and Combined Insurance demonstrates that the actual features of the job do not themselves determine whether the work will be defined as most appropriate for men or women. Rather, these job features are resources for interpretation that can be drawn on by workers, their superiors, and other audiences.

Despite this flexibility in the interpretation of gender appropriateness, in these two work settings the association of the work with either women or men was made to seem natural, an expression of the essential natures of women and men. Even though the workers' behavior was largely dictated by routines they had no part in creating, and even where the job drew on traits associated with both femininity and masculinity, job segregation by gender was interpreted largely as an outgrowth of inherent gender differences in attitudes and behavior. In trying to make sense of the fact of gender segregation, workers drew on taken-for-granted beliefs about the qualities and preferences of women and men. The prevalence of either men or women in a job became evidence that the job demanded specifically masculine or specifically feminine qualities and that the job-holders chosen must be those best suited for the work. For the public, as well as for workers, gender segregation of service jobs contributes to the general perception that differences in men's and women's social positions are straightforward reflections of differences in their natures and capabilities (see West and Zimmerman 1987: 146).

OVERVIEW

Routinizing interactive service work inevitably sets up tensions concerning the identity and individuality of workers, and, to a lesser extent, of customers as well. The sorts of identity issues created for workers vary, however, with the type of work and the type of relations with customers that are organized by the company. The possible ways of handling these tensions or of reconciling conflict between workers' preferred self-images and the identities imposed on them by their routines are likewise structured by the organization of the work. How possible is it to hold one's self in reserve while on the job? How compromising is it to a worker's feelings of dignity and individuality to embrace the routine? How far is it possible to interpret the role in ways that are compatible with a self-identity the worker is willing to accept?

The identities of workers in all sorts of jobs are shaped by the work they do, but the routinization of interactive service work tends to give employers more explicit and, in some areas, more extensive rights to define workers' looks, demeanor, attitudes, and outlooks. Braverman (1974), in his account of the history of work routinization, emphasized that deskilling jobs was the most important goal and outcome of employers' efforts to rationalize work. The jobs I have described have been deskilled to some extent. McDonald's window workers need fewer skills than do waiters or waitresses in conventional restaurants, and Combined's agents need fewer skills than do insurance agents who sell a wide variety of products without formal scripting, although the agents' training did give them skills that let them control their work more effectively. Nevertheless, a focus on skills does not capture some of the most significant features of the routinization of interactive service work. The qualities that allow workers to succeed in these jobs, and that employers try to control, are personal attributes, character traits, interactional styles, and the like. Some aspects of these dimensions can be regarded as skills, but only in an ambiguous and complicated sense. For instance, if workers are required to control their emotions on the job, would one call their loss of decision-making authority over their own behavior deskilling? Or would one say that the job requires the skill of self-control? The ability to get along well with people can easily be regarded as a skill, but what about the ability to tolerate abuse?

The concept of deskilling, appropriate as it is for understanding the standardization of tasks and the reduction of job complexity, does not illuminate the distinctive aspects of the routinization of interactive service work. Employers of these types of workers may find that to routinize work they must undertake the transformation of their employees' identities, ways of thinking, and sources of motivation, much as, for instance, religious orders and armies transform their recruits. Until now, research on work routinization has tended to downplay the relevance of social psychological theory, except in denouncing the attempts of managers of the human relations school to manipulate their workers. To understand the full impact of routinization in interactive service work, more serious attention to issues of identity, authenticity, and individuality is required. Investigations of workers' subjectivity must take into account not only employers' efforts to shape workers' consciousness but also workers' determined agency in providing justifications and interpretations of their experiences.

7

Conclusion

The term "factory hand" poignantly reveals how little relevance the minds and spirits of workers have for some industrial employers. Service organizations, too, have pursued policies of routinization that lessen their dependence on workers' intelligence and skill, but such employers cannot make do with mere hands. "Now hiring smiling faces," a Kentucky Fried Chicken outlet advertises, and the shift in synecdoche signals differences between the processes and ramifications of routinization in service work and manual work. The selves of service workers are bound up with their work in ways quite different from those of workers who interact with objects or data rather than people.

In trying to mold interactions to their own purposes, service employers shape the self-conceptions and self-presentations of their workers, often quite straightforwardly. The service-recipients who are involved in these interactions also feel the effects of organizationally imposed routines. As Goffman noted (1983: 14):

> In contemporary society almost everyone has service transactions every day. Whatever the ultimate significance of these dealings for recipients, it is clear that how they are treated in these contexts is likely to flavor their sense of place in the wider community.

The cultural influence of routinizing service work thus goes beyond its impact on workers and its requirement that service-recipients cooperate with organizational logic during service encounters. To understand these ramifications of routinized service work, we must ask what lessons customers as well as workers are taught by their participation in scripted interactions, and what effects those experiences have on their beliefs about themselves, on their relations to others, and on the culture at large.

The most significant implications of routinizing interactive service work derive from the two distinctive features of such work emphasized throughout this book. These are the features that lead employers to try to hire, and continually reproduce, smiling faces. First, service-recipients participate in the work processes of interactive service workers, and it is for their benefit that managers of some kinds of services expect workers to smile. Second, the quality of the interaction between worker and service-recipient is integral to the delivery of many kinds of services. Smiling (or other affective display) is therefore part of the work, not necessarily a reflection of a worker's mood or disposition (Hochschild 1983).

These two properties of interactive service work can greatly expand the scope of organizational control efforts associated with routinization. Control strategies are broadened to include people other than employees, because interactive service routines depend on the cooperation of service-recipients. They too are subjected to organizational practices aimed at standardizing their behavior.[1] Whether they play along with the role scripted for them or try to evade it, they are likely to find that some of the assumptions that guide ordinary interactions have been altered or suspended. Organizational control practices expand in depth as well, as employers treat more and more of the selves of their workers as relevant to their capacity to perform the job. Workers' appearance, moods, emotions, and habits of mind are all considered fair game for employer intervention when self-presentation and interactive style are integral parts of the work task.

The threats to identity felt by service workers whose jobs require emotional labor have been well analyzed by Hochschild (1983), who also hints at the uneasiness felt by service-recipients unsure whether they are dealing with a person behaving in a genuine manner or with an actor following a script. Less attention has been paid to the broader cultural impact of routinized interactive work. Scripted service work accustoms both workers and service-recipients to participation in interactions that violate basic norms. These interactive norms reflect central cultural values, and they help give coherence to social life and to individual identity. When they are disrupted in the service of organizational goals, the ramifications are felt by

1. This control of service-recipients' behavior seems ironic in light of the emphasis placed on consumption as a sphere of choice and self-expression (see, e.g., Halle 1984). To develop mechanisms that represent the interests of service-recipients is an important challenge for proponents of workplace democracy.

everyone who takes part in service interactions, that is, by almost everyone. The influence of employers' control strategies thus extends far beyond the workplace.

The legitimacy of service organizations' management of customers' and workers' behavior and emotional responses remains somewhat ambiguous. Their right to manipulate is rarely openly disputed, yet the manipulation often provokes unease or resentment in both workers and service-recipients. The details of scripted service routines seem laughable—the Combined Shuffle, the friendly interactions timed with a stopwatch, the slick rebuttals that overwhelm opposition—but they are also disquieting to many participants and cultural observers. When I have shared examples from my research with colleagues, friends, and students, I have noticed them shaking their heads as they laughed, conveying a sense of helpless chagrin. The cynical manipulativeness of the scripts implies a disrespect for service-recipients that is both funny and alarming, especially to those who recognize that they have often succumbed to similar manipulations themselves. Some of the laughter, though, is directed at the service workers, who are perceived as sacrificing their autonomy and self-respect by enacting scripts. That sacrifice should arouse compassion as well as contempt, however. Scripted service routines can be clever or ludicrous, clumsy or effective, but it is hard to escape the uncomfortable sensation that they threaten participants' dignity and promote a reductive view of human relations.

The efforts of service organizations to routinize human interactions violate important cultural standards about the status of the self, standards that honor authenticity, autonomy, sincerity, and individuality. Although these values are compromised daily in countless ways, they are ideals most Americans take seriously.[2] In routinized service interactions, the collision between ideals and practices is particularly marked, and the uncomfortable contradictions are hard to ignore. Service routines compromise the identities of workers most obviously, but the principles and self-conceptions

2. In speaking of widely held ideals I do not mean to attribute uniformity and consensus to American society. Subcultures vary in their degree of allegiance to cultural values and in the codes of behavior through which those values are expressed. Furthermore, people of different classes, genders, races, and ethnic groups differ in the means available to them for enacting the values they do hold in common. Since I did not systematically investigate service-recipients' responses to routinization, my discussion of the manipulation of cultural values by service organizations is necessarily general and speculative.

of service-recipients are challenged as well as they are forced to respond to organizational manipulation.

Authenticity implies connection with what is understood to be a stable core of self, a true self, estrangement from which produces painful feelings of falsity and emotional detachment.[3] Interactive service organizations compromise workers' sense of authenticity when they teach workers what they should feel in particular circumstances and discredit other reactions (see Hochschild 1983). The standards by which emotional responses are judged in these circumstances is not authenticity but practical effect: do they impede or enhance the workers' ability to provide the kind of service demanded of them? Workers are encouraged to suppress, disregard, or reinterpret feelings that the organization finds unhelpful.

Speech and behavior that do not directly reflect the individual's self-perceived authentic self are acceptable under many circumstances, indeed often required. Conscious sculpting of self-presentation or even personality may compromise authenticity, but if it is the individual who directs these adjustments they need not undermine her or his dignity. When others exact such adjustments, however, submission can seem humiliating, a surrender of fundamental prerogatives. The Western liberal tradition strongly upholds the autonomy of the self. It puts the individual at the center of its value system and accords that individual a zone of privacy within which self-determination is guaranteed. The American political tradition stresses freedom from interference by the state, but it allows employers greater leeway in exercising authority over workers' behavior, on the principle that the employment relationship was entered into voluntarily. Still, the legitimacy of employers' interference with workers' selves is also precarious. "The human personality is a sacred thing," Durkheim (1974 [1924]: 37) wrote; "one dare not violate it nor infringe its bounds." Interactive service organizations do dare to infringe the bounds of their workers' personalities as a matter of course, but not without sparking resentment. Employers' assertion of control over workers' appearance, words, and self-presentation seems intrusive to many workers and observers, and efforts to reshape demeanor, attitudes, and feelings are often seen as

---

3. See Wouters (1989) for one relevant critique of this conception of selfhood. He questions the assumption that a self untainted by internalized emotion rules or other kinds of social learning could exist, let alone represent the "true" self.

attacks on workers' dignity. Not surprisingly, workers frequently defend their right to a sphere of noninterference, responding to control efforts with displays of role distance intended to show that they are "not capitulating completely to the work arrangement in which [they find themselves]" (Goffman 1961b: 114).

Authenticity and autonomy are ideals for the individual's relation to the self. In relations with others, sincerity is highly valued, but not implacably required. Tact, courtesy, and convention all temper sincerity as an ideal. Indeed, few of us would want to live unshielded from some of the sincere feelings of our associates. The demands of civility notwithstanding, sincerity remains a standard by which Americans judge themselves and others. They do not want to think of themselves as fake. They disparage flatterers, pretenders, and all who present an unconvincing façade, and they worry about being taken in by less transparent façades (Lamont 1992). Although most adults recognize limits to the practicality of sincerity, they generally agree that it is dishonorable to disguise feelings, intentions, or characteristics in order to present oneself in an undeservedly flattering light or to put others at a disadvantage.

Interactive service routines often require workers to be insincere, variously calling on them to feign interest or disinterestedness, carefree cheeriness or shocked sympathy, as the occasion demands. Sometimes the insincerity is intended not to hoodwink but to gratify service-recipients, by providing a pleasing style of interaction, though service-recipients may or may not appreciate the attempt. If in some settings insincerity is merely "making an effort" for other people's benefit, in others it is an effort to "take them in" for one's own—or one's employer's—benefit. Social disapproval is more virulent in the latter instance, but service-recipients may regard workers who practice either kind of insincerity with contempt, and so may the workers themselves. In our culture, even insincerity in the service of kindness or politeness can be seen as compromising one's integrity, and some feel that dissimulation, regardless of intention, expresses disrespect for oneself if not for others.

Authenticity, autonomy, and sincerity allow the development and expression of the unique self that is culturally ascribed to every person. Individuality is highly honored in American culture (even though conformity is richly rewarded), and this value is especially hard to reconcile with routinized interactions. The meaning of individuality is considerably narrowed when people are encouraged to express it through their selection of mass-produced commodities, yet treatment that emphasizes that one is merely one of a mass remains offensive. Routinized interactive service affronts the individuality of both worker and service-recipient. It assumes that workers' individuality is not substantial enough or worthy enough of deference to interfere with their adoption of qualities designed for them by others. And it further assumes that service-recipients, grouped according to market segment, will be able and willing to fit into standard procedures and accept standardized treatment. Organizations sensitive to the danger of offending service-recipients by failing to acknowledge their individuality may script personalizing touches as part of service routines. These embellishments do not ensure individual treatment of customers, but they do signal recognition of the importance of that ideal. To some service-recipients, however, such engineered personalization is as self-invalidating as computer-generated junk mail with the recipient's name printed in strategic places.

When they undertake the routinization of human interactions, then, service organizations promulgate an understanding of selfhood that conflicts with other socially validated constructions of the self. In the organizational framework, human personality is regarded as highly flexible. It is, not an inviolable core, but a resource that can be reshaped to meet the demands of various settings. People may legitimately adopt an instrumental stance toward their selves, and individuals and organizations may legitimately treat others instrumentally. Furthermore, the construction of routines for dealing with service-recipients takes for granted, in Fussell's phrase, "the uniform identity of human creatures" (1975: 185). People are understood to be essentially similar, even though they prefer to be treated as individuals. The uniformities are substantial enough to allow the use of relatively inflexible interactive routines, and idiosyncrasies and desires for personal treatment can be accommodated through minor adjustments of the routine and through the emotion work of employees. These conceptions of the nature and importance of selfhood coexist with cultural ideals that sanctify the uniqueness of each person, value spontaneity and frankness, and privilege individual self-definition.

Everyone knows that these cultural ideals do not necessarily guide behavior. They know that self-interest frequently determines how people treat each other, that people alter their self-presentation to create an impression appropriate for the social situation, that membership in most kinds of organizations requires acting in accordance with organizational interests. Routinized service interactions are nonetheless unnerving, because they raise questions for participants about their rights as individuals and about their competence to maneuver in a world where the standards are shamelessly manipulated. People want to believe that they can distinguish between instrumental and expressive behavior, between manipulation and spontaneity. They feel that behavior and demeanor should reflect character and feeling, and they judge themselves and others by that standard. Such terms as "robot" and "brainwashing" express both contempt for and fear of situations in which organizational considerations dominate individual agency.

Nevertheless, as I have stressed throughout this book, routinization is not necessarily resisted by either workers or service-recipients. Research that focuses narrowly on the alienating and dehumanizing aspects of routinization highlights the power of management to dominate but does not reveal the complicated and fluctuating play of interests among managers, workers, and service-recipients. By paying attention to both the positive and the negative features of routinization in given circumstances, we can more readily understand the often ambivalent responses of workers and consumers. Both groups accept routinization in part, because it provides them with practical benefits. Depending on the context, service routines can help workers to do their job, can boost their confidence, can limit the demands made upon them, can give them leverage over service-recipients, and can offer psychic protection from demeaning aspects of the job. Correspondingly, in various situations, routinization can provide service-recipients with more reliable, less expensive, or speedier service, can protect them from incompetence, can minimize the interactive demands on them, and can clarify what their rights are.[4]

In addition to these practical incentives to cooperate with organizational routines, both workers and service-recipients are often influenced by ideological lures and justifications for employer strategies. For although the routinization of interactive service work challenges the values of authenticity, autonomy, sincerity, and

---

4. Note that some of these outcomes are benefits only because the interactions take place within a framework of unequal power.

individuality, service organizations often draw on these and other widely shared values to bolster the legitimacy of their control efforts. In the process, the values themselves may be diminished. For example, the lines "We want to treat every customer as an individual in sixty seconds or less" and "Be Kevin" draw their meaning from the values of individualism and authenticity, yet they are embedded in processes that flatly contravene those ideals, using them only instrumentally.

Phrases such as these from my fieldwork stayed on my mind throughout the writing of this book because they encapsulated for me the combination of the preposterous and the poignant that gives routinized interactive service work its tragicomic quality. In the values evoked and manipulated, scripted sentences like these capture something, not just about routinization, but also about the character of contemporary American life: the can-do belief in efficiency applied to obligatory familiarity; the faith in people's capacity for self-transformation put to profitable use; the insistence on individuality coexisting with domination by an imposed corporate culture. Even as the effects of routinizing interactive service work reverberate beyond the workplace, then, the particular shapes that the scripted routines take reflect wider cultural preoccupations, not just employer interests.

Both McDonald's and Combined Insurance draw on the American preference for friendliness and informality and for the egalitarianism they imply, a cultural characteristic notable at least since Tocqueville's time (1969 [1835]). Their routines are structured to include a show of bonhomie or personal connection, on the assumption that service-recipients resent dealings with impersonal bureaucracies in which they are "treated like a number." Whereas other cultures might see indiscriminate friendliness as presumptuous, invasive, and an attack on legitimate social distinctions, here those who resist friendly overtures risk condemnation for snobbery or coldness. By and large, although Americans may criticize the falseness of routinized friendliness, they rarely criticize the idea that friendliness is desirable in relations between workers and service-recipients.[5] However, service organizations and workers often use such overtures to invoke a

---

5. Judith Martin, a.k.a. Miss Manners, is an exception. She sees that invoking norms of friendship makes it more difficult for service-recipients to insist on satisfaction (1985: 45–49).

sense of reciprocity that puts pressure on service-recipients to play along obligingly with the standardized script in order not to insult the apparently friendly worker. Although many workers dislike forced friendliness, some who resent being in the position of serving others may be reassured by the assertion of equal status that friendly overtures imply. Since subordinates typically do not have the right to initiate intimacy or informality (Goffman 1956: 481–82), routines that call for a friendly and informal approach can undercut the sting of servility or the indignity of having to please others who may not wish to please in return.

McDonald's and Combined Insurance share appeals to individuality and friendliness, but they differ in the values they draw on to support routinization. Since workers at McDonald's are so tightly controlled and its customers have so many alternatives available to them, making routinized interactions acceptable to customers is a more significant ideological challenge for the company than is accommodating workers to standardization. The enormous success of McDonald's suggests that it has succeeded in associating itself with values that have wide appeal. One reading of the garishness of most McDonald's stores, the requirement that customers do some of the work, the emphasis on convenience and speed rather than on fine dining, and the lack of attentiveness of the staff once the meals are served is that these are low-class establishments that do not offer the status rewards customers pay for at more expensive restaurants. Certainly that interpretation is a common one. Yet the very lack of formality, exclusivity, and class pretension appeals to the egalitarian strain in American culture.

Fantasia's work on the reaction to American-style fast-food establishments in France (1991) brings into focus the democratic ethos McDonald's sells. French teenagers he interviewed reported valuing McDonald's "American atmosphere" of informality and freedom, a novelty to them. At McDonald's, these young people feel free of the strict rules of decorum that constrain their behavior in what they regard as stuffy French restaurants. The emphasis is on fun rather than elegance. Customers do not have to order complete meals, can dress informally, can eat with their hands, can talk loudly. As Fantasia emphasizes, the association of McDonald's with freedom is ironic in light of its homogenizing influence, strict controls on labor, and domination of the industry. Yet Americans too see something democratic in McDonald's, if not in allowing masses of people to influence decision making, then at least in providing an experience that is available to virtually everyone. Moreover, service routines provide an implicit guarantee that everyone will be treated equally.

Tocqueville feared that Americans' zeal for egalitarianism might make them relatively inattentive to threats to their liberty posed by a strong central power (1969 [1835]: 57). The power he feared was that of a despotic state. The kinds of limitations on individuals' behavior imposed by corporate routines and mass consumer culture are less dramatic than those Tocqueville warned against, but they, too, can be made tolerable by an apparent egalitarianism, a minimization of distinctions among groups.[6] Unlike government, McDonald's is able to present itself as a realm of personal choice. Customers need not participate in McDonald's routines unless they judge that the attractions of its food, prices, informality, and speed outweigh any limits on choice and any impersonality the routine imposes. Finally, Americans' commitment to efficiency as an important good helps legitimize McDonald's requirement that customers comply with organizational routines.

Combined's sales routines are themselves designed to bring customers into compliance. The company's most important ideological task is to persuade its agents, whose work is largely unsupervised, to accept a standardization that encompasses many aspects of their identity. Like McDonald's, the company achieves its goal in part by implying that its experts have worked out the best possible system for carrying out the work, making it sensible for participants to choose to comply with routines. Combined Insurance puts a marked emphasis on personal choice. Its rhetoric stresses not submission to corporate rules but individual commitment to self-reformation (see Biggart 1989). The value of autonomy is reconciled with adherence to company norms of personality, style, and thought through a discourse stressing agents' responsibility for changing themselves into more successful people. The company presents itself as offering the opportunity to succeed to anyone willing to accept the challenge of self-transformation. Its language resonates deeply with familiar and

6. American political culture is markedly concerned with minimizing distinctions between elites and "the people." It is notable that during the 1991 hearings on Clarence Thomas's nomination to the Supreme Court, Thomas drew on McDonald's to emphasize his identification with ordinary Americans. Arguing that he would not be devastated if his nomination were defeated, he listed "getting a Big Mac at McDonald's" as one of the homely activities to which he would gladly return (quoted in Dowd 1991).

time-honored themes in American culture: that everyone is entitled to a chance to make good; that success is within the grasp of anyone with the requisite initiative, perseverance, and faith; that individuals have the power to redeem themselves, to make a fresh start (see Biggart 1983).

This appeal to personal transformation based on will and hard work makes acceptance of highly detailed routines palatable, and it goes further to infuse these routines, the everyday stuff of life, with deep meaning. Calvinists, Weber taught us, found work intensely meaningful because they treated success in business as evidence that they were among those elected by God to escape damnation. Christian asceticism helped to bring into being an economic system that requires everyone to engage in disciplined, rationalized work, whether or not the work provides personal fulfillment or emotional solace. Weber argued, therefore, that "the Puritan wanted to work in a calling; we are forced to do so." Combined's agents, among many others, must indeed submit to rationalized work, but to them the work is not an "iron cage" drained of meaning (Weber 1958 [1904–5]: 181). Instead, every sales talk is an opportunity to demonstrate strength of character. The workers are encouraged to interpret their success not as a measure of God's pleasure but as a result of personal attributes for which they themselves can take the credit, an even headier affirmation.

Goffman spoke of a special type of risky activity, "action," during which the individual has the chance "to lay himself on the line and place himself in jeopardy during a passing moment." Moments of action lie outside "the safe and silent places, the home, the well-regulated role in business" (1967: 268) and provide opportunities for heroic self-expression. For Combined's agents, ordinary sales calls are "where the action is," in Goffman's sense, precisely because they have been trained to understand these interactions as symbolically important chances to prove their character by overcoming attempts to block their will. Even highly rationalized work is thus imbued with personal meaning. Combined Insurance does not take this motivating force for granted. It is careful to shape and reinforce the agents' understanding of the personal fatefulness of their day-to-day work, providing meanings that are useful to the business as well as inspiring to the agents.

If organizational strategies for routinizing interactive service work violate some important cultural values, then, they draw on others.

Appeals to equality and friendliness, personal choice, efficiency, and the possibility of self-redemption undercut resistance to the extension of bureaucratic control over more aspects of individual identity and personal interaction. These ideological supports, along with the practical benefits routinization can offer workers and service-recipients, help explain the ambivalence many people feel about routinized service work. Although scripted interactions offend against the values that sanctify individual selfhood, they provide, in various settings, some apparent and some real compensations.

Even if routines offer some benefits to some people, the routinization of interactive service work always engages participants in activities that call taken-for-granted principles into question. As Goffman has amply documented, cultural ideals such as authenticity and individuality are expressed in minute interactive practices that uphold the sacredness of the self (1956). These practices, supported by moral imperatives, serve to "[make] society safe for interaction" (1957: 52). Goffman brings to our awareness, often by drawing attention to violations of them, rules of conduct we usually act upon unthinkingly. Interactive service scripts can do the same thing. The danger is that the routines undermine the reality on which social norms rest even as they take advantage of the existence of those norms.

Service organizations that script interactions do not play fair. They give the appearance of respecting the standard rules of interaction while actually manipulating them. As Goffman noted, "The mutual accommodation that orders human traffic can . . . be seen to render vulnerable those who take it for granted" (1967: 250). This lesson is pointedly reinforced when service-recipients find that they put themselves at a disadvantage if they act according to the social norms that service organizations self-interestedly invoke. For example, Combined's prospects found that they paid a price if they politely accepted the "face" and "line" presented by agents and treated them with the customary civility that grants others the benefit of the doubt (Goffman 1956: 479).[7] When the agents "established rapport" through companionable chatter, they took the line

---

7. Goffman defines "line" as "a pattern of verbal and nonverbal acts by which [a person] expresses his view of the situation and through this his evaluation of the participants, especially himself." "Face," he says, is "the positive social value a person effectively claims for himself by the line others assume he has taken during a particular contact" (Goffman 1955: 213).

that they were friendly and trustworthy people who would not take advantage of the prospect, yet they did so precisely in order to make it more difficult for prospects to defend themselves against the manipulations of the script.

The agents did not give prospects the benefit of the doubt in return by allowing them to sustain the line they chose to take. Rather, in many cases they willfully misread prospects' meaning, as when they responded to a dismissive "I already have insurance" with "I'm glad to hear that. That shows me that you understand the value of insurance. As I was saying . . . " I came to recognize a particular expression that crossed the faces of some Combined Insurance prospects at moments like these. It was a half-resigned, half-exasperated egg-on-the-face look that seemed to say, "You got me." It appeared when prospects recognized that they had been successfully manipulated, had fallen for the agent's line. A grudging smile sometimes communicated acknowledgment of the agent's skill in taking advantage of the prospect while apparently honoring the rules of respectful treatment of others. If these prospects looked resigned, it was because they were unwilling to shatter the polite surface of the interaction that had misled them. Although aware that they were being imposed upon, they respected the social conventions too much to be openly discourteous. At these moments, agents and prospects communicated on two levels simultaneously, having come to a mutual agreement to play their roles as though the interaction could be taken at face value, although each recognized that the other was aware of the underlying power play. However, not all prospects were willing to behave as though such interactions were supported by underpinnings of fairness and solicitude that were in fact patently missing. Some instead spoke sharply to agents or simply ended the interaction.

In most social interactions, participants are bound by the obligations of the "ceremonial idiom" to conduct themselves in ways that reinforce the participants' dignity and affirm the communal value of the sacredness of the individual (Goffman 1956: 477). Service-recipients, understandably, often treat interactions with workers as a special category of encounter in which these obligations do not hold. There are other situations in which the obligations are not binding. For example, one may treat another as a non-person (Goffman 1956: 483) when passing a stranger on the street, and one may refuse to give interactional support to the line of a suspected swindler. The situation in scripted interactive service work, though, is ambiguous enough to make many service-recipients unsure of their interactive obligations and to provoke varied responses. Some customers respond to a cheerful greeting from a McDonald's worker with smiles and mild pleasantries, while others do not acknowledge the greeting at all. The former uphold the obligation to treat others as "ritually delicate objects" (Goffman 1955: 224), but the latter do not admit any such duty under the circumstances.

People who treat McDonald's workers with indifference may simply be rude—that is the workers' usual explanation—but apparently many customers feel that such behavior is appropriate. These customers, knowing that the workers' friendliness is as likely to reflect corporate policy as fellow-feeling, adjust their interpretations and reactions accordingly. The difference of interpretation reflects unsettled questions. Do the rules of interaction that protect participants' selves hold when one party is acting on behalf of an organization? Do they hold when the organization, or the interactant, is manipulating the rules? Is it legitimate to express disapproval of perceived violations of the ideals of authenticity, autonomy, sincerity, and individuality by refusing to play along with routines one finds offensive? Is it fair to express such disapproval at the expense of a worker who is trying to do the job well (or, conversely, at that of a customer who is trying to cooperate)? Why should one risk rebuff by taking a personal approach to a worker or customer who might not agree that service interactions carry obligations of mutual acknowledgment and courtesy?

Service interactions present uncertainties for both workers and service-recipients, either of whom may find that the line they choose to take with respect to the interaction is rejected by the other or proves to be foolhardy. Service organizations intentionally blur the status of the interactions they script, drawing on norms of friendly, noninstrumental encounters in situations in which those norms leave service-recipients vulnerable to manipulation and workers vulnerable to rejection or easy discrediting. These are dangerous waters. Does regular immersion in them affect people's overall willingness to adhere to the moral rules and provide the reaffirming gestures that bolster individuals' sense of self and acknowledge mutual acceptance of communal values?

Repeated experiences of placing oneself at a disadvantage by inappropriately honoring interactive conventions surely undercuts the social force of those conventions. Instead of being generalized obligations, they come to be understood as appropriate to some situations and inappropriate to others. The social world is altered as people learn that they should be careful about giving others the benefit of the doubt and treating their self-respect with gentle consideration, rather than extending these courtesies routinely. More people maintain a defensive unwillingness to enter into the spirit of interaction, waiting to be persuaded that their suspicions of the others' intentions are groundless instead of assuming goodwill. Workers are especially apt to suffer when they are asked to play roles that provoke service-recipients to suspend the norms protecting the face of the other, yet prevent the workers from openly defending their own dignity.

Service organizations attempt to have it both ways, to treat workers and service-recipients as relatively uniform entities and to convey appreciation of individuality and respect for the integrity of the self. To counteract the impersonality of bureaucratic encounters, these organizations design routines and train workers to simulate personal engagement. Yet, by involving workers and service-recipients in interactions that treat such engagement instrumentally, they promote habits of interaction that make it less likely that people will extend to each other the kind of affirmation that supports both individual identity and social cohesion, support which, Goffman argued (1956: 493), is indispensable:

> Each individual is responsible for the demeanor image of himself and the deference image of others, so that for a complete man to be expressed, individuals must hold hands in a chain of ceremony, each giving deferentially with proper demeanor to the one on the right what will be received deferentially from the one on the left. While it may be true that the individual has a unique self all his own, evidence of this possession is thoroughly a product of joint ceremonial labor, the part expressed through the individual's demeanor being no more significant than the part conveyed by others through their deferential behavior toward him.

If service organizations, through routinization, undermine the ground rules of interaction, some of the links in this chain of ceremony are weakened. People may reasonably judge, then, that it is safer to confine their ceremonial labor to smaller circles of relations. Diminishing expectations of connection and support in the public sphere in turn help bring into being a public sphere that is relatively unnourishing of the self and of social relations.[8]

Although service routines are designed with quite specific purposes in mind, they exert a general influence on the society. Because the routinization of interactive service work orders the behavior of service-recipients as well as of workers, "the long arm of the job" (Lynd and Lynd 1929) stretches out to affect community life quite directly. Sociologists of work typically see relations of inequality at work as affecting the broader society through their impact on workers' economic power and consciousness, both individual and collective.[9] Sociologists of culture, by contrast, tend to downplay workplace relations and instead to concentrate on other means by which economic elites exert social control.[10] But when the principles of routinization are extended to interactive service work, an additional dimension of cultural influence becomes available to employers. Because routinized service work orders the behavior of service-recipients as well as that of workers, employers' strategies for controlling the labor process themselves affect the cultural milieu. The Marxist argument that consciousness is shaped at the point of production is applicable here, but service-recipients as well as paid workers are present. Service-recipients are enmeshed in relations of

8. Drawing boundaries between areas where it is and is not safe to accept interactions at face value proves to be difficult, however. Some service organizations try to disguise instrumental relations with the trappings of personal connection and obligation, and others insinuate the logic of commercial relations into existing personal relations. For example, some insurance companies (Oakes 1990) and most direct-sales organizations (Biggart 1989) count on their employees or distributors to exploit their own personal and familial relationships by turning them into business relationships. People who come into contact with these workers may find themselves in scripted interactions that take advantage of their loyalty or their trust in what they thought were noncommercial settings.

9. Burawoy (1979), for example, insists on the primacy of the relations of production in shaping workers' subjectivity and thus constraining the possibilities for broad social change. Many researchers have looked outside the workplace to demonstrate that paid work affects families and communities. The material conditions of family life, from standard of living to daily scheduling (Gerstel and Gross 1987; Luxton 1980; Lynd and Lynd 1929), the relative power of women and men (Finch 1983; Hochschild with Machung 1989), the possibilities for involvements outside of work (Margolis 1979), and the values guiding child-rearing (Kohn 1969) are all shaped by the conditions of paid work.

10. Students of mass culture, education, and politics have argued that businesses direct the interests, goals, and attitudes of the public by controlling the media, by creating needs and the commodities that supposedly fill those needs, by using their economic power to influence government, and by framing the boundaries and terms of discourse.

production on their own time, and the boundaries separating production, consumption, and sociability break down.

It is obvious that employer-created routines shape how consumers and workers behave during these service interactions. That influence extends outward as well, affecting patterns of relations beyond the point of production. Participation in scripted service interactions provides training in cynicism and defensiveness that affects people's understanding of social relations, including their sense of their own rights and power, their expectations of other people, and their beliefs about their obligations to others.

Various groups and individuals apply these lessons differently. As was demonstrated in the analysis of gender segregation of jobs, the meaning of social circumstances for participants' identities depends on their own interpretations. However, the interpretations of participants and audiences are structured and constrained by organizationally created social facts and by the range of ideas available in the culture.

Routinized service interactions extend the logic of instrumental economic rationality to more and more aspects of the self and to ever additional kinds of social relations. Yet it is important not to overstate the negative power of routinization. Routinizing service interactions does not make self-expression or real human contact impossible. Many of the encounters between workers and customers at McDonald's and between agents and prospects of Combined Insurance were experienced by both parties as real social exchanges. Moreover, it is clear that neither customers nor workers necessarily want service interactions to demand or provide deep involvement. Because such interactions are so frequent, many people prefer to conduct them without much expenditure of emotional energy. Service routines that are undemanding of personal engagement can nevertheless establish a floor of civility and competence for which many customers have reason to be grateful. Interactive routines can also protect workers, limiting the psychic costs of dealing with the public by allowing workers to interpret customer hostility and condescension as responses to the routine, not to them personally.

Since routinization can provide security as well as constraints for both workers and customers, to regard the imposition of routines merely as oppression and depersonalization is to ignore much of the evidence. Nevertheless, the standardization of human interactions does encroach on social space not previously dominated by economic rationality. It shifts the meanings of such fundamental values as individuality and authenticity, raising troubling issues of identity for workers and customers. Through the standardization of the selves of workers and the treatment of customers, service businesses promote an instrumental orientation toward others and toward the self. Corporate and bureaucratic definitions of moral behavior and of self-actualization gain cultural force as workers are trained to consider these ways of thinking essential for success on the job, and as service-recipients respond defensively.

Moreover, participants in service routines must learn to negotiate interactions in which they can no longer take for granted the usual moral framework for dealing with others. By disrupting the ground rules that govern interaction, the routinization of interactive service work alters the character of relations among people in and out of the marketplace. We may wonder whether civility, trust, and personal liberty and integrity can be written into the scripts.

APPENDIX 1

Researching Routinized Work

Since this project focused on interaction, control, and the manipulation of appearances and responses, in my fieldwork I was perhaps more than usually conscious of issues that all fieldworkers have to consider: How much is their presence altering the situation? How far are they piercing the front that respondents may wish to maintain? Are they taking advantage of people? Are they being taken advantage of? How are their emotional reactions affecting their data-gathering?

Consciousness of these issues does not eliminate them as problems any more than confessing to difficulties in the collection of data produces better data. Such consciousness can at least remind the researcher to consider probable omissions and biases, though, and confession puts readers in a better position to gauge the trustworthiness of the account. Virtually all candid tales of fieldwork describe some mix of careful planning, serendipity, blunder, and idiosyncratic predilections, and mine is no different (see Van Maanen 1988). In this appendix I will explain how I chose my research sites and went about the research and describe some problems that arose in the course of the study.

This book began as my doctoral dissertation, but even before I started graduate school I had had considerable experience with and interest in service work, routinization, and acting, and both my ideas about service work and my choices of research methods reflect those experiences. Having worked at various times as a cashier, a waitress,[1] and an actor, I was comfortable with the idea of consciously taking on roles and I generally liked dealing with the public. I had some memories of appalling treatment by customers and bosses, but I never felt that there was anything inherently demeaning about service jobs, not even in the required demonstrations of deference.

I first began thinking seriously about the problems of routinizing

---

1. I use this gender-specific term because "waiter" and "waitress" frequently designate, not only the gender of the jobholder, but also the style of service and type of restaurant (Hall 1990).

interactions when, immediately after I graduated from college, I worked as a research assistant on a large telephone survey. The study director had hired me to do a qualitative study of the process of gathering quantitative data. My assignment was to listen in on telephone interviews to see whether they were going smoothly, whether there were problems with the questionnaire, and where the researchers needed to be especially cautious in interpreting data. I became fascinated by the sheer impossibility of interviewers accomplishing their work if they meticulously followed the antiseptic routine deemed necessary to collect reliable data. Not only was my belief in the crisp accuracy and objectivity of quantitative data forever shattered, but I came to see that the messiness did not result from poor research design or incompetent interviewing. The interactive requirements of gaining cooperation, maintaining rapport, clarifying misunderstandings, and addressing unexpected contingencies were too complex for any preplanned script to fit all calls. Interviewers who were able to balance objectivity and precision with responsiveness to interviewees were most likely to get valid data. I am still grateful to the survey supervisor who insisted that I conduct at least one interview myself to get a feel for the pressures of the job.

These experiences, as well as many exasperating and amusing experiences as a service-recipient, influenced which questions struck me as interesting and which procedures seemed reasonable when I began this study. It was clear to me that participant-observation was the only way I could get the kind of data I wanted on the subtleties of interaction that were central to the study. Workers' self-reports in surveys or interviews could not provide enough contextual information to convey the experience of doing interactive service work. My experiences also persuaded me that I could get an adequate (if not exhaustive) sense of service-recipients' preferences and reactions without directly interviewing them, since workers' interpretations and my own observations of their demeanor and behavior could provide a great deal of information. Once I had decided that I wanted the research to contrast at least two types of routinized interactive service work and to include interviewing and participant-observation, my next task was to locate suitable research sites and gain access. Because I wanted to be able to interview managers as well as to meet workers, I would need official cooperation.

I knew from the beginning that I wanted one of the case studies to be of McDonald's. The company was a pioneer and exemplar of routinized interaction, and since it was locally based, it seemed like the perfect place to start. McDonald's had other ideas, however, and only after tenacious pestering and persuasion did I overcome corporate employees' polite demurrals, couched in terms of protecting proprietary information and the company's image. Finally, a previously unyielding executive in the human resources department offered to set up an interview for me with a training manager. She said that he would only be "willing to talk in generalities" and added that she doubted that any further research could be arranged.

Once I showed up at the management training facility, Hamburger University (described in detail in Chapter 3), my luck changed. The training manager (or "professor," as he was called) immediately offered to give me a tour of the facility, told me that I would be welcome to attend classes there, asked whether I would be interested in working at a McDonald's restaurant to gather more information, and offered to get in touch with the regional headquarters to make arrangements for my placement. With his help, I was able to get started right away. In fact, it became apparent that placing outsiders in McDonald's outlets was quite routine; there was even a regional coordinator of "special placements." That coordinator wished me a good "in-store experience" and put me in touch with the owner of a local franchise, who proved quite agreeable to my proposal.

The next snag came when I had finished my work at Hamburger University, had been trained to work behind the counter, had put in my work shifts (looking at least ten years younger in uniform), and was ready to begin interviewing workers. I had agreed to show the franchise owner the interview questions before beginning, and although he had no objection to them, he told me that he had felt obliged to send them along to the regional headquarters for approval. I seemed to have quite a bit of trouble getting my phone calls to him accepted after that. When I did get through, the store owner told me that permission for the interviewing had been denied, and he referred me to headquarters; the manager at headquarters who had arranged my placement in turn referred me to the head of the region. Although I had previously spoken to this manager about my study and had made clear that I planned to interview workers, he now said that interviewing had not been part of the agreement, and he flatly refused to allow me to talk with workers.

The regional manager was adamant, but I had been fortified by Howard S. Becker's advice to fieldworkers in such situations: act as though all you can hear is "yes" or "maybe." The manager argued that he did not have the right to allow me to do anything that would make workers uncomfortable and that he had the "obligation to safeguard the reputation and image of our company and our operators and employees." I doggedly persisted, countering that I had no wish to put workers on the spot, that only workers who chose to participate would be interviewed and that they could decline to answer any question, and that complete confidentiality would be maintained. He softened somewhat, saying that I could do the interviews if he maintained the right to review my writings and refuse permission for publication. I said that it would be very helpful for him to review what I wrote to provide explanations or alternative accounts for points he felt I had misinterpreted, but that I could not give him the authority to prevent publication. He blustered quite a bit about his responsibility to the company and its employees; I refrained from pointing out that the workers were in fact employed by the franchise owner, who had no objection to the interviews. Instead, I affected certainty that McDonald's workers' comments would reflect the company's commitment to good employee relations and told him, truthfully, that it was my intention to contrast McDonald's with an organization that was not dedicated to pleasing the service-recipients, such as a bill-collecting firm or a public agency. My mention of a comparison that seemed to put McDonald's in a positive light apparently persuaded him that I did not necessarily intend to malign the company, and he was able to back down without losing face by saying that he did not remember my having mentioned before that it was a comparative study. Finally, he gave me permission to go ahead with the interviews on the condition that he would have the opportunity to respond to transcripts of the interviews from which all identifying details had been removed and to read my writing before publication. As it happened, by the time I completed the interviewing and transcription the manager had been transferred to another part of the company, and no one else in the office expressed interest when I offered to send the interview transcripts. I did send a copy of my dissertation to the man who replaced him as regional manager, but I received no reply.

When dealing with managers in person during my research at Hamburger University and at the franchise, I generally used a manner that I hoped conveyed straightforwardness and seriousness about my work, but I was not above taking advantage of whatever benefits I could derive from my personal and social characteristics. For example, my relatively low social status as a young woman and a student sometimes seemed to inspire in the men I met a chivalrous desire to be helpful, an attitude I cultivated by adopting, when convenient, a manner that combined perky enthusiasm with humble gratitude. With workers, I was most concerned that I convey an attitude of respect and even identification, since my status clearly set me apart from the majority of them. How they responded to me—a highly educated white woman, older than most of the workers but still in school, able to deal with managers on terms different from their own but apparently disposed, as an erstwhile coworker, to take their own point of view—varied quite a bit. Some were guarded, made shy or resentful, I supposed, by the race and class divide. Some liked having a chance to voice their opinions to an adult who seemed to be interested in the details of their work lives. Depending on their age, gender, race, class, and personal style, they flirted with me, showed off for me, avoided me, humored me, ignored me, teased me, confided in me, asked for favors or information from me, or tolerated me. By and large, though, they seemed to respond to my questions with candor.

The restaurant's managers did not schedule the interviews or indicate in any way that the crew people were required to cooperate. I obtained interviews by spending hours hanging around the crew room, asking workers whether they would be willing to be interviewed. Most of the questions concerned relations with customers, I explained, adding that they would be free to skip any questions they preferred not to answer. By and large, they apparently translated my explanation of why I was conducting the research into "working on a paper for school."

Most workers had no objection to being interviewed, and a few were quite eager to be included in the study. In general, those with whom I had worked behind the counter consented most readily. A few workers who declined at first decided to participate after they had gotten used to my presence or, occasionally, after they had listened in on part of an interview with a fellow worker. Five workers, all black women in their teens or twenties, did decline to be interviewed. Two voiced no objection to participating but always seemed to be in a rush to leave after their shifts; three who talked with me informally on a variety of occasions said they did not want to be interviewed.

The interviews themselves were structured but allowed room to pursue topics of particular interest to the workers. Almost all of them took place in the crew room located in the restaurant's basement, and they generally lasted about half an hour. I conducted, or at least started, a few interviews during workers' breaks, but most were held after workers had finished their shifts—that is, on their own time. I tape-recorded the interviews (unless the worker objected, in which case I took notes) and transcribed them myself. It was not uncommon for other crew people to come in and out of the crew room during an interview, occasionally chiming in with comments of their own. The effect of these coworkers' presence on the interviews is hard to gauge. It may have inhibited some workers, but it seemed to stimulate others to give more complete answers, since some enjoyed being in the spotlight and others were aware that incomplete answers or those that did not reflect the workers' usual behavior could be challenged. In any case, I had no means of enforcing privacy, though if a worker seemed uncomfortable continuing the interview while others were present I interrupted it until we were alone. When a manager came into the crew room, I either delayed completing the interview or stuck to nonsensitive questions.

Informal interaction with workers provided a good means of judging the adequacy of the interview data—it was not uncommon, for instance, to hear complaints that had not been mentioned in response to my formal questioning. Hanging out in the crew room was especially important in helping me get a sense of the peer culture that had been created by the workers, which clarified for me why so many of them told me that what they liked most about working there was "the people."

An even more useful supplement to the interviews was my experience working behind the counter. I learned far more about relations between customers and workers by doing the job than I did by asking questions. Much as I tried to make my questions about interactions with customers and workers' responses to them quite specific, pressing for concrete examples, it was often hard to get workers to articulate their experiences. The reasons concern both the interview process and the work process. In some cases I simply could not establish enough rapport to get the workers to enter into the spirit of the conversation. In these disappointing interviews, the respondents did their best to stick to such minimal responses as "Uh huh" and "I guess so." Other workers were willing enough to participate but gave unrealistic accounts of their attitudes toward their jobs and their customers. No respondent told me, for instance, "I strongly resent having to be nice to customers, so I am usually brusque or sullen," but I certainly saw some workers behave that way.

One of the most important limitations of the interview data derives from the nature of the job and the types of phenomena of interest. Most of my questions concerned customer contact: I asked about variations from the routine, about dealing with difficult customers, and about workers' responses to customers. However, the interactions between workers and customers at McDonald's are over almost as soon as they begin, and others are immediately under way. Since most are very similar, they tend to blend into one another in memory. Workers may remember exceptionally nice or exceptionally obnoxious customers, but for the most part the interactions are immediately forgotten, leaving only a general impression of a good day or a bad one, a slow shift or a busy one. I was sometimes able to get respondents to provide detailed information by asking a series of questions or giving examples of what I meant, but even these efforts were not always sufficient. For example, in my field notes I carefully recorded instances of customers who were not completely familiar with McDonald's routines—a woman who offered me a tip; a man who insisted on getting a Danish long after we had stopped serving breakfast—but it was very difficult for the workers I interviewed to call such minute incidents to mind. Indeed, I myself might not have remembered them, had I not been making a special effort to do so.

Furthermore, not all of the variation in workers' behavior and demeanor in response to different types of customers was the result of conscious decision-making. Only especially self-aware workers were able to report in detail how they adjusted their routines to meet particular circumstances. And, since these variations usually involved rather subtle shifts of tone which are not generally the subject of discussion, only especially articulate workers could explain them to me.

For these reasons, watching other workers on the job and paying careful attention to my own behavior and feelings were important means of supplementing the relatively sketchy and generalized responses to my interview questions. I cite my own work experiences frequently in Chapters 3, 5, and 6, not because I believe that my reactions were typical (I am sure they were not), but as evidence of the sorts of pressures workers face on the job. During the research I used my own experiences of discomfort, pleasure, and irritation as guides to significant features of the service interactions and as prompts to check how others reacted to similar situations.

Participant-observation was also essential for obtaining information on how managers treated workers and how workers treated each other on the job. In addition, working behind the counter at McDonald's was the best means of gathering information on the varieties of customer behavior. My attempts to observe worker-customer interactions from the customer side of the counter were relatively unsuccessful. From that vantage point I could watch how customers sorted themselves into lines and indicated their readiness to order, and I could see how the workers appeared to customers, but it was usually impossible to overhear the interactions without seeming intrusive.

Of course, not all McDonald's franchises and company-operated stores work precisely the way the franchise I studied did. As most McDonald's customers know, the stores vary in how they are run and in how pleasant they are to visit. My impression is that the research site was closer to a model McDonald's than to an average one, in that it was very tightly supervised, its owner and managers followed corporate advice closely, and it did not suffer from labor shortages that required it to compromise on standards for worker behavior. Many McDonald's stores are less scrupulous in maintaining company standards of cleanliness, friendliness, and efficiency.

My fieldwork on routinization at McDonald's was designed to provide both an overall view of the company's intentions and methods and a detailed look at how the routines were implemented in one setting. Since I studied only one McDonald's store, concentrated on daytime shifts, and interviewed only some of the window workers, the research could have been extended in several ways. Chapter 3 provides further discussion of how representative the franchise I studied and the workers I interviewed were. Although I cannot claim to give an exhaustive account of the possible ramifications of routinization at McDonald's, I am confident that my fieldwork provided sufficient data to bring to light the types of difficulties that are raised by this approach to routinization and the range of stances and strategies with which workers respond.

I wanted my second research site to provide a variety of contrasts to McDonald's, but my choice of Combined Insurance was serendipitous. I was acquainted, through mutual friends, with an actuary who worked for Combined Insurance, and when I mentioned my research topic to him he promptly said, "You should study my company." His brief account of the scripting of Combined's agents and of the Positive Mental Attitude philosophy that guided the company immediately interested me, and I easily gained permission to go ahead with the research once he had set up appointments for me with people he knew in the marketing research department.[2] Because these contacts all worked in Combined's life insurance division, I was assigned to a training class in that area. I later learned that although similar training methods and sales approaches were used in the company's other divisions, the routinization of the life agents was somewhat less rigid than it was for agents in the company's largest division, accident insurance.

At Combined Insurance, as at McDonald's, I was open with managers, trainees, and workers about my research. When I was first assigned to my training class, the trainer suggested that I not tell the other trainees that I was there as a researcher, so that they would treat me as one of them. I preferred to make my status clear, both because for practical and ethical reasons I did not like the idea of carrying out such a deception and because I wanted to be free to ask my classmates questions about their backgrounds, reactions to the training, and expectations for their careers.[3] I do not think that my presence as a researcher changed the training classes in any significant way; everyone was too serious about teaching or learning the skills necessary for success to be overly concerned with what I was making of the process.

I took part in class as though I were going to become an insurance agent, memorizing the sales presentations, rehearsing proper movements, and participating in role plays. (Indeed, my trainer and

---

2. In contrast to the reactions of McDonald's managers, my contact reported that the first responses of a Combined Insurance executive to his description of my proposed research "ranged from 'Well, I don't see any negatives' to 'Gee, that sounds fascinating.'"

3. The trainer's fear was that the trainees would be reluctant to include me in their study sessions if they thought I had a lesser stake in learning the material well. It soon became clear, though, that I was closer to being a ratebuster than a laggard. Not only could I memorize the presentations more easily than the other students (my experience as an actor helped me there), but I took far more extensive notes in class than anyone else did. The trainer pointed this difference out to my classmates, to my embarrassment, telling them that they should be even more motivated to work hard than I was, since my income was not going to depend on knowing the material.

classmates all thought I had a great future in sales and could not imagine why I would want to stick with graduate school instead of making a fortune.) There was time for informal talk with the trainees before class started each morning and during lunch and coffee breaks. The main limitation on my involvement with the training was that I did not stay at the hotel with the other trainees. My contacts tried to get the company to put me up there but found that it was too expensive. I did attend a weekend study session the trainees held at the hotel.

As at McDonald's, my personal characteristics shaped the range of informants' responses to me. A game played in class one day made me especially conscious of how my classmates saw me. The game, presumably intended to hone trainees' competitive drive and to force them to think fast on their feet, was familiar to me. We stood in our places, the trainer started the game by counting "one," and we continued counting around the circle. When the next number in sequence either had the digit seven in it or was a multiple of seven, the player had to say "buzz" instead of the number. Anyone who made a mistake and buzzed instead of counting or counted instead of buzzing was out. The game went on until the only ones left standing were a large, loud, middle-aged Texas man and myself. At that point he walked up to me to continue the game at close range. We went on counting, he towering over me and quickening the pace, until I hesitated when I should have buzzed and he was declared the winner. The class laughed uproariously and shouted that he had won through intimidation, noting that he could use his height and force of personality similarly in the field. It seemed to me that the merriment derived in part from the tension some of the men felt about having a young woman in the group who was better educated than they and who apparently found it relatively easy to do well in class. Some seemed to admire me for it, others to be made uneasy by it, and their treatment of me ranged from avuncular to respectful to nervous.

There was also some tension with my trainer. He was in a position of authority over the class, and he clearly wished to impress and inspire its members by stressing his success. My sponsorship by his superiors in the company put him in a different relation to me, and he seemed to be concerned to assert his authority in his own domain. That authority came into question when he insisted that I abide by a pledge the trainees had to sign that required, among other things, that we make no use of the sales materials except in our work for Combined Insurance. I had no desire to disclose trade secrets, but I had every intention of quoting those materials in my work and had permission to do so from people who outranked the trainer. He was angry when, as diplomatically as possible, I told him so, and he insisted that I sign the pledge. My allies in management instructed me to go ahead and sign, assuring me that they would back me up if there were ever any difficulties about the use of organizational materials. I was careful thereafter to be properly deferential in dealing with the trainer, who also seemed eager to demonstrate that there were no hard feelings.

When the training was over, the trainer and the regional sales manager both strongly encouraged me to obtain a temporary license so that I could try my hand at selling. That proved to be impractical, however. The Combined Insurance department in charge of overseeing agents' licensing did not want to sponsor anyone for a temporary license who did not plan to get a permanent one. I have no doubt that I would have gotten a deeper understanding of the agents' work if I had tried it myself, but when I began accompanying agents on sales calls I found myself experiencing many of the tensions and difficulties of the job even as an observer.

As was discussed in Chapter 4, the sales team to which I was assigned was typical in some ways, but it had unusually high sales. I later came to believe that the regional manager had deliberately refrained from assigning me to a team that would have been more convenient for me but that had members he knew to be unethical. As at McDonald's, then, my participant-observation of routinization in action was not in an average setting, but in one the corporation regarded highly. The regional manager at first declined to give me permission to observe more than one agent in the field. He wanted me to accompany only the sales manager of the team I eventually studied. His fear was not that I would reveal embarrassing information or interfere with the sales calls but that I might demoralize the agents by negative lines of questioning. Combined Insurance regards the agents' Positive Mental Attitude as crucial, and the regional manager told me that I could cost the company employees if I "blew their attitudes" by asking questions such as "How does it feel to be turned down five times in a row?" or "Do you often work a whole morning without making any money?" In the course of our conversation he was mollified by my evident sensitivity to the problem—I did not want to transform the situation I was trying to study—and agreed to let me observe the other agents if I would be careful not to promote negativity.

My main difficulties at Combined Insurance were with the team's sales manager, who evidently had not been consulted about my studying his team. The district manager, at the direction of the regional manager, instructed me to join the team for a breakfast meeting before its members separated to begin their rounds in surrounding towns. While the other agents were friendly, if a bit wary, at this meeting, the sales manager quite obviously regarded me as a nuisance. Throughout the week and a half I spent with the team, he never went out of his way to be helpful and in fact subjected me to considerable inconvenience. For instance, on two consecutive days I drove an hour and forty-five minutes to meet him, only to be stood up, left sitting in a hotel lobby with no way to get in touch with him. Eventually, I fulfilled my plan of observing each team member at work, including the manager, and even was granted a long interview by him, but our relations were never cordial. I fantasized vengeance but, having no leverage over him, I could express my resentment only by withholding the smiling agreeableness and shows of respect that marked my dealings with the other agents. In doing so I merely matched his own flat affect, so whether he knew or cared what I thought of him I do not know. I was rather gratified to hear the other agents mock his attempts to assert authority. Several of them had superior sales records, and some intimated to me that he had used unethical sales practices in the past but had been given another chance.

The other agents were more polite, but several of them were reluctant to have me accompany them on their sales calls.[4] One agent, Kevin, told me straightforwardly that I could come with him, but if he found that my presence was affecting the calls he would have to drop me off somewhere. Once the calls were under way, all the agents, including Kevin, seemed comfortable with me. Some treated me as a an equal, and others used the boastful manner frequently adopted by young men and strongly encouraged in Combined's insurance agents.

---

4. A couple of the agents feared that I planned to take notes during the calls, since they had seen me taking notes during a meeting. Once I learned of this concern, I was able to assure them that I had no intention of doing so.

The issue of whether my presence would significantly change the nature of the work was a serious methodological one. For one thing, I assumed that prospective customers would wonder who I was. As it happened, only one of the customers we called on ever asked about me; she asked whether I was learning to sell. Some of the agents introduced me by name at the beginning of a call, sometimes referring to me as "my associate," but others did not even do that much. The customers all seemed to take for granted that I had some legitimate reason for tagging along, and they oriented themselves to the agent, who was doing all the talking. It was actually not uncommon for agents to have someone accompany them on their calls—agents spend their first week in the field working with a manager, and even after that a manager may go on calls with one who is having trouble selling; some agents also choose to work together on occasion, taking turns giving presentations.

The agents were most concerned, quite legitimately, with the effect my presence would have on the sales calls, a concern I shared for different reasons. They were worried about making sales; I was worried about contaminating the data. Kevin was afraid he would have a harder time maintaining control of the interactions if I were there. He feared that prospects "might look to you for an out" when he was trying to close a sale. At the end of the day, though, Kevin told me that my presence "didn't change anything." "I would have let you know" if it had been a problem, he said. This assurance, and the other agents' apparent belief that their calls were going much as usual, gave me confidence that the picture I was getting of the variety of sales situations was generally accurate. The agents were too intent on making sales to have put up with much disruption.

Nevertheless, it was not quite true that my presence "didn't change anything." First, the agents were well aware that they had an audience. If any of them did engage in unethical sales practices on occasion, they would no doubt have refrained from doing so while I was observing them. My presence did encourage one or two of the agents to work more diligently than they might have done otherwise. Josh, who made a very large sale in the morning, told me that he would probably have been satisfied with his day's income and quit work for the day if he had been alone, but he felt obliged to give me a chance to see him work. I had the sense that at least one of the agents, who otherwise would have taken a break, kept working because he wanted to make a good impression.

During the sales calls I tried to be unobtrusive, but I certainly would not claim that my presence had no effect. On the simplest level, there were logistical complications. Combined's agents were trained to try to arrange to seat themselves side by side with prospective customers, preferably at a table. It was sometimes hard for me to figure out where to sit so as not to interfere with this tactic, as in this instance:

> There are only two chairs at Doris's kitchen table. I hesitate, but she tells me to sit down. Unfortunately, this leaves her standing—not a good selling situation.

Moreover, I could not completely escape participation in the interactions. If a prospect addressed a comment to me, my response, even if it was a failure to respond, would have some effect on the prospect's feelings about the sales call. For the most part, by behaving in the way that felt natural to me in this sort of situation (that is, a situation where one wants something from someone), I supported the agents' efforts to establish a pleasant tone to the calls. I found myself smiling ingratiatingly at prospects, laughing at their jokes, and participating in small talk, partly because I would have felt uncomfortable not doing so and partly because I felt that failure to do so would have made the agents' work more difficult.

This behavior was largely uncalculated. On sales calls I found myself identifying strongly with the agents. I felt nervous about whether we could get through the door; I felt deflated when we met with rudeness; I felt anxious when someone interrupted the sales talk, and I thought about what I would do in the agent's place to smooth the situation over. This response was not entirely attributable to identification with the agents—I wanted a chance to see all sorts of interactions, and I would not learn much if we never got through a door. But having taken the training course, I found that I was thinking like an agent even when I was also thinking like a researcher. When prospective customers were rude or abrupt I experienced some of the disappointment and irritation the agents did, and when they made a sale I shared in their elation.

During the interactions, then, I was likely to behave in ways that were marginally helpful to agents, since I tried to take my cues from them and to pattern my behavior on theirs. On a few occasions I got carried away and intervened more actively to keep the calls running smoothly. One such situation involved a difficult sale, where the husband was clearly interested in the policies, while the wife continually stated her objections. After quite a long discussion, the husband finally decided to buy a policy for each of them—the decision-making power was his—and the agent began filling in the applications. In training class we had been taught that it was important for the agent to keep talking while doing this paperwork, because a long silence would give the customer an opportunity to think of reasons to change his or her mind about taking the policy. When this agent, Tom, failed to fill in the silence, I started making polite small talk about the couple's dog, flower garden, and decor. I spoke up not so much because I was afraid that the sale would be lost, but because the tense atmosphere—an argument between the man and woman seemed entirely possible—was too much for me. Tom later thanked me for keeping up the chatter, which, he said, he should have done himself, but I chided myself for not having had the discipline to wait and see what happened when the agent did not actively control the situation.

I was similarly impulsive in another situation when the agent seemed to have gotten way off track. We called on a couple who were watching the Donahue show on television. They politely turned the set off when we sat down, but, to my amazement, Chuck suggested that they turn it back on, since he found the show interesting. They did so, and we sat and watched for a while. Chuck expressed derisive astonishment at the opinions of Donahue's guest, although our hosts gave no indication of whether they agreed with her. When a commercial came on, I turned to the prospective customers and jokingly said, "Well, we just stopped by to watch some television," at which point Chuck reclaimed the floor and proceeded to give the sales presentation. Again, my feeling that the agent was handling the situation badly and creating awkwardness overrode my intention to remain as neutral as possible. These incidents, evidence that my presence to some degree altered the situations I was trying to study, are also evidence that although I did not get as full a sense of what it was like to be an agent as I would have if I had done the job myself, I did feel acutely the pressure to manage interactions effectively that is a major factor in the agent's job.

Altogether, I observed fifty-five attempted sales calls on which an adult answered the door, and thirty sales presentations or attempts to renew a policy. Nine of those thirty attempts were successful, resulting in the sale of four new policies and the renewal of five existing policies. I would have preferred to have spent more time in the field with agents, and I would probably have pressed for the opportunity to do so had my relations with the sales manager been less brittle. As it happened, I did see enough of a range of calls to get a sense of the degree to which the agents varied their routines and to see agents make both successful and unsuccessful efforts to control prospects' behavior by using the techniques the company had taught them.

My fieldwork let me experience firsthand at least some of the pressures and pleasures that are associated with working on people. It also helped me understand the range of interpretations and responses that participation in organizationally scripted encounters prompted in workers and service-recipients. My experiences as a fieldworker were exasperating, fun, exhausting, and eye-opening. They were also indispensable, I think, in illuminating the distinctive features of work that involves management of the self and other people.

APPENDIX 2

Revising the Script at
Combined Insurance

I began my study of Combined Insurance at a time when the company was preparing to institute major changes in its life insurance division. I learned from my interviews with managers that the planned changes were in response to significant problems. Among the most pressing of these were excessive agent turnover, declining sales, and low persistency rates (the proportion of policyholders who renew their policies). As one executive drily put it:

> When you're losing your sales personnel very rapidly, when you're losing your customers very rapidly, you really have a rather important drag on your growth rate.

To deal with this situation, the life division, under the guidance of outside consultants, was making major changes to bring it more closely into line with prevalent industry practices.

First, the company would introduce new, more flexible products. These policies could provide much larger amounts of insurance than existing ones, and they could be tailored to meet the requirements of customers in a variety of ways. Second, the new products would be sold, not with a quick, high-energy monologue, but with an approach called Financial Needs Analysis that had long been used in other companies. Instead of trying to sell a particular product by appealing to prospects' emotions, the agents would present themselves as professionals who would analyze prospective customers' particular financial needs. They would elicit information on prospects' financial situations and goals, then demonstrate how Combined's life insurance policy could help them reach those goals.[1]

Although the routines I learned and observed are no longer in use in the life insurance division, the description and analysis of the

---

1. Unlike professional financial planners, Combined's agents could not offer information or advice on a variety of types of investments. The company's assumption is that the people in its traditional market, who are not very affluent, should have financial plans based on life insurance rather than more sophisticated investments.

sales system presented in Chapter 4 are still applicable to the work of most Combined Insurance agents. Significant changes have been made in the life division, but the company has not tampered with the success of the highly profitable accident division, which adheres strictly to the old routines. Even in the life division there is considerable continuity between the old and the new practices, although the new policy and sales routine did represent a change in direction. Positive Mental Attitude instruction, for example, is still an important component of training, as are many of the techniques of body language and demeanor detailed by the company's founder. Moreover, the new system also makes use of scripting. The sales routine has a basic structure and standard, memorized components, even though it is not an unvarying monologue. Essentially, the agents choose from a menu of scripted interactions based on the prospects' responses. The work, then, is still highly routinized.

I gathered information about the new sales system at two points. At the time of my initial fieldwork at Combined Insurance I interviewed several managers involved in planning the transition. One of them went through the new sales routine with me, using a prototype of the "Factfinder" interview guide and other sales materials. Another, who had just joined the company to help reshape the life division, gave me his outsider's perspective on Combined's ways of doing things, helping me to place the company in the wider context of the life insurance industry. (This executive sat in on some of the same training classes I did so that he could learn about existing company practices and culture.) He also showed me a videotape of an important meeting at which the outside consultants who were guiding the changes demonstrated their system to top managers and answered their questions.

In 1989, two years after my initial research, I returned to Combined Insurance to learn what I could about how the transition had gone. Had the life division's problems been ameliorated? What had been the effects of providing agents with more flexible routines? Had Combined Insurance abandoned its unusual commitment to standardization? I interviewed four managers at that time, two of whom I had spoken with in 1987.[2] The director of marketing and the director of sales for half of the country were both able to provide an overview of changes in the division, and the director of sales could also

2. I taped and transcribed these interviews myself.

speak as a guinea pig, because he had been regional manager in the territory that was the first to work with the new system. The current regional manager of that area had joined the company after the changes had been instituted, and he could both compare Combined Insurance with other companies and observe the differences between agents trained under the new and the old system. The manager of an Eastern region was able to tell me about the transition in progress rather than retrospectively, because his region was among the last to introduce the new policy and sales system. This second round of interviewing turned out to be useful in a number of ways, including satisfying my curiosity about what had happened to the agents I had known.[3] I also heard updates on the performance of the division and got some sense of how changes ordered by top management were played out at lower levels of the organization.

The introduction of the new policy and sales routine had been accompanied by several other kinds of changes. The managers of the life division had been persuaded that they needed a different type of person to sell the new products, one who was less interested in quick money and more concerned with establishing a long-term career. The division also needed people who were capable of making decisions, since both the sales presentation and the policies would have to be adjusted in response to the answers provided by prospective customers. To find such people, the company had adopted a much more elaborate recruitment system than had previously been in place. Applicants were carefully screened and tested, were given a better sense of what the requirements of the job were than they had been in the past, and went through a four-to-eight-week "precontract period" during which they carried out a series of assignments, observed the work, and were themselves observed before they were actually hired and trained. By increasing the resources devoted to recruitment and selection, the company aimed to break the self-perpetuating cycle in which high turnover rates produced a constant need to hire more agents quickly without being very particular about their qualifications, a pattern which inevitably contributed to high turnover rates. Under the new system, it was hoped, most turnover would take place before the agents were actually

---

3. None of the trainees from my class was still with the company. The two top agents on the team I studied (described in Chapter 4) were now district managers winning national awards and netting substantial earnings, and the rest of the team members, including the manager, were no longer with the company.

hired, so that fewer resources would be wasted training people who were not cut out for insurance sales.

Major changes in the means of recruitment and in the type of workers hired meant that I could not easily distinguish between those changes in the division's performance that were attributable to increased flexibility in the work process and those that were attributable to changes in the work force. Moreover, these two types of changes were closely intertwined, since a variety of alterations in the agents' job were designed to make it more appealing to the stable, career-oriented people the division hoped to attract.

In many respects, agents working under the new system have a different job than their predecessors did, and they have different expectations about how their careers will develop. Whereas promotion to sales manager had previously been the main way for agents to improve their status and earnings, the career of the agent is itself now supposed to provide scope for development. The flexibility of the new policies means that agents can find it worthwhile to work continually to add to their knowledge about insurance, which in turn can allow them to include more affluent people among their clientele.

The idea that agents have clienteles is itself a new development at Combined Insurance. Under the new system, agents can develop relationships with prospects during the longer, more interactive sales calls, and they are expected to provide ongoing service to customers instead of just selling policies that other agents will later try to renew. Agents' relations with their customers have been altered by changes in the incentive system as well. Under the revised commission program, agents are paid throughout the life of the policy, which encourages them to maintain ongoing contact with customers and undercuts the temptation to use unethical practices to make quick sales. The commission system also provides incentives for long-term employment with Combined Insurance, as do the changes that make the job more lucrative. The higher face values available for the new policy can yield higher commissions, and the company planned to phase out the old system of collecting premiums in the field, which required a great deal of unproductive travel and cut into agents' selling time.

Combined Insurance had previously encouraged its life insurance agents to think of themselves as salespeople, both directly in training and implicitly through the structure of the work and reward systems. The division's managers believe that the newly organized job, with its increased scope for decision making and its opportunities and incentives to build a clientele and expand both knowledge and earnings, will make it easier for employees to think of themselves as insurance professionals.

Although the wide-ranging changes in the agents' job made it hard for me to draw comparisons between the two sales systems, the process of change did provide me with opportunities to gather more complete information and more varied opinions about the old system than I could otherwise have gotten. In training classes and in the field during my original research, the precepts of Positive Mental Attitude clearly biased the evidence I could gather. Trainers built up the confidence of fledgling agents by assuring them that the system worked wonderfully, and agents themselves, to keep their own spirits up, tried to focus on its successes. Those I interviewed at that time who were involved in developing the new system, by contrast, obviously had a different assessment of the strengths and weaknesses of the old one. They were bound to focus on its defects as they tried to gain support for replacing it, and I got a less determinedly optimistic view of the existing operation when they explained what they hoped to accomplish by overhauling the workings of the life division. Similarly, those looking back on the abandoned system in 1989 had reason to stress the limitations of the old system and the strengths of the current one.

These interviews revealed that at least some managers had a low opinion of Combined's traditional work force and believed that it was only the high degree of routinization that had made such employees acceptable in the past. Two of the managers implied that more intelligent agents are needed under the new system. One, commenting on the increased importance of product knowledge for agents, said candidly:

> Hey, they gotta be smarter, too. I don't want to imply that we hired nothing but dummies in the past, but there certainly was a very low level of importance attributable to their own basic mental capacity. Not today. I mean, we couldn't take just somebody who—not a puppet. . . . In the past . . . they had a formula that was so tightly derived that they strictly had to follow the path. . . . They didn't have to think almost, OK? All they had to do was to go into the routine

that they had. And today, the individual is being forced to comprehend what's going on, and not follow the formula so strictly that they just go through the same motions time and time again.[4]

The interviews also illuminated the relation among routinization, agent character, and organizational prestige. Although even relatively unknowledgeable agents could succeed under the old, highly routinized sales system, some managers believed that that system drew people whose character or style could undermine sales and persistency. Honesty and professionalism were problematic areas, because the focus on quick sales attracted people who were interested in quick money. One manager who had built his career under the old system admitted that Combined Insurance might have had in the past a "peddler-type image in the community," rather than the image of "a professional, service-oriented sales organization." Giving the agents a stake in the persistency of the policies they sold and encouraging them to go back to the same customers "eliminates some of the huckstering" that was a temptation to agents whose interest in short-term profits sometimes overrode their commitment to ethics. This manager had heard that Pat Ryan, the new company president, wanted to upgrade the prestige of the organization by professionalizing its image.

A manager who had come to Combined Insurance from another company was reluctant to be overly critical of the company's past practices, but he clearly hoped to attract higher-caliber people who would want smarter, more sophisticated associates than they would have found in the past:

> Remember, [the old] system produced one of the most results-oriented, profitable businesses the insurance industry has ever noticed. [Hiring a lot of people who did not work out] was a cost of doing business. It also played into most stereotypes that most companies and most graduating seniors and professional-oriented type of people want to shy away from. "I don't want to go into a system where they throw ten against the wall and one strong [one] will survive. I think I've done more than that. I want a results-oriented, merit-based system, and I'd like to be able to look around at my peer group and see people with socks." [I laugh out loud, as does he.]

---

4. The director of sales disagreed that the new system required significantly more decision making than the old one did, arguing that the agents had always had to adjust their pitch to suit the circumstances.

By investigating the changes in the work of the agents, then, I learned that Combined Insurance, like many companies before it, had found that minimizing both the need for skill or intelligence and intrinsic job rewards through routinization can create difficulties in attracting, keeping, and managing a work force. By changing the nature of the sales system and attracting different sorts of workers, the life division hoped to improve its reputation in the industry and in the communities it served, as well as to enhance its profitability more directly.

Although in the second round of interviews I gathered information about the performance of the life division under the new system, the significant changes in recruitment methods, hiring standards, incentive systems, career design, and, to a lesser extent, target market that accompanied the redesign of the sales routine make it impossible to judge how much of the change in performance is attributable to the increased flexibility of the work process. The changes in the life division did lead to improvements in areas of concern to management, although the director of marketing was disappointed with the scale of improvement as of 1989.[5] Others were more enthusiastic, but it was clear that the changes had not been easy to institute. According to one manager, many agents left the company or moved to the accident division rather than adopt the new selling style. Another reported that some agents sold the new policy using the old "product selling" approach instead of the "needs selling" approach. That is, they continued to pitch a standard product rather than design a policy to suit prospects' self-determined needs.

Under the new hiring system, far fewer agents joined the company, and turnover rates declined from about 150–180 percent to 100 percent in a two-year period. Managers reported, however, that even with this improvement the division was still "not close to the industry standard" in retaining agents. Agents had reason to be happier with their jobs, since average income had increased; several managers mentioned that the most common reason for quitting had been dissatisfaction with earnings. An executive had told me in

5. Throughout 1990, Combined's life insurance division continued to struggle with problems related to these changes (*Aon Corporation Annual Report* for 1990: 5): "Sales of [the new] product improved during 1990, but not at a rate sufficient to offset the run-off of field-renewed traditional products. Thus, the volume of life business in the domestic market was marginally lower for the year. To address this problem, new emphasis has been placed on field renewals by life agents to improve renewal rates and new-sales proficiency."

1987 that the average life-division agent earned $200 per week, or less than $10,000 per year. Two years later, he reported that average annual earnings were up to $20,000. The manager of the region that had most recently adopted the new system had already seen dramatic improvements. He told me that the average person in his region (including both sales managers and agents) was making $150 more a week than the previous year, and that the average agent's annual earnings would rise from $15,000–22,000 to $18,000–28,000 that year. Some managers believed that the new selling system also made the agents' work more satisfying in itself, since, more plausibly than in the past, they could think of themselves as providing a service to those who bought (see Oakes 1990).

The changes in the life division that improved the agents' job also seemed likely to improve the persistency of their sales. Although the director of marketing told me that there was as yet no measurable alteration in the division's persistency rates (it was too soon to track policies for more than a few quarters), the two regional managers I spoke with were sure that customers who bought their policies under the new selling system were much more likely to renew them. One reported a "skyrocketing jump" of 20 percentage points per quarter in persistency, and the other said that there was a "day and night" difference in how persistent sales were under the two systems. He hoped that the improvement in persistency rates would be sustained in the long term, since customers who had participated in determining what kind of policy would be best for them would presumably be more likely to renew than those who had been swept along by a quick sales talk.

My investigation of the changes at Combined Insurance was useful in shedding light on the weaknesses of the old system and in providing additional information about the possibilities for making interactive routines more flexible. The substantial degree of scripting retained under the financial-needs-analysis system, however, and the continued practice of tightly standardized product-selling in the accident division are evidence that even autonomous workers and resistant service-recipients can be managed through a strategy of routinization.

References

Acker, Joan
1990   "Hierarchies, Jobs, Bodies: A Theory of Gendered Organiza-
        tions." *Gender & Society* 4: 139–58.
Advertising Age
1990   "Adman of the Decade: McDonald's Fred Turner: Making All
        the Right Moves." (January 1): 6.
1991   "100 Leading National Advertisers: McDonald's." (September
        25): 49–50.
Albrecht, Karl
1988   *At America's Service: How Corporations Can Revolutionize the Way
        They Treat Their Customers.* Homewood, Ill.: Dow Jones-Irwin.
Albrecht, Karl, and Ron Zemke
1985   *Service America! Doing Business in the New Economy.* Homewood,
        Ill.: Dow Jones-Irwin.
Aon Corporation Annual Report
Various years   Chicago, Ill.
Barrows, Sydney Biddle, with William Novak
1986   *Mayflower Madam: The Secret Life of Sydney Biddle Barrows.*
        New York: Arbor House.
Beechey, Veronica
1988   "Rethinking the Definition of Work: Gender and Work."
        Pp. 45–62 in Jane Jenson, Elizabeth Hagen, and Ceallaigh
        Reddy, eds., *Feminization of the Labor Force: Paradoxes and Prom-
        ises.* New York: Oxford University Press.
Benson, Susan Porter
1986   *Counter Cultures: Saleswomen, Managers, and Customers in Ameri-
        can Department Stores, 1890–1940.* Urbana, Ill.: University of
        Illinois Press.
Berg, Eric N.
1991   "An American Icon Wrestles with a Troubled Future." *New York
        Times* (May 12): sec. 3, 1.
Berk, Sarah Fenstermaker
1985a   *The Gender Factory: The Apportionment of Work in American House-
        holds.* New York: Plenum.
1985b   "Women's Work and the Production of Gender: A Reciprocal
        Relation." Paper presented at the annual meeting of the Amer-
        ican Sociological Association, Washington, D.C.

257

Bertagnoli, Lisa
1989a   "McDonald's: Company of the Quarter Century." *Restaurants and Institutions* (July 10): 32–60.
1989b   "Inside McDonald's." *Restaurants and Institutions* (August 21): 44–70.
Biggart, Nicole Woolsey
1983   "Rationality, Meaning, and Self-Management: Success Manuals, 1950–1980." *Social Problems* 30: 298–311.
1989   *Charismatic Capitalism: Direct Selling Organizations in America.* Chicago: University of Chicago Press.
Blauner, Robert
1964   *Alienation and Freedom.* Chicago: University of Chicago Press.
Boas, Max, and Steve Chain
1976   *Big Mac: The Unauthorized Story of McDonald's.* New York: New American Library.
Braverman, Harry
1974   *Labor and Monopoly Capital: The Degradation of Work in the Twentieth Century.* New York: Monthly Review Press.
Burawoy, Michael
1979   *Manufacturing Consent: Changes in the Labor Process Under Capitalism.* Chicago: University of Chicago Press.
Butterfield, Steve
1985   *Amway: The Cult of Free Enterprise.* Boston: South End Press.
Byrne, Harlan S. (HSB)
1990   "Aon Corporation: It Stands Apart from Traditional Insurers." *Barrons* (April 12): 62–63.
Chandler, Alfred D., Jr.
1962   *Strategy and Structure: Chapters in the History of the American Industrial Enterprise.* Cambridge, Mass.: M.I.T. Press.
Chase, Dennis
1991   "P & G Gets Top Marks in AA Survey." *Advertising Age* (January 29): 8, 10.
Chase, Richard B.
1978   "Where Does the Customer Fit in a Service Operation?" *Harvard Business Review* 56 (Nov.–Dec.): 137–42.
Chaudhry, Rajan
1989   "Burger Giants Singed by Battle." *Nation's Restaurant News* (August 7): F36.
Chodorow, Nancy
1978   *The Reproduction of Mothering: Psychoanalysis and the Sociology of Gender.* Berkeley: University of California Press.
Cialdini, Robert B.
1984   *Influence: How and Why People Agree to Things.* New York: William Morrow and Company.
Cockburn, Cynthia
1983   *Brothers: Male Dominance and Technological Change.* London: Pluto Press.

1985   *Machinery of Dominance: Women, Men and Technical Know-How.* London: Pluto Press.

Combined International Annual Report
1986   Chicago, Ill.

Connelly, Maureen, and Patricia Rhoton
1988   "Women in Direct Sales: A Comparison of Mary Kay and Amway Sales Workers." Pp. 245–64 in Anne Statham, Eleanor M. Miller, and Hans O. Mauksch, eds., *The Worth of Women's Work: A Qualitative Synthesis.* Albany: State University of New York Press.

Cooley, Charles Horton
1902   *Human Nature and the Social Order.* New York: Charles Scribner's Sons.

Cziepel, John A., Michael R. Solomon, and Carol F. Surprenant
1985   *The Service Encounter: Managing Employee/Customer Interaction in Service Businesses.* Lexington, Mass.: Lexington Books.

Dalby, Liza Crihfield
1983   *Geisha.* Berkeley: University of California Press.

Davis, Fred
1959–60 "The Cabdriver and His Fare: Facets of a Fleeting Relationship." *American Journal of Sociology* 65: 158–65.

Desatnick, Robert C.
1987   *Managing to Keep the Customer: How to Achieve and Maintain Superior Customer Service Throughout the Organization.* San Francisco: Jossey-Bass.

DeVault, Marjorie L.
1991   *Feeding the Family: The Social Organization of Caring as Gendered Work.* Chicago: University of Chicago Press.

Dewar, Thomas R.
1978   "The Professionalization of the Client." *Social Policy* 8: 4–9.

Dowd, Maureen
1991   "The Thomas Nomination: In Ugly Atmosphere, the Accusations Fly." *New York Times* (October 12): 1.

Durkheim, Emile
1974 [1924]
    "The Determination of Moral Facts." Pp. 35–62 in *Sociology and Philosophy,* trans. D. F. Pocock. Glencoe, Ill.: Free Press.
1965 [1915]
    The Elementary Forms of the Religious Life. Trans. Joseph Ward Swain. New York: Free Press.

Edwards, Richard
1979   *Contested Terrain: The Transformation of the Workplace in the Twentieth Century.* New York: Basic Books.

Fantasia, Rick
1991   "American Commodities as Cultural Goods: The 'Place' of Fast-Food in France." Unpublished manuscript, Smith College, Northampton, Mass.

Finlay, William, and Jack K. Martin
1991   "Attitudes vs. Skill: Technology and Hiring Decisions in Electrical and Textile Plants." Paper presented at the annual meeting of the American Sociological Association, Cincinnati, Ohio.

Finch, Janet
1983   *Married to the Job: Wives' Incorporation in Men's Work.* London: Allen and Unwin.

Fishman, Pamela M.
1978   "Interaction: The Work Women Do." *Social Problems* 75: 397–406.

Forbes
1990   "Ranking the Forbes 500." (May 1): 246–86.

Fortune
1990   "The Service 500." (June 4): 304–31.
1991   "Fortune Global Service 500: The 50 Largest Retailing Companies." (August 26): 179.

Friedman, Andrew
1977   *Industry and Labour: Class Struggle at Work and Monopoly Capitalism.* London: Macmillan.

Frye, Marilyn
1983   "Sexism." Pp. 17–40 in *The Politics of Reality.* Trumansberg, N.Y.: The Crossing Press.

Fuller, Linda, and Vicki Smith
1991   "Consumers' Reports: Management by Customers in a Changing Economy." *Work, Employment, and Society* 15: 1–16.

Fussell, Paul
1975   *The Great War and Modern Memory.* New York: Oxford University Press.
1980   *Abroad: British Literary Traveling Between the Wars.* New York: Oxford University Press.

Garfinkel, Harold
1967   *Studies in Ethnomethodology.* Englewood Cliffs, N.J.: Prentice Hall.

Garson, Barbara
1975   *All the Livelong Day: The Meaning and Demeaning of Routine Work.* New York: Doubleday.
1988   *The Electronic Sweatshop: How Computers Are Transforming the Office of the Future into the Factory of the Past.* New York: Simon and Schuster.

Geist, William E.
1987   "Citadel of Fury: Anger Strikes Out at the Auto Pound." *New York Times* (February 28): 33.

Gerstel, Naomi, and Harriet Engel Gross
1987   *Families and Work.* Philadelphia: Temple University Press.

Gibson, Richard, and Robert Johnson
1989   "Big Mac Plots Strategy to Regain Sizzle." *Wall Street Journal* (September 29): B1.

Glazer, Nona Y.
1984   "Servants to Capital: Unpaid Domestic Labor and Paid Work."
          Review of Radical Political Economics 16: 61–87.
Glenn, Evelyn Nakano, and Roslyn L. Feldberg
1979a   "Proletarianizing Clerical Work: Technology and Control."
          Pp. 51–72 in Andrew Zimbalist, ed., *Case Studies on the Labor
          Process*. New York: Monthly Review Press.
1979b   "Women as Mediators in the Labor Process." Paper presented
          at the annual meeting of the American Sociological Associa-
          tion, Boston, Mass.
Gloria Marshall Figure Salons
N.d.   "Encouraging Phrases to Use for Patron Whose Weight Is *over*
          Projection." Typescript.
Goffman, Erving
1955   "On Face-Work: An Analysis of Ritual Elements in Social Inter-
          action." *Psychiatry* 18: 213–31.
1956   "The Nature of Deference and Demeanor." *American Anthropol-
          ogist* 58: 473–502.
1957   "Alienation from Interaction." *Human Relations* 10: 47–60.
1961a   "The Medical Model and Mental Hospitalization: Some Notes
          on the Vicissitudes of the Tinkering Trades." Pp. 321–86 in
          *Asylums: Essays on the Social Situation of Mental Patients and Other
          Inmates*. Garden City, N.Y.: Anchor Books.
1961b   "Role Distance." Pp. 83–152 in *Encounters: Two Studies in the
          Sociology of Interaction*. Indianapolis, Ind.: Bobbs-Merrill.
1961c   "The Underlife of a Public Institution: A Study of Ways of
          Making Out in a Mental Hospital." Pp. 125–70 in *Asylums:
          Essays on the Social Situation of Mental Patients and Other Inmates*.
          Garden City, N.Y.: Anchor Books.
1967   "Where the Action Is." Pp. 149–270 in *Interaction Ritual: Essays
          on Face-to-Face Behavior*. Garden City, N.Y.: Anchor Books.
1977   "The Arrangements Between the Sexes." *Theory and Society*
          4: 301–31.
1983   "The Interaction Order." *American Sociological Review* 48: 1–17.
Goldman, Marshall
1990   Presentation at colloquium on Reforming the Soviet Economy.
          University of Pennsylvania, May 17.
Greenberger, Ellen, and Laurence Steinberg
1986   *When Teenagers Work: The Psychological and Social Costs of Adoles-
          cent Employment*. New York: Basic Books.
Gutman, Herbert
1977   *Work, Culture and Society in Industrializing America*. New York:
          Vintage Books.
Hall, Elaine J.
1990   "Waitering/Waitressing: Engendering the Work of Table Ser-
          vers." Paper presented at the annual meeting of the Eastern
          Sociological Society, Boston, Mass.

Halle, David
    1984   *America's Working Man: Work, Home, and Politics Among Blue Collar Property Owners*. Chicago: University of Chicago Press.
Harris, Thomas A.
    1969   *I'm OK, You're OK: A Practical Introduction to Transactional Analysis*. New York: Harper and Row.
Heskett, James L., W. Earl Sasser, Jr., and Christopher W. L. Hart
    1990   *Service Breakthroughs: Changing the Rules of the Game*. New York: Free Press.
Hill, Napoleon, and W. Clement Stone
    1960   *Success Through a Positive Mental Attitude*. New York: Pocket Books.
Hochschild, Arlie Russell
    1983   *The Managed Heart: Commercialization of Human Feeling*. Berkeley: University of California Press.
Hochschild, Arlie, with Anne Machung
    1989   *The Second Shift: Working Parents and the Revolution at Home*. New York: Viking.
Hostage, G. M.
    1975   "Quality Control in a Service Business." *Harvard Business Review* 53 (July–Aug.): 98–106.
Howard, Robert
    1985   *Brave New Workplace*. New York: Viking.
Hughes, Everett C.
    1984 [1951]
            "Work and Self." Pp. 338–47 in *The Sociological Eye*. New Brunswick, N.J.: Transaction Books.
    1984 [1970]
            "The Humble and the Proud: The Comparative Study of Occupations." Pp. 417–27 in *The Sociological Eye*. New Brunswick, N.J.: Transaction Books.
International Bartending Institute
    N.d.   "Presentations for Personal Interview." Typescript.
Joffe, Carole
    1986   *The Regulation of Sexuality: Experiences of Family Planning Workers*. Philadelphia: Temple University Press.
Kanter, Rosabeth Moss
    1977   *Men and Women of the Corporation*. New York: Basic Books.
Katz, Elihu, and S. N. Eisenstadt
    1960   "Some Sociological Observations on the Response of Israeli Organizations to New Immigrants." *Administrative Science Quarterly* 5: 113–33.
Keegan, John
    1976   *The Face of Battle*. Harmondsworth, England: Penguin.
Kessler, Ronald
    1985   *The Life Insurance Game*. New York: Holt, Rinehart and Winston.

Kessler, Suzanne J., and Wendy McKenna
1978   *Gender: An Ethnomethodological Approach.* Chicago: University
         of Chicago Press.
Knights, David
1990   "Subjectivity, Power and the Labour Process." Pp. 297–335 in
         David Knights and Hugh Willmott, eds., *Labour Process Theory.*
         London: Macmillan.
Knights, David, and Hugh Willmott, eds.
1990   *Labour Process Theory.* London: Macmillan.
Koepp, Stephen
1987a   "Big Mac Strikes Back." *Time* (April 13): 58–60.
1987b   "Pul-eeze! Will Somebody Help Me?" *Time* (February 2): 48–55.
Kohn, Melvin
1969   *Class and Conformity.* Homewood, Ill.: Dorsey Press.
Kroc, Ray, with Robert Anderson
1977   *Grinding It Out: The Making of McDonald's.* Chicago:
         Contemporary Books.
Kusterer, Ken C.
1978   *Know-How on the Job: The Important Working Knowledge of
         "Unskilled" Workers.* Boulder, Colo.: Westview Press.
Lally-Benedetto, Corinne
1985   "Women and the Tone of the Body: An Analysis of a Figure
         Salon." Paper presented at the annual meeting of the Midwest
         Sociological Society, St. Louis, Mo.
Lamont, Michele
1992   *Money, Morals, and Manners: The Culture of the French and
         American Upper Middle Class.* Chicago: Univeristy of Chicago
         Press.
Lawson, Helene
1991   "Learning to Suspect and Betray: The Transformation of Car
         Sales Women." Paper presented at the annual meeting of the
         Midwest Sociological Society, Des Moines, Iowa.
Levitt, Theodore
1972   "Production-Line Approach to Service." *Harvard Business
         Review* 50: 41–52.
Life Assurance Association of Japan
1988   *Life Insurance Business in Japan, 1987/8.* Tokyo.
Lipsky, Michael
1980   *Street Level Bureaucracies: Dilemmas of the Individual in Public
         Service.* New York: Russell Sage.
Littler, Craig R.
1990   "The Labour Process Debate: A Theoretical Overview,
         1974–1988." Pp. 46–94 in David Knights and Hugh Willmott,
         eds., *Labour Process Theory.* London: Macmillan.
Littler, Craig R., and Graham Salaman
1982   "Bravermania and Beyond: Recent Theories of the Labour
         Process." *Sociology* 16: 251–69.

Love, John F.
1986   *McDonald's: Behind the Arches*. New York: Bantam Books.
Lovelock, Christopher H., ed.
1988   *Managing Services: Marketing, Operations, and Human Resources.*
        Englewood Cliffs, N.J.: Prentice Hall.
Lovelock, Christopher H., and Robert F. Young
1979   "Look to Consumers to Increase Productivity." *Harvard Business
        Review* 57 (May–June): 168–78.
Luxenberg, Stan
1985   *Roadside Empires: How the Chains Franchised America*. New York:
        Viking.
Luxton, Meg
1980   *More Than a Labour of Love: Three Generations of Women's Work in
        the Home*. Toronto: Women's Press.
Lynd, Robert S., and Helen Merrell Lynd
1929   *Middletown: A Study in American Culture*. New York: Harcourt,
        Brace and World.
McCallum, J. Richard, and Wayne Harrison
1985   "Interdependence in the Service Encounter." Pp. 35–48 in
        John A. Czepiel, Michael R. Solomon, and Carol F. Surpren-
        ant, eds., *The Service Encounter: Managing Employee/Customer
        Interaction in Service Businesses*. Lexington, Mass.: Lexington
        Books.
McDonald's Annual Report
Various years   Oak Brook, Ill.
Majors, Richard
1989   "Cool Pose: The Proud Signature of Black Survival." Pp. 83–87
        in Michael S. Kimmel and Michael A. Messner, eds., *Men's
        Lives*. New York: Macmillan.
Malinowski, Bronislaw
1954 [1948]
        Magic, Science and Religion. Garden City, N.Y.: Doubleday
        Anchor.
Margolis, Diane Rothbard
1979   *The Managers: Corporate Life in America*. New York: William
        Morrow.
Martin, Judith
1985   "Now That Society Is Abandoned, One's Only Friend Is
        One's Bank." Pp. 45–49 in *Common Courtesy: In Which Miss
        Manners Solves the Problem That Baffled Mr. Jefferson*. New York:
        Atheneum.
Matza, Michael
1990   "Write 'em Up, Move 'em Out." *Philadelphia Inquirer Magazine*
        (May 13): 14–20.
Mead, George Herbert
1934   *Mind, Self, and Society*, ed. Charles W. Morris. Chicago: Univer-
        sity of Chicago Press.

Melosh, Barbara
1982   "The Physician's Hand": Work Culture and Conflict in American
        Nursing. Philadelphia: Temple University Press.
Milgram, Stanley
1965   "Some Conditions of Obedience and Disobedience to Author-
        ity." Human Relations 18: 57–76.
Milkman, Ruth
1987   Gender at Work: The Dynamics of Job Segregation by Sex During
        World War II. Urbana, Ill.: University of Illinois Press.
Miller, Russell
1984   Bunny: The Real Story of Playboy. London: Michael Joseph.
Mills, C. Wright
1951   White Collar: The American Middle Class. New York: Oxford
        University Press.
Mills, Peter K.
1986   Managing Service Industries: Organizational Practices in a Post-
        industrial Economy. Cambridge, Mass.: Ballinger.
Montgomery, David
1979   Workers' Control in America: Studies in the History of Work, Tech-
        nology, and Labor Struggles. Cambridge: Cambridge University
        Press.
Normann, Richard
1984   Service Management: Strategy and Leadership in Service Businesses.
        Chichester: John Wiley and Sons.
Norwood, Stephen H.
1990   Labor's Flaming Youth: Telephone Operators and Worker Militancy.
        Urbana, Ill.: University of Illinois Press.
Noyelle, Thierry J.
1987   Beyond Industrial Dualism: Market and Job Segmentation in the New
        Economy. Boulder, Colo.: Westview Press.
Oakes, Guy
1990   The Soul of the Salesman: The Moral Ethos of Personal Sales. Atlan-
        tic Highlands, N.J.: Humanities Press International.
Ouellet, Lawrence J.
1986   "Work, Commitment, and Effort: Truck Drivers and Truck-
        ing in Small, Non-Union, West Coast Trucking Companies."
        Ph.D. dissertation, Sociology Department, Northwestern
        University.
Parcel, Toby L., and Marie B. Sickmeier
1988   "One Firm, Two Labor Markets: The Case of McDonald's in
        the Fast-Food Industry." Sociological Quarterly 29: 29–46.
Paules, Greta Foff
1991   Dishing It Out: Power and Resistance Among Waitresses in a New
        Jersey Restaurant. Philadelphia: Temple University Press.
Peters, Tom, and Nancy Austin
1985   A Passion for Excellence: The Leadership Difference. New York:
        Random House.

Piper, Watty
  1930   *The Little Engine That Could.* Retold by Watty Piper from *The Pony Engine* by Mabel C. Bragg. New York: Platt and Munk.
Prottas, Jeffrey
  1979   *People Processing.* Lexington, Mass.: Lexington Books.
Prus, Robert
  1989a   *Making Sales: Influence as Interpersonal Accomplishment.* Newbury Park, Calif.: Sage Publications.
  1989b   *Pursuing Customers: An Ethnography of Marketing Activities.* Newbury Park, Calif.: Sage Publications.
Reiter, Ester
  1991   *Making Fast Food: From the Frying Pan into the Fryer.* Montreal: McGill-Queen's University Press.
Reverby, Susan M.
  1987   *Ordered to Care: The Dilemma of American Nursing, 1850–1945.* Cambridge: Cambridge University Press.
Rollins, Judith
  1985   *Between Women: Domestics and Their Employers.* Philadelphia: Temple University Press.
Roman, Murray
  1979   *Telephone Marketing Techniques.* New York: AMACOM (American Management Association).
Rosenthal, Herma M.
  1989   "Inside Big Mac's World." *Newsday* (June 4): magazine section, 8–12, 16, 19, 24–25.
Sabel, Charles F.
  1982   *Work and Politics: The Division of Labor in Industry.* Cambridge: Cambridge University Press.
Schein, Edgar H.
  1956   "The Chinese Indoctrination Program for Prisoners of War: A Study of Attempted 'Brainwashing.'" *Psychiatry* 19 (May): 149–72.
Schroedel, Jean Reith
  1985   *Alone in a Crowd: Women in the Trades Tell Their Stories.* Philadelphia: Temple University Press.
Seligman, Martin E. P.
  1990   *Learned Optimism.* New York: Alfred A. Knopf.
Seligman, Martin E. P., and Peter Schulman
  1986   "Explanatory Style as a Predictor of Performance as a Life Insurance Agent." *Journal of Personality and Social Psychology* 50: 832–38.
Sennett, Richard, and Jonathan Cobb
  1972   *The Hidden Injuries of Class.* New York: Knopf.
Silpakit, Patriya, and Raymond P. Fisk
  1985   "'Participatizing' the Service Encounter: A Theoretical Framework." Pp. 117–21 in Thomas A. Bloch, Gregory D. Upah, Valarie A. Zeithaml, eds., *Services Marketing in a Changing Environment.* Chicago: American Marketing Association.

Simon, Ruth
  1986   "Turning Mongrels into Greyhounds." *Forbes* (September
           22): 80.
Simpson, Richard L.
  1985   "Social Control of Occupations and Work." *Annual Review of
           Sociology* 11: 415–36.
Smith, Adam
  1982 [1776]
           The Wealth of Nations. New York: Penguin.
Smith, Joan
  1984   "The Paradox of Women's Poverty: Wage-earning Women and
           Economic Transformation." *Signs* 10: 291–310.
Spradley, James P., and Brenda J. Mann
  1975   *The Cocktail Waitress: Woman's Work in a Man's World*. New York:
           John Wiley and Sons.
Steinem, Gloria
  1983   "I Was a Playboy Bunny." Pp. 29–69 in Gloria Steinem, *Out-
           rageous Acts and Everyday Rebellions*. New York: Holt, Rinehart
           and Winston.
Stinchcombe, Arthur L.
  1990a   "Work Institutions and the Sociology of Everyday Life."
           Pp. 99–116 in Kai Erikson and Steven Peter Vallas, eds., *The
           Nature of Work: Sociological Perspectives*. New Haven, Conn.: Yale
           University Press.
  1990b   *Information and Organizations*. Berkeley: University of California
           Press.
Stone, W. Clement
  1962   *The Success System That Never Fails*. Englewood Cliffs, N.J.:
           Prentice Hall.
Swerdlow, Marian
  1989   "Men's Accommodations to Women Entering a Nontraditional
           Occupation: A Case of Rapid Transit Operatives." *Gender &
           Society* 3: 373–87.
Therrien, Lois
  1991   "McRisky." *Business Week* (October 21): 114–22.
Thomas, Barbara J.
  1990   "Women's Gains in Insurance Sales: Increased Supply, Un-
           certain Demand." Pp. 183–204 in Barbara F. Reskin and
           Patricia A. Roos, *Job Queues, Gender Queues: Explaining Women's
           Inroads into Male Occupations*. Philadelphia: Temple University
           Press.
Thompson, Paul
  1989   *The Nature of Work: An Introduction to Debates on the Labour
           Process*, second edition. London: Macmillan.
Tocqueville, Alexis de
  1969 [1835]
           Democracy in America, ed. J. P. Mayer, trans. George Lawrence.
           Garden City, N.Y.: Anchor Books.

Trilling, Lionel
    1972   *Sincerity and Authenticity.* Cambridge, Mass.: Harvard University Press.
Van Maanen, John
    1988   *Tales of the Field: On Writing Ethnography.* Chicago: University of Chicago Press.
Van Maanen, John, and Gideon Kunda
    1989   "'Real Feelings': Emotional Expression and Organizational Culture." Pp. 43–103 in L. L. Cummings and Barry M. Staw, eds., *Research in Organizational Behavior* 11. Greenwich, Conn.: JAI Press.
Walker, George Lee
    1985   *The Chronicles of Doodah.* Boston: Houghton Mifflin.
Weber, Max
    1946 [1919]
            "Politics as a Vocation." Pp. 77–128 in H. H. Gerth and C. Wright Mills, trans. and eds., *From Max Weber.* New York: Oxford University Press.
    1958 [1904–5]
            The Protestant Ethic and the Spirit of Capitalism, trans. Talcott Parsons. New York: Charles Scribner's Sons.
Wener, Richard E.
    1985   "The Environmental Psychology of Service Encounters." Pp. 101–12 in John A. Czepiel, Michael R. Solomon, and Carol F. Surprenant, eds., *The Service Encounter: Managing Employee/Customer Interaction in Service Businesses.* Lexington, Mass.: Lexington Books.
West, Candace, and Don H. Zimmerman
    1987   "Doing Gender." *Gender & Society* 1: 125–51.
Wharton, Amy S., and Rebecca J. Erickson
    1990   "The Emotional Division of Labor: Women's Work and Family Life." Paper presented at the annual meeting of the American Sociological Association, San Francisco, Calif.
Whyte, William F.
    1946   "When Workers and Customers Meet." Pp. 123–47 in William F. Whyte, ed., *Industry and Society.* New York: McGraw-Hill.
Wildavsky, Ben
    1989   "McJobs: Inside America's Largest Youth Training Program." *Policy Review* 49: 30–37.
Williams, Christine
    1989   *Gender Differences at Work: Women and Men in Nontraditional Occupations.* Berkeley: University of California Press.
Willis, Paul
    1977   *Learning to Labor: How Working Class Kids Get Working Class Jobs.* New York: Columbia University Press.

Willmott, Hugh
    1990   "Subjectivity and the Dialectics of Praxis: Opening up the Core
              of Labour Process Analysis." Pp. 336–78 in David Knights and
              Hugh Willmott, eds., *Labour Process Theory*. London: Macmillan.

Wolfe, Tom
    1979   *The Right Stuff*. New York: Bantam Books.

Wouters, Cas
    1989   "The Sociology of Emotions and Flight Attendants:
              Hochschild's *Managed Heart*." *Theory, Culture and Society* 6:
              95–123.

Zelizer, Viviana A. Rotman
    1979   *Morals and Markets: The Development of Life Insurance in the United
              States*. New York: Columbia University Press.

Zemke, Ron, with Dick Schaaf
    1989   *The Service Edge: 101 Companies That Profit from Customer Care*.
              New York: NAL Books.

Index

Designer: Janet Wood
Compositor: Star Type
Text: 10/13 Palatino
Display: Palatino
Printer   Haddon Craftsmen
Binder: Haddon Craftsmen